Great
CAR
COLLECTIONS
of the World

Great
CAR
COLLECTIONS
of the World

Edward Eves and Dan Burger

GALLERY BOOKS
An imprint of W H Smith Publishers Inc
112 Madison Avenue, New York City 10016

This book was devised and produced by
Multimedia Publications (UK) Ltd

Editors: Edward Bunting and Valerie Passmore
Production: Karen Bromley
Design: John and Orna Design
Picture research: J. Baker and Paul Snelgrove

First published in the United States of America 1986 by
Gallery Books, an imprint of W H Smith Publishers Inc.,
112 Madison Avenue, New York, NY 10016

ISBN 0 8317-4067-1

Typeset by Rapidset and Design Limited
Origination by Peninsular Repro Service Limited
Printed by Cayfosa, Barcelona, Spain

Contents

Introduction 8

Australia
Birdwood Mill National Motor Museum 9
Gilltraps Auto Museum 13
York Motor Museum 16

Austria
Vienna Museum of Industry and Trade 19

Belgium
Provincial Automobile Museum 22

Canada
Canadian Automotive Museum 26
National Museum of Science and Technology 30

Czechoslovakia
National Museum of Technology 33
Tatra Technical Museum 35

Denmark
Ålholm Automobile Museum 38

France
Henri Malartre Motor Museum 42
National Automobile Museum (Schlumpf) 47
National Museum of Compiègne Castle 52
National Technical Museum 56

Germany, Democratic Republic (East Germany)
Transport Museum 59

Germany, Federal Republic (West Germany)
Automobile and Technical Museum 62
Daimler-Benz Museum 66
German Motor Museum 71
North German Motor and Technical Museum 73

Italy
Alfa Romeo Museum 77
Carlo Biscaretti di Ruffia Automobile Museum 81
Quattroruote Collection 84

Netherlands
Autotron Drunen 87

New Zealand
Len Southward Museum 91

Norway
Norwegian Technical Museum 94

Sweden
Allan Söderström Automobiles 96
Svedino's Car and Aircraft Museum 99

Switzerland
Swiss Transport Museum 103

Union of Soviet Socialist Republics
Moscow Polytechnical Museum 106

United Kingdom
British Motor Industry Heritage Trust Museum, Syon
   Park 108
Donington Collection 112
Midland Motor Museum 116
Museum of British Road Transport 119
National Motor Museum (Beaulieu) 125

United States of America
Auburn-Cord-Duesenberg Museum 130
Behring Museum 134
Bellm's Cars and Music of Yesterday 137
Crawford Auto-Aviation Museum 142
Briggs Cunningham Automotive Museum 147
Henry Ford Museum and Greenfield Village 151
Gilmore-Classic Car Club Museum 157
Harrah's Automobile Collection 161
Imperial Palace Auto Collection 166
Indianapolis Motor Speedway Hall of Fame
   Museum 172
Merle Norman Classic Beauty Collection 175
Alfred P. Sloan Museum 179
Brooks Stevens Automotive Museum 184
Swigart Museum 187
Texas Science Center Automotive Collection 192
Volo Antique Auto Museum 197

Index 200

Endpapers: **The dramatically lighted main entrance hall of the National Motor Museum at Beaulieu, England, contains a range of British-built cars dating from 1906 to the present day**

Half title page: **Rolls-Royces from the Rainsford Collection in Birdwood Mill Museum, South Australia**

Facing title page: **This custom-built 1928 Minerva is only one of 35 automotive jewels which shimmer in the soft light of the Grand Salon Showroom of the Merle Norman Classic Beauty Collection in Sylmar, California**

Picture credits page: **Mercedes-Benz W125 Grand Prix at the *Musée nationale*, Mulhouse, France**

Facing contents page: **Rare and typical of the period: a beautiful 1939 Mercedes-Benz cabriolet in the Daimler-Benz Museum, Germany**

Introduction

In planning this book, the first decision that had to be made was: what determines a great car collection? There are, of course, many collections of character and distinction around the world – some 200 in the United States alone. Choosing just 50 collections involved some difficult decisions. Criteria would include quality, quantity, historical significance, accessibility and singularity.

Most collections have a particular theme that dominates the entire display: the place of the motor car in society for example, as at Beaulieu in Britain or Volo in Illinois, or the history of a particular make, as at Ford in Dearborn, Michigan, or Alfa-Romeo in Milan, or the bringing together of vehicles produced in a certain area, as at Auburn-Cord-Duesenberg in Indiana or at Henri Malartre near Lyons in France. Others have gained recognition because they cover automotive history from beginning to end. It is decidedly difficult to define quality to the satisfaction of everyone. Even worse is the attempt to impose a rigid common standard on all. On the other hand, though, quality is always recognizable when it's there, and when it's not.

Naturally the number of cars in a collection has a bearing on whether it should be included, although quantity alone does not ensure greatness among our selections. Several collections contain over 200 automobiles and many others display over 100 cars. The Harrah Automobile Collection at one time numbered over 1500 automobiles. Although that number has been reduced to approximately 500 vehicles, the collection remains one of the world's largest and most respected and most frequently visited. Yet this takes nothing away from the smaller collections we have included among our selections.

Another influential criterion is a sense of history. This goes beyond the obvious factors of age and chronology. For instance, the Auburn-Cord-Duesenberg Museum in Indiana, housed in the 1930s art deco factory showroom of the Auburn Automobile Company, creates an atmosphere which perfectly complements the cars on exhibit. The Henry Ford Museum's auto collection is only a portion of the stupendous assembly of Americana which Ford began collecting in the late 1920s. Undoubtedly, the preservation of a historical setting augments the presentation of the automobiles. In several instances, it was unfortunate that inaccessibility excludes fine collections.

The BMW and Porsche collections in West Germany have been omitted because it was felt that the number of cars was too restricted. Peugeot's burgeoning collection in France has also been excluded because it can only be seen by appointment. So too is Fiat's fascinating Centro Historico in Turin. The collections presented in this book are regularly open to the general public.

The craftsmanship involved in the restoration of antique automobiles has reached new levels of excellence, as new technology and traditional hand-labor combine to recreate the motor cars of the past. Many of the collections have their own restoration facilities and employ a crew to restore and maintain the cars. The Briggs Cunningham Collection in California is renowned for its superbly maintained cars which are regularly driven. Restoration work has become a true science and some contend it has gone beyond its intended limits by 'over-restoring' cars or presenting an auto in better than new condition.

Finally, let us not forget that automobiles are dynamic objects, designed for locomotion, not for pedestals. Ideally every museum should take at least one vehicle from every period represented and put it in a condition in which it can be run on the road. We specifically asked the museums we approached how many runners they have, and the trend in this direction is very encouraging.

Note on exhibit listings

Holdings in any collection are likely to change from time to time depending on the acquisition policy of the museum or owner. The lists published in this book are therefore subject to change but are included in order to give at least a general guide to the scope of the collections as they were in early 1986.

Australia

BIRDWOOD MILL NATIONAL MOTOR MUSEUM

Birdwood, South Australia 5234. Telephone: (085)-685-006.
Location: In the small town of Birdwood 33 miles (53 km) north of Adelaide.

This collection, now established as the Australian National Motor Museum, was started in 1964 by Jack Kaines who bought an empty flour mill initially to house his collection of motor cycles. The next year he and his friend Len Vigar opened the mill as a motor museum. This was the era of a surge of interest in old cars in Australia and the original building quickly filled up with cars and motor cycles. A separate building had to be erected to house the original Jack Kaines motor cycle collection and make room for the new influx.

In the ensuing years there were changes of ownership and it was feared that the collections would be split up and sent to other states or perhaps overseas. In 1976, therefore, the South Australian government stepped in and bought what had become the most important vehicle collection in Australia and the buildings housing it. A year later the new main display pavilion was opened.

In the first place the policy of the museum was to encourage private collectors to loan items for display. Many prominent collectors became involved, notably the Rainsford family, whose collection, started by Eric Rainsford in 1952, formed the backbone of the museum. To a great extent it is thanks to these individuals that the display is of such high quality.

The automobile played an essential role in the opening up of Australia, just as it had in the USA; for most of the century the country has been second only to America in the density of car ownership. Thus the policy of the museum is to display vehicles of Australian origin or makes which have played a part in the development of the country, and the range of exhibits depicts the pioneering spirit which has helped create modern Australia.

This museum also shows how many historic vehicles have been preserved by the benevolently dry climate in Australia. There is no need to salt roads against frost and vehicles suffer corrosion only if they are run on the beach or parked close to the sea. For this reason some of the exhibits at Birdwood are in original condition after more than 60 years except for a fresh coat of paint and perhaps larger section tires to cope with rough roads in the outback.

Items which catch the eye are the Shearer steam car, the third car to be built in Australia, and the 1908 Talbot 25 tourer. The latter, driven by Dutton and Aunger, was the first vehicle to travel from Adelaide to Darwin in 1908 and is being restored in readiness for a repeat trip in the year 2008. From the same period also comes a rare-for-Australia limousine body on a 1912 40/50 Rolls-Royce Ghost chassis and a brace of delightful Edwardian Daimlers dating from 1910, one a landaulet and the other a nice double tonneau. Both are in almost original condition. Yet another worthy British import is 'Sundowner', the 14/40 Bean in which Francis Birtles made the pioneering drive from London to Australia in 1925.

At the turn of the century motoring conditions in Australia were very much the same as in the USA and large numbers of Fords, Dodges, Chryslers and other less well known makes were imported because of their suitability for the terrain. There are excellent examples of these and of the older breed of British sports cars, notably pre-GM Vauxhalls, which gave yeoman service before being discarded. Maybe this predilection for Vauxhalls laid the foundation for the GM-Holden operation in southern Australia where Holdens were leading coachbuilders before being taken over by GM and turned into a manufacturing plant. Very properly the first, one-millionth and two-millionth Holdens are in the collection.

Jack Brabham's Australian designed Brabham-Repco is unique in having won the driver both the World Drivers' Championship and the Manufacturers' Championship in 1966

Birdwood is in Holden territory and holds one of the biggest collections of this GM controlled marque. Here is the first production Holden in a suitable setting

This brings home the fact that Birdwood is not a repository for golden oldies; there are several modern racing cars, including Jack Brabham's Brabham-Repco BT19, which was the first car bearing its driver's name to win a World Championship. Many well-loved classics which will become historic in their turn, like the Morris Minor, have not been forgotten. The 175 vehicles here help to make Birdwood one of the world's best-balanced collections.

Below left: **Birdwood's 1914 Dixi R12 is the sole survivor of this model from the Eisenach factory which eventually made the first BMW cars**

Below: **Based on a horse-buggy, the steam-powered 1899 Shearer is the oldest running vehicle in Australia**

Above: **This British Talbot 25 hp was the first car to cross Australia from south to north, in 1908. In England the same model created a world first when it put 100 miles into the hour**

Alvis
Saracen personnel carrier (outside) (1954)

American-La France
fire ladder (1943)

Associated Daimler
breakdown lorry (1926)

Aston Martin
1½-liter long wheelbase tourer (1934)
1½-liter short wheelbase tourer (1933)

Austin
Lancer Mk II (in store) (1960)
A30 saloon (1956)
1800 rally car (1968)
A50 saloon (1955)
Sheerline limousine (1951)
A40 saloon (1950)
Seven doctor's coupe (1936)
Seven single-seat special (1930)
Seven Chummy tourer (1929)

Aveling & Porter
steam roller (outside) (1920)

Bean
'The Sundowner' (1926)

Bedford
Krospel mobile store (in store) (1951)
30 cwt truck (in store) (1937)

Bentley
R-Type (1954)
4½-liter tourer (1930)
6½-liter tourer (1929)

Bristol
401 saloon (1949)

BSA
13.9 hp tourer (1914)

Buick
sedan (1939)

Cadillac
unspecified (1965)

Caravan
(1939)

Carlton
single-cylinder tonneau (1903)

Chevrolet
Six Holden sedan (1931)
tourer (1927)
Superior tourer (1925)
490 tourer (1919)

Chic
prototype chassis (1924)

Chrysler
Valiant hardtop (1970)
Valiant Series B (1962)
Floating Power sedan (1933)

Citroën
light-15 saloon (1957)
C3 Cloverleaf (1926)

Clément-Bayard
4-cylinder 2-seat tourer (1913)

Cooper-Bristol
Formula 2 racer (1953)

Crestmobile
air-cooled (1902)

Daimler
2½-liter Barker drophead (1949)
15.9 hp double phaeton (1910)

Daimler (UK)
Ferret scout car (1952)
Dingo scout car (1938)

De Dion Bouton
15/20 double phaeton (1906)
Model K runabout (1903)

Dennis
fire engine (1927)

Dixi
18 hp tourer (1914)

Dodge
Phoenix (in store) (1964)
Kingsway (in store) (1956)
hearse (1919)
4-cylinder tourer (1916)

Elfin
MR9 racer (1982)
Mono 600 (1964)

Erskine
roadster (in store) (1927)

Fiat
500 station sedan (1966)
500 Topolino (in store) (1949)
130 (1977)
500 Topolino (1949)
501 tourer (1924)

Flinders
electric Mk II-Fiat 127 (in store) (1977)
electric Mk I (in store) (1970)

Ford
Model A sedan (Club Corner) (1930)
Model A roadster (Club Corner) (1928)
Model A coupe (Club Corner) (1928)
Model A tourer (Club Corner) (1928)
Consul saloon (in store) (1959)
Zephyr saloon (in store) (1954)
Thames panel van (in store) (1954)
Prefect saloon (in store) (1946)
Model T tourer (restoring) (1923)
Falcon (1960)
Jeep (1942)
V8 chassis only (1933)
Model T roadster (1923)
Model T tourer (1921)

Halladay
not specified (1912)

Healey
Elliott saloon (1949)

Holden
EK sedan (in store) (1961)
FC station sedan (in store) (1958)
Statesman Caprice (1984)
Commodore-Repco rally winner (1979)
dragster (1976)
Torana GTR-X (1970)
HK brougham (two-millionth car) (1968)
EH sedan (1964)
EJ saloon (millionth car) (1963)
48/215 (1949)
Number One car (1948)

Holt
Caterpillar ZH (outside) (1920)

HRG
Aerodynamic (in store) (1948)

Hudson
Super-Six 7-seat phaeton (restoring) (1925)

Humber
saloon (1927)
not specified (1926)
7½ hp 2-seater (1909)

HWM
Jaguar-engined single-seater (1952)

International
D2 30 cwt truck (in store) (1938)

International Harvester
Buggy (1910)

Jaguar
E-Type coupe (1966)
XK 120 (1948)

Jensen
FF 4-wheel drive coupe (1969)

Karrier
street sweeper (1930)

Lancia
Aurelia 2500GT coupe (1956)
7th series Lambda (1927)

Leyland
Mini saloon (1978)
Force 7V mock-up (1977)
Force 7V (1977)

Locomobile
steam car (1900)

Mazda
3-wheel pick-up (1960)

Merryweather
fire engine (in store) (1923)

Messerschmitt
3-wheel cabin scooter (1958)

Métallurgique
(1910)

MG
TC 2-seater (in store) (1947)
MGA 2-seat roadster (1960)
ZA saloon (1955)
TF 2-seat sports (1955)
TD 2-seat sports (1952)
YT-Type tourer (1950)
SA saloon (1936)

Morgan
JAP-engined 3-wheeler (1933)

Morris
Mini-Moke rally car (1968)
Minor 1000 saloon (1955)
Minor tourer (1949)
Series E saloon (1948)
Eight tourer (1937)

McDonald
Diesel roller (outside) (1962)

Nash
Ambassador Eight (1934)

Oldsmobile
curved dash (1903)

Overland
Model 79 tourer (1917)

Packard
4th series Single-six tourer (1927)
Six sedan (1927)

Pelladini
Steam-sports (1976)

Peugeot
203 saloon (1952)
Type 9 chassis No. 724 (1897)

Pierce-Arrow
Club brougham (1933)

Porsche
356B coupe (1960)

Renault
750 rear-engine (in store) (1951)
12 hp tonneau (1910)

Riley
Kestrel saloon (1936)

Renault
12 hp tonneau (1913)

Rolls-Royce
Silver Cloud III cabriolet (1962)
Phantom III limousine (1938)
Twenty tourer (1926)
40/50 Ghost sedanca (1923)
40/50 Ghost open-drive limousine (1912)
40/50 Ghost tourer (1912)

Rover
chassis (in store) (1909)
P4 saloon (1950)
Ten roadster (1932)
8 hp runabout (1907)

SS
Airline saloon (1934)

Shearer
steam carriage (1899)

Sigma
Turbo (1979)

Skoda
440 (in store) (1961)

Standard
Ten saloon (in store) (1957)
Phase 3 Vanguard (1957)

Studebaker
tourer (in store) (1923)

Summit
Acme suspension tourer (1924)

Sunbeam
16/40 tourer (1923)

Talbot (GB)
25 hp Adelaide-Darwin overland (1908)

Toyota
2000GT (1969)

Triumph
Vanguard Spacemaster (in store) (1954)

Vanden Plas
Princess R saloon (1965)

Vauxhall
14/40 saloon (1925)
23/60 tourer (1923)
30/98 E-Type tourer (1923)
A-Type tourer (1912)

Volkswagen
Beetle saloon (1956)

Wichita
truck (Berliet radiator) (1923)

Willys-Overland
sedan (1939)

Wolseley
limousine (1936)

Zeta
500 sports (1965)
324 cc saloon (1965)
saloon (1963)

GILLTRAPS AUTO MUSEUM

Box 128, Palm Beach, Queensland 4221. Telephone: (075)-53-1659.

Location: Dreamworld, Dreamland Parkway, Coomera, Queensland.

The well-styled Pritchard steam car in the Gilltraps collection is of great technical interest

This, one of the oldest of the antipodean museums, had its beginnings in Rotorua, New Zealand, in 1954. The founder was an Irish immigrant, George E. Gilltraps, who opened a small museum next to his business premises to display a burgeoning collection of cars which he had started in 1949 with the acquisition of a Stanley Steamer. Subsequently, he made arrangements for a more permanent collection to be established on Australia's Gold Coast and this was opened in 1959.

One of the features of the Gilltraps Yesteryear World, as it was originally christened, was that all the cars were drivable and were in regular use giving rides to visitors. As George Gilltraps said, 'I was privileged to witness and take part in the transition from the use of animal power to mechanical for mankind's needs in transportation and agriculture. I felt that it would be a wonderful and worthwhile project to gather together and preserve for the enlightenment of future generations a living history of the changeover. Not in the cold, cemetery-like atmosphere of a city museum but as a living, breathing display. . .' George Gilltraps gave up his successful car and machinery business to further this aim.

The Gilltraps Auto Museum has a small collection of cars by Australian standards, about 30 in all. However, they are all meticulously restored and main-

tained in good running order; each is unique and of considerable historical interest. For example, the famous 12 hp Darracq 'Genevieve' has found her home in this place. This type was being built by the Portello factory of ALFA in Milan immediately before the Italian-designed ALFA went into production.

At the other end of the scale, but in direct line of descent from Alfa Romeo, is one of the very few Ferrari Squalos built to the original Formula 1 2½-liter unsupercharged specification. This not entirely successful model appeared immediately before the gift of the Lancia Formula 1 racing team to Ferrari gave his design office a shot in the arm.

One car which deserves to be seen in action is the prototype Pritchard steam car. Built in 1979, it has a well-styled modern saloon body around a very advanced steam generator and engine. The 1915 Detroit Electric 55 was built by Anderson Electric of Detroit and was in regular use by its original owner until after the Second World War.

Only one car is not fully restored: one half of a Model T Ford has been restored and the other half left 'as found' to illustrate the art of the restorer.

One of the most famous veteran cars of all time, the 1904 Darracq 'Genevieve', star of the film of that name, has found its home at the Gilltraps Museum

A 1918 example of the Australian Six. One of the most serious attempts to produce an Australian national car, it was in production from 1918 to 1930.

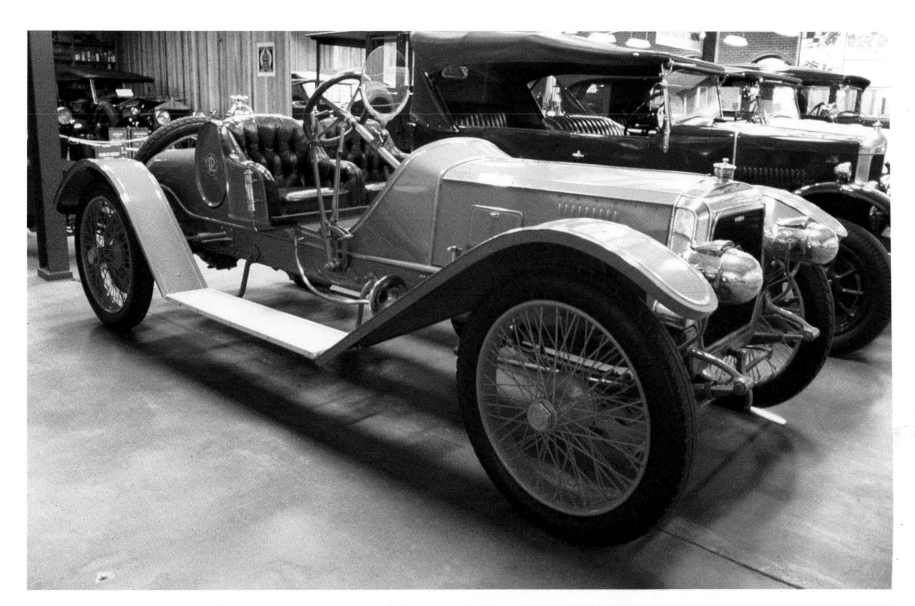

A sturdy raceabout from Panhard
Levassor made in 1910, when the
firm was already approaching its
twentieth year.

Albion
  Model T tourer (1923)
  12 hp tonneau (1902)
Auburn
  convertible phaeton (1936)
Austin
  1800 saloon (1968)
  Seven Chummy (1923)
Australian Six
  tourer (1918)
Cadillac
  Model K runabout (1907)
Chic
  chassis only (1923)

Clément-Bayard
  8/11 hp runabout (1908)
Darracq
  12 hp runabout (1904)
De Dion Bouton
  Model E tonneau (1900)
Detroit Electric
  Model 55 brougham (1915)
Ferrari
  Super Squalo Grand Prix (1955)
Ford
  1896 runabout replica (modern)
  Special single-seater (1939)
  Model N runabout (1906)

Franklin
  IOB tourer (1923)
Holden
  sedan (1948)
Morris
  Oxford De Luxe 2-seater (1914)
Panhard Levassor
  X12 raceabout (1910)
  Model A tonneau (1903)
Peugeot
  172 roadster (1923)
Pritchard
  prototype steamer sedan (1979)

Rolls-Royce
  40/50 hp Ghost dual-cowl tourer (1923)
Stanley
  SV252 fixed-head tourer (1925)
Summit
  chassis only (1925)
Triumph
  Super-Seven saloon (1927)
Twombley
  Tandem (1914)
Vulcan
  25 hp Roi des Belges (1908)
Volkswagen
  Beetle chassis (1954)

YORK MOTOR MUSEUM

Avon Terrace, York, Perth, Western Australia.

Location: York village lies about 40 miles (64 km) inland from Perth; the museum is situated in the main street.

York motor museum, founded by Peter Briggs, occupies a building in the town's main street and houses the founder's collection of approximately 150 vehicles. This is claimed to be the finest collection of sports and racing cars in Australia. All the vehicles are maintained in first class running order and a number of them take part in an annual event called the Castrol York Flying Fifty. Nominally this is a parade of cars but it tends to develop into a race.

There are a great many unrestored and historic vehicles in Australia and at the time of writing many are still coming into the museum for restoration. It should not be assumed that all the vehicles on the museum list are fully restored although the ones on display most definitely are.

Although the emphasis is on sporting types the museum can boast a number of historic vehicles like their 1 hp 1899 Renault and the 1910 8 hp Clément tourer, not to mention a delightful single-cylinder Cadillac double phaeton. York Museum also houses one of the rare Bedelia cyclecars decked out in non-vintage colors and a completely original 1914 40/50 hp Silver Ghost Rolls-Royce open-drive limousine — said to have been Claude Johnson's personal car. It is an admirable foil to a magnificent straight-eight Tipo 8 Isotta-Fraschini tourer.

The sporting slant to the collection is typified by a good selection of MGs, including the N Type MG Magnette which George Eyston drove in the 1934 TT, a Project 109 flat-16 cylinder 3-liter BRM, and, a long way from home, the old Indianapolis Offenhauser Dr Sabourin Special which raced in 1954 but failed to complete the course. One vehicle whose fame has reached as far as Europe is Charlie Dean's Maybach Special, considered by the pundits to be one of the best specials ever produced. Built in three different versions, the ultimate development is to be seen here.

The cars are displayed in three main halls and an external courtyard and the vehicles in each hall are related to a specific era in motoring history.

This 1923 Tipo 8 Isotta-Fraschini was the product of a company destined to become famous for its aviation engines. It is powered by the world's first production straight-eight engine

AC
Cobra sports roadster (1966)
12/24 2-seater with dickey (1924)
Alfa Romeo
2600 Berlina (1967)
RLS tourer 3rd series (1923)
Allard
J1 2-seater team car (1946)
Alta
1.5-liter supercharged GP single-seater (1952)
Alvis
TA21 Grey Lady drophead coupe (1954)
Amilcar
CGS boat-tail 2-seater (1925)
Amphicar
Argo all-terrain vehicle
Argyll
shooting brake (1912)
Aston Martin
DB6 Volante coupe (1967)
DB6 Volante convertible (1967)
1½-liter SV sports 2-seater (1923)
1½-liter long wheelbase tourer (1933)
Austin
Racer pedal car (1937)
Princess Vanden Plas landaulet (1953, 1955)
Seven Holden 2-seater (1925)
Austin-Healey
3000 Liège-Rome-Liège replica (1960)
Australian Six
5-seater tourer (one of four) (1919)
BRM
Formula 1 Project 83 (no engine) (1966)
Formula 1 Project 109 H16 (1967)
Bedelia
Tandem cyclecar (1914)
Bentley
4¼-liter Franay drophead (1936, 1937)
4¼-liter convertible (1937)
4½-liter supercharged (1930)
4½-liter sports (1927)
Bentley (Derby)
3½-liter saloon (1934)
BMW
Batmobile racing saloon
Brabham
BT33-2 Formula 1 (1970)
Bugatti
Type 52 Baby electric
Type 23 Brescia roadster (1923)
Cadillac
Eldorado Biarritz convertible (1958)
Model M victoria tourer (1906)

Carter Electric
3-wheeler (1938)
Chevrolet
tourer (1928)
Chrysler
New Yorker sedan (1948)
Model 50 display chassis (1925)
Clément
tonneau (1901)
Connaught
L.2 prototype sports racer (1948)
Cooper-Climax
Type 39 Bobtail 1½ liter sports (1951)
Cooper-Ford
Formula Junior single-seater
Cosworth
4 X 4 Formula 1 (no engine) (1969)
Crossley
Type 2 tourer (1921)
De Dion
tricycle with trailer (1898)
taxi-landaulet (1905)
opera coupe (1906)
Dennis
fire engine (1926)
Ferrari
195 Mille Miglia Berlinetta (1950)
250GT Lusso coupe (1962)
Ford-engine LM replica (1967)
Fiat
12/15 hp patent landaulet (1902)
500 Topolino coupe (1939)
FN
tourer (1912)
Ford
Model T roadster, Flood body (1923)
RS2600 Capri racer (1972)
Prefect utility (1951)
Model T boat-tail racer
Model T torpedo runabout (1910)
Frazer Nash
TT replica (1935)
Le Mans replica (1948)
Frazer Nash-BMW
328 sports roadster (1937)
Glas
Goggomobil mini-car (1956-69)
Go-Kart
rocket-powered
Hawker
V8 mid-engined special (1938, 1962)
Hispano-Suiza
Alfonso XIII roadster (1913)
H6B tourer (1926)

Holden
FJ ambulance (1955)
A9X Torana ex-Bob Morris (1977)
FX prototype (1953)
Repco.Formula Junior experimental (1953)
Holsman
gas buggy (1906)
Honda
S.800 sports (1965)
Horch
8-cylinder cabriolet (1931)
HRG
1½-liter sports 2-seater (1947)
International
charabanc (1912)
Invicta
1½-liter 121/45 tourer (1933?)
4½-liter sports 4-seater (1933)
Isotta-Fraschini
Tipo 8 tourer (1923)
Jaguar
12-cylinder E-Type roadster (1974)
D-type Le Mans (1954, 1957)
Lightweight E-Type roadster (c1964)
Lagonda
LG45 drophead coupe (1937)
Lanchester
40 hp 6-seat tourer (1927)
Lancia
Stratos rally car (1974)
Stratos rally car (1975)
Lambda tourer (1926)
Leyland
charabanc (1924)
Lola
Type 506 single-seat racer (1970)
Lotus
64 4-wheel drive Indianapolis (1969)
XI 1100 cc sports racing (1957)
March
Formula 1 ex-Jackie Stewart (1970)
Maserati
300S sports racer (1956)
Maybach Special
Mk 3 racing (1955)
Mercedes-Benz
300SL gullwing (1955)
Messerschmitt
3-wheel cabin scooter (1958-61)
MG
TC special sports 2-seater (1948)
J3 supercharged sports 2-seater (1934)
Mk IV 2-seater with dickey (1928)
MGA twin-cam 2-seater (1960)

NE TT-Type ex-GET Eyston (1934)
TC sports roadster (1947)
TC single-seat special (1949)
M-type 2-seater (1930)
Morgan
Plus-8 2-seat sports (1980)
Aero 3-wheeler
Morris
Minor 1000 convertible (1948)
Oxford sports 2-seater (1926)
Mini-Cooper 2-door saloon (1964)
Napier
N1 15 hp Colonial tourer (1912)
Offenhauser
Indianapolis race car (1955)
Oldsmobile
curved dash roadster (1902)
Peugeot
Model 9 vis-à-vis (1896)
Model BB Bébé (1911)
Phanomobil
3-wheeler (1925)
Pontiac
Silver Streak sedan (1939)
Porsche
911SC cabriolet (1983)
Renault
1½ hp runabout, tiller steering (1898-9)
Riley
Brooklands model (1927)
Rolls-Royce
40/50 hp Barker landaulet (1914)
40/50 hp Alpine Eagle replica (1914)
Twenty tourer (1923)
Rugby
tourer (1925)
SS
Jaguar 100 2-seater (1938)
Jaguar 100 sports 2-seater (1937-9)
Toyota
S800 2-seat coupe (1967)
GT2000 coupe (1967)
Volkswagen
Beetle (1946)
Williams
Saudia Formula 1 FW07 (1979)
Wolseley
8-cylinder tourer (1928)
Worth
dogcart (1898)

Alan Jones drove this Williams FW07, serial 04, to four victories in his 1980 World Championship year

Right: **The first Aston Martin cars were strictly speaking Bamford and Martins. York museum's side-valve engined racing two-seater, built in 1923, is the 28th car**

Left: **World speed record holder George Eyston drove this NE-type MG Magnette in the 1934 Tourist Trophy Race (*Above*). Later it scored many successes in Australia and is now in York Motor Museum**

Austria

VIENNA MUSEUM OF INDUSTRY AND TRADE

Technisches Museum für Industrie und Gewerbe in Wien, Mariahilfer-strasse 212, 1140 Wien. Telephone: 89-31-08/9 or 83-36-18.

Location: In central Vienna. Mariahilfer-strasse runs outwards from the junction of the Burgring and the Opernring. Bus route 4, or tram routes 52 and 58, take you to the museum.

A rare unmodified 1920
Austro-Daimler 6/25 hp sporting
tourer

This is one of the older European technical museums, having been founded in 1918. In common with the Musée National des Techniques in Paris and the Deutsches Museum in Munich, the Vienna establishment is all-embracing in its coverage. However, particular emphasis is put on the automobile section and pains have been taken to acquire as many Austrian vehicles as possible. So, although the museum possesses a mere 48 vehicles, 24 of these are of Austrian origin and for this reason the collection should not be missed.

Undoubtedly the *pièce de résistance* here is the controversial Markus-Wagen which, with its four-stroke engine, mechanically operated valves and electric ignition, was hidden by its owners during the Nazi occupation in case the new rulers might destroy it as evidence of Austrian inventive flair. Siegfried Markus was a dilettante Austrian scientist; of the four vehicles he built only the museum car survives. Originally thought to have been built in 1874 it is interesting to see that it now bears an 1888 date tag. In the same collection is one of the inevitable 1885 Benz Patent Motorwagen replicas to provide a comparison.

There are several very early Austrian cars in this inventory. Among them is the small car (Kleinwagen) built in 1898 by the brothers Gräf which is notable for its use of front-wheel drive. Another eminent Austrian was the tinsmith's son Ferdinand Porsche whose first job with the Lohner engineering works in 1900 resulted in the Lohner-Porsche electric car with motors mounted in the hubs of the wheels. An example of this car can be seen in the museum along with a 1901 Lohner-Porsche petrol-electric car, an experimental vehicle of the same type built by the designer in 1922, a 1920 Austro-Daimler tourer and a 1925 Austro-Daimler ADR chassis, all from the drawing board of the young genius from Bohemia. Another brilliant designer from that part of Austria which became Czechoslovakia was Hans Ledwinka whose Tatra 57 can be seen here. Also on display are products of Steyr, Gräf und Stift and the rare Perl-Suprema.

Above: **The 1909 Lohner-Porsche Elektromobil was one of Ferdinand Porsche's earliest creations. The electric motors were built into the front wheel hubs**

Top: **The controversial 1888 Markus: at one time it was thought to have been built in 1873, which would have made it the first practical automobile in the world**

Akkuwagen
chassis only (1899)
Austro-Daimler
ADR show chassis (1925)
6/25 hp tourer (1920)
Austro-Fiat
Type C1 chassis (1908)
Benz
Viktoria (1893)
Comfortable 2-seater velo (1893)
chassis only (1890)
Dreirad 3-wheeler (1885, 1886)
Daimler (Canstatt)
Reimenwagen (1894)
Ditmar & Urban
tourer (1914)
Egger-Lohner
Elektromobil chassis (1899)
ESA
sporting cyclecar (1917)

Fiat
522 27CV saloon (1931)
Fross Büssing
subsidy lorry (1907, 1918)
Gebrüder Gräf
front-wheel drive Kleinwagen (1898)
Gräf und Stift
VK II (1925)
Duke of Cumberland's car (1911)
Hispano-Suiza
Alfonso XIII (1913)
Knoller-Friedmann
steam car (1904)
Lloyd
400 saloon (1955)
Locomobile
steam runabout (1900)
Lohner-Porsche
petrol-electric town car (1906-10)
petrol-electric car (1901-5)

Lux
runabout (1906?)
Markus
carriage, 4-stroke engine (1888)
Mercedes-Benz
2½-liter W196 Grand Prix (1954, 1955)
170H rear-engine (1936)
Nesselsdorfer
runabout (1899)
NSU-Fiat
500 Topolino (1940)
Perl-Suprema
runabout (1925)
Phanomobil
Cyclonette 3-wheeler (1912)
Piccolo
runabout (1903)
Porsche
experimental petrol-electric (1922)

Serpollet
steam car (1897)
Steyr
1500A chassis (1945)
55 Baby coupe (1938)
220 coupe 2260 cc (1938)
Type V chassis only (1924)
Tatra
Type 52 chassis (1927)
Voisin
C7 (1925)
Volkswagen
Type 11 de luxe saloon (1962)
Beetle cutaway chassis (1960)

The 1938 Steyr 220 Cabriolet in the Viennese collection is typical of the advanced designs being produced by Central European designers in the 1930s

Belgium

PROVINCIAL AUTOMOBILE MUSEUM

Provinciaal Automobilmuseum, Keltcherhoef, 3530 Houthalen. Telephone: 011-38-02-11.

Location: Off Highway E314 at exit 30 taking the Hasselt-Eindhoven road into Houthalen. In the town head for Zwatberg and the museum is at a crossroads 5 km (3 miles) out of town. By train to Ghent and then by bus (route 31).

In 1944 Ghislain Mahy, a young car dealer, bought an old FN motor cycle and the wreck of a Ford Model T for the princely sum of 150 Belgian francs – $8 at the time. The pleasure he gained from restoring them provided the inspiration for a collection which now numbers 850 vehicles, arguably the largest in Europe and certainly one of the biggest in the world. These cars are stored in Ghent in an old permanent circus building which is not open to the public. A changing selection of 250 of the best of them is sent regularly to Houthalen where an automobile museum was set up by the Limburg provincial government in 1970. The most important cars are permanently at Houthalen.

Although it can boast the world's largest Ford assembly plant Belgium now has no indigenous make. In earlier times, it had a thriving industry producing such illustrious marques as Minerva, Excelsior, FN, Nagant, Vivinus and many others. Examples of all except Excelsior can be found in the Houthalen catalog. It is especially pleasing to find a really representative collection of Minervas – at one time the Hon. Charles Rolls was the British concessionaire – including the limousine used by Albert, King of the Belgians shortly before World War I. There are nine different FN models spanning 1901 to 1934 but sadly only a single Vivinus (from 1900).

Apart from those already mentioned the Mahy Collection is especially proud of its 1906 Fondu limousine and the Alfa Romeo RLSS Gran Premio model, listed here as the Targa Florio from which it was derived, which is said to be the very car with which Willy Cleer, a German Alfa Romeo agent, took third place in the Formule Libre German Grand Prix at Avus in 1926.

Another sporting oldy is a Delahaye which took part in the 1912 Monte Carlo Rally, while for sheer elegance the Delage D8/160 with a cabriolet body by d'Itieren of Brussels would be hard to match. The cars are attractively displayed in a well-lit modern building and are grouped by country.

Houthalen has an outstanding selection of Delahayes of all ages: this is a sporting 1938 Type 135M with Chapron coachwork

Above: **A 1924 3/4½-liter Bentley in a museum is a rarity. This was a popular conversion in Britain in the immediate pre-1939 years**

Right: **A 1923 Nagant type 1000C in a sylvan setting in the forests surrounding the Houthalen Provincial Museum**

A World War II Volkswagen Schwimmwagen in an appropriate setting

List represents only one sample public exhibition

Alfa Romeo
    6C/2500SS Pininfarina (1948)
    RLSS works Targa Florio (1923)
Alva
    Type C doctor's coupe (1913)
Austin
    Seven Swallow saloon (1931)
Automoto
    M3 quadricycle (1899)
Belga-Rise
    BR8 8-cylinder limousine (1934)
Bellanger
    Type A Series 1 (1920)
Benjamin
    Type R 7/22CV boat-tail (1925)
Bentley
    Mk VI Continental prototype (1948)
    Mk VI Vanden Plas saloon (1948)
    3/4½-liter Vanden Plas speed model (1928)
Benz
    16/40PS Karpatensieger (1915)
Black
    118 Stanhope surrey (1908)
Léon Bollée
    voiturette tricycle (1895)
Bugatti
    Type 44 tourer (1930)
    Type 23 Brescia 2-seater (1922)
Buick
    Model 41 sedan (1939)
    90L limited limousine (1938)
    8-cylinder sedan (1937)
    35/57 8-cylinder sedan (1935)
    90L Master 8-cylinder limousine (1932)
    Model 40 phaeton (1930)
    Master 6-cylinder 2-seater with dickey (1926)
    30 4-cylinder roadster (1913)

Cadillac
    Series 355D roadster luxe (1934)
    341 Fleetwood cabriolet (1928)
    Model 314 phaeton (1927)
    Model 57 Pershing car (1918)
    Model 57 V8 tourer (1917, 1918)
    Model K 10 hp runabout (1906)
Chenard-Walcker
    Type T2 (1913)
Chevrolet
    Model 36 town sedan (1936)
    34-5559 sport sedan (1934)
    Confederate de luxe (1932)
    'Independence' ice cream (1931)
    Superior 2-door sedan (1925)
    Superior roadster (1925)
    490 tourer (1923)
Chrysler
    Airstream roadster (1935)
    Model 70 roadster (1925)
    Model 70 tourer (1924)
Citroën
    Type 7A Traction Avant (1934)
    C3 Cloverleaf (1925)
    C2 Matthijs Cloverleaf (1925)
    C2 tourer (1924)
    B2 Luxe 10CV (1923)
Clément-Bayard
    4 M 5 roadster (1913)
    AC 2 Vter double phaeton (1905)
Cord
    Model 812 Beverley sedan (1937)
    Model 812 phaeton (1937)
Cottereau
    10/12CV tonneau (1904)
Luc Court
    14CV 4-cylinder (1914)
Daimler (GB)
    30 hp 3/4 landaulet (1922)

Darmant
    DS 3-wheeler (1927)
Darracq
    TT 13 (1913)
    O12 double phaeton (1912)
    C11 torpedo (1911)
De Dion Bouton
    DX tourer (1913)
    Type DX tourer (1913)
    Type BG double phaeton (1908)
    Type AL Populaire (1906)
    Type L (1902)
    Type G No. 533 Tilbury (1901)
    M9 tricycle (1899)
    Type G vis-à-vis (1901)
Delage
    D8/120 d'Itieren drophead coupe (1939)
    D6/11 (1934)
    CO tourer (1920)
    Type T Series 7 2-seater (1910)
Delahaye
    135 Vanden Plas Belge (1948)
    135M Chapron Sport (1938)
    Type 58 Double Berline (1911)
    fire engine (1907)
Delaunay-Belleville
    Type V Belvalette limousine (1911)
Dennis
    fire engine (1929)
De Soto
    SD floating power (1933)
    Model K chassis (1928)
Dixi
    3/15 hp Austin Seven license (1928)
Dodge
    fire engine (Van Denil) (1937)
    Model A (1923)

Donnet-Zedel
    Type G 7CV de luxe (1926)
Essex
    Super Six sedan (1930)
    Six sedan (1929)
    Six tourer (1925)
Fiat
    8CV coupe (1952)
    500 Topolino (1936)
    514MM 2-seater Mille Miglia (1931)
    521 torpedo (1929)
    509A (1928)
    503 (1927)
    505A 6-seater torpedo (1924)
    501 (1924)
    510 original body (1921)
    Tipo 52B M2 charabanc (1916)

FN
    Prince Baudouin saloon (1934)
    1.400 S wooden body (1930)
    1.400 Weymann cabriolet (1930)
    1.300 Sport (1925)
    1.800 S (1924, 1925)
    2700 AT coupe de ville (1919)
    2.000A limousine (1908)
    3.5 hp 4-cylinder motor cycle (1905)
    4CV tonneau (1901)
Fondu
    Type CF Decunsul body (1906)
Ford
    Series 81A 3.6-liter V8 (1938)
    Series 74 2.2-liter V8 (1937)
    C 4-cylinder (1934)
    A Tudor de luxe sedan (1932)
    A town sedan (1930)
    Model T 4-speed speedster (1927)
    Model T cabin truck (1926)
    Model T coupe (1925)
    Model T tractor (1924)

Victor Decunsel of Brussels built the surprising pitch-pine limousine body for this 1906 Type CF Fondu. Interior fittings are in ivory

Model TT 1 ton truck (1924)
Model T Belgian-built (1924)
Model T Tudor sedan (1924)
Model T torpedo tourer (1922)
Model T tourer (1921)
Model T center-door sedan (1919)
Model T tourer (1918)
Model T (1911)
Model N (1906)

Franklin
Series 9B (1918)

Germain
Daimler-Belge 2-cylinder brake (1900)

Graham
75 Kellner-Venlo (1935)
819 Blue Streak aerodynamic (1933)
621 convertible with dickey (1929)

Grégoire
Type 134 15CV staff car (1921)
Type 132 10/14 hp 5-seater (1914)

Hansa
C 4-cylinder tourer (1914)

Hispano-Suiza
K6 Chapron saloon (1935)

Horch
931 4-seat cabriolet (1939)
850/51 landaulet (1936)
780 straight-eight (1932)

Hudson
Model J super-six tourer (1917)

Humber
11.4 hp tourer (1922)

Imperia
TA-8 Hotchkiss-engine (1948)
TA 9BS Adler-engine (1937)
8-25 sleeve-valve (1932)

Jaguar
XK120 roadster (1952)

Jensen
CV8 coupe (1950)

La Salle
Model 60 convertible sedan (1939)

Lacroix de Laville
Type 2 6CV 3-wheeler (1906)

Lancia
Astura Pininfarina drophead (1932)

Lanz
two-stroke ½-diesel tractor (1917)

Le Zèbre
A4 5CV 2-seater tourer (1911)

Maybach
SW38 LWB sports cabriolet (1937)
SW38 touring cabriolet (1936)

MB
1100 Cîme engine (c1929)

Mercedes
28/95 hp coupe de ville (1922)

Mercedes-Benz
170S cabriolet (1950)
170V saloon (1939)
300 Mannheim (1931)

Messerschmitt
KR200 3-wheel cabin scooter (1957)

Minerva
Type M4 10CV (1934)
SP Auto Traction fire engine (1934)
Type AR limousine (1932)
Type AL 8-cylinder Le Baron (1930)
Type AE faux-cabriolet (1929)
Type AG chassis only (1926)
Type AD touring cabriolet (1925)
Type OO Vanden Plas Tulip (1921)
Type KK coupe de ville (1914)
Type KK ambulance (1914)
Type X 26CV tourer (1911)
Type WT landaulet (1911)
2CV single-cylinder motor cycle (1903)

Nagant
Type 1000C torpedo (1923)
Type 7000J 18/24CV (1910)

NSU
K101 Kettenrad 3-track (1942)

Oldsmobile
Special 40 sedan (1940)
F36C sedan (1936)
F35C sedan (1935)
curved dash (1904)

Omega
Series A course (1929)

Opel
1.8 liter saloon (1931)
8/20 tourer (1911)

Packard
Clipper 8 limousine (1946)
Model 120C roadster (1937)
Model 115C (1937)
Model 1100 roadster (1934)
Model 1101 ambulance (1933)
Model 900 roadster (1932)
Model 645 sedan (1929)
Model 443 limousine (1928)

Panhard Levassor
X77 Dynamic 140 (1937)
X26 Driguet limousine (1915, 1922)
X26 limousine (1914)
U2 limousine (1907)

Paterson
Model 6-42 (1916)

Peugeot
Type VLV electric (1942)
201 saloon (1930)
VD2 V4 (1915)
Bébé BP1 runabout (1913)
Type 135 sedanca (1911)
Type 68 tonneau (1905)

Peugeot-Lion
Type VC1 tonneau (1909)
Type VA single-cylinder (1906)

Piedboeuf
M18 motor cycle (1903)

Pierron
Type 1, Ballot engine (1912)

Plymouth
Model U roadster (1930)
Model PF (1934)
Model U sedan (1929)

Pontiac
Six sedan (1939)
Six sedan (1938)

Prunel
Type A tonneau (1900)

Renault
Nervasport 8-cylinder sport (1932)
MT 6CV (1924)
I tourer (1921)
HG torpedo tourer (1920)
AX Phaetonia (1912)
AX (1909)
V1 racer replica (1908)
X1 Voiture de Maître limousine (1908)
Type C Tilbury runabout (1900)

Rochet-Schneider
Series 11.000 coupe chauffeur (1913)

Rolls-Royce
Phantom III saloon (1937)
20/25 Hooper landaulet (1934)
40/50 hp PI binder coupe (1926)
40/50 hp open-drive limousine (1920)
40/50 hp Silver Ghost (1911)

Rovin
D3 light car (1950)

Sizaire et Naudin
Grand Tourisme (1910)

Standard (GB)
9 hp Rhyl (1913)

Stanley
Model 735 Steamer (1921)

Star
Comet saloon (1930)

Studebaker
35 Model AA tourer (1913)

Suère
Type K 6CV chassis only (1925)

Sunbeam
Alpine 90 sports saloon (1954)

Vivinus
7CV (1900)

Voisin
C24 Carène (1933)
Type C Charmant saloon (1928)

Volkswagen
Schwimmwagen (1943)

Volugrafo
Bimbo mini-car (1946)

Wanderer
307/27 Glaser body (1939)
5/15PS Püppchen tandem-seat (1915)

Canada

CANADIAN AUTOMOTIVE MUSEUM

99 Simcoe Street, Oshawa, Ontario L1H 4G7. Telephone: 416-576-1222.

Location: In central Oshawa.

A 1908 model F McLaughlin. These Canadian cars were built using Buick running gear, and were noted for their fine finish

Occupying two floors of a purpose-built building this museum was founded in 1962 as a non-profit making automotive museum intended to demonstrate the influence of the motor car on the development of Canada. To put the vehicles into historical perspective they are displayed in contemporary settings which include such items as domestic washing machines and printing presses.

There are in effect two collections at Oshawa. One is the official one which contains many historic cars, the other is the property of the manager, J F Innes. These 50 or so vintage cars form a hire fleet for film work and are mentioned because some of them are put on show when not otherwise engaged.

Although the oldest car in the collection proper is an 1898 Fisher Electric, it is vehicles like the Orient Buckboard and the Redpath Messenger which truly reflect the progress of mechanical transport in Canada. The Orient is a fascinating American pioneer four-wheeler with a wooden plank chassis. There was no springing in the normal sense, road shocks being absorbed by the natural springiness of the wooden frame. The Redpath was a more conventional, for the time, single-cylinder runabout powered by an 1170 cc engine. Built in Toronto, it ceased production in 1907 when the factory was burned down.

The museum's 1914 Galt is another fascinating Canadian car: Galt made petrol cars until 1913 when the company failed and was immediately revived to manufacture petrol-electric vehicles. It is not clear whether the Oshawa Galt is one of these. However we can be certain about the two Canadian Brooks steam cars. One of them, a 1924 model, is complete with its original fabric body and the other, from 1926, is in chassis form. Steamers dating from the mid-1920s are always a fascinating study because of the ingenuity used to make steam-raising and driving the car as quick and easy as starting and driving a petrol car. The International Auto Wagon, built by the company which eventually became the International Harvester Company, is yet another Canadian pioneer make. These cars, equipped with high wheels to cope with rough colonial roads, were also marketed with an IHC label; one of them is to be found in New Zealand in the Len Southward museum.

A fine example of a 1929 Packard Eight. This marque reigned supreme in the American luxury market in the 1920s

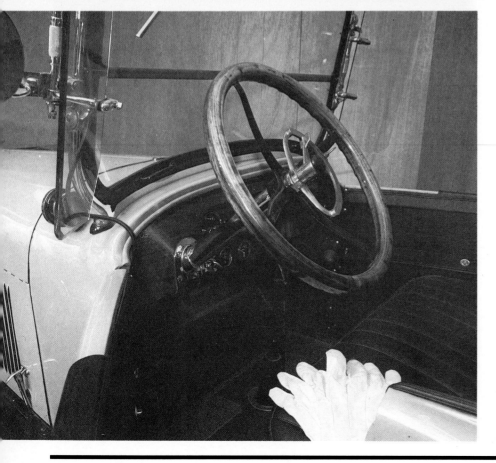

Top left: **Canadian-built Buicks retained the McLaughlin name on a Buick radiator**

Top right: **Gray-Dort cars, like this 1921 tourer, were Canadian-built American Dorts, using four-cylinder Lycoming engines**

Left: **Buick took over McLaughlin in 1918 to produce cars like this 1922 McLaughlin-Buick tourer**

AC
2-seat tourer (1924)
Allard
cabriolet (1949)
Amphicar
convertible amphibian (1965)
Auburn
phaeton (1936)
Austin
Princess limousine (1960)
Brooks
steam car chassis (1926)
steam car chassis (1924)
Cadillac
Model 30 speedster (1911)
single-cylinder runabout (1903)
Carter Car
tourer (1911)
Chevrolet
Corvette (1954)
truck (1931)
International Six tourer (1929)
sedan 'tornado victim' (1926)
sedan (1926)
tourer (1924)
Snowmobile (1918)
tourer (1915)
Crossley
convertible (1947)

Dodge
sedan (1950)
sedan (1938)
tourer (1924)
coupe (1918)
Durant
sedan (1928)
Fisher
electric runabout (1898)
Ford
Mustang (1965)
Model T coupe (1924)
Model TT oil tanker (1918)
Model T tourer (1915)
Model T roadster (1929)
Francis-Barnett
2-stroke motor cycle (1931)
Frontenac
unrestored coupe (1932)
Galt
Canada Tourist (1914)
Gardner (USA)
phaeton (1931)
GM
X-car body only (1980)
Gray-Dort
tourer (1921)
Harley-Davidson
scooter (1960)

Hudson
Super-Six sedan (1928)
International Harvester
Auto Wagon (1911)
Marquette
unrestored sedan (1929)
Maxwell
roadster (1915)
Meteor
Tudor (1949)
McLaughlin
tourer (1922)
tourer (1918)
tourer (1912)
tourer (1908)
Morris
Oxford 2-seater (1926)
Oakland
sedan (1929)
Orient
buckboard (1902)
Overland
coach (1925)
Plymouth
K car (1981)
Pontiac
sedan (1926)
Rauch & Lang
electric coupe (1917)

Redpath
Messenger (1903)
Reo
pick-up truck (1937)
chassis only (1908)
Rolls-Royce
saloon, model unspecified (1927)
Singer
roadster (1934)
Star
saloon (1927)
Talbot (UK)
roadster (1936)
Willys
Whippet coupe (1926)
Wolseley
tourer (1912)

Innes Collection of Motion Picture Cars

Buick
Riviera 2-door (1978)
Wildcat 2-door hardtop (1962)
Cadillac
hearse (1949)
2-door de ville (1979)
4-door de ville (1977)
2-door sedan (1974)
hearse (1965)
4-door hardtop (1960)
Case
steam roller (1917)
Checker
Blue Cab (1981)
Marathon (1978)
Yellow Cab (1978)
Stretch Cab (1976)
cab (1976)

Chevrolet
van-bodied 2-ton truck (1981)
2-door sedan (1974)
2-door hardtop (1967)
convertible (1965)
2-door sedan (1952)
sedan (1947)
tourer (1922)
Dodge
convertible (1969)
highway tractor and trailer (1967)
2-door hardtop (1957)
half-ton stake truck (1946)
Ford
police car (1978)
Mustang convertible (1968)
Bronco (1967)
2-door sedan (1947)
universal carriers (1942-4)
roadster (1929)

GMC
3-ton dump truck (1946)
Harley-Davidson
motor scooter (1960)
Hudson
sedan (1927)
Jeep
military (1942)
Leyland
single-deck London Transport bus
(1934)
Maxwell
roadster (1915)
Mercedes-Benz
220 saloon (1971)
Metz
Speedster (1914)
Speedster (1912)
Morris
Minor 2-door saloon (1957)

Oldsmobile
Regency 4-door (1977)
convertible (1964)
Paige
dump truck (1921)
Pontiac
ambulance (1969)
sedan (1947)
Rambler
wagon (1964)
Rolls-Royce
40/50 hp saloon (1927)
Victor
electric golf car (1958)
White
half-track (1944)
Willys-Knight
sleeve-valve sedan (1929)

NATIONAL MUSEUM OF SCIENCE AND TECHNOLOGY

2380 Lancaster Road, Ottawa, Ontario K1A OM8. Telephone: (613)-991-3083.

Location: In the city of Ottawa. Traveling west on Queensway (417), turn left at exit to St Laurent Boulevard: Lancaster Road is the second main intersection on the left.

This is a national museum dedicated to all the sciences with an automotive section that is impressive in size and quality. Ninety vehicles are on the inventory, many of which are unique and each of which has played some part in the development of motor transport in Canada. It is to be hoped that the present policy of displaying 12 vehicles at any one time will be changed.

Probably the museum's most treasured automobile, if it can be called that, is the steam carriage built by Seth Taylor in 1867. It is claimed to be the first self-propelled road vehicle in Canada, which had to wait another 36 years for its first production car, the diminutive Le Roy runabout. Another interesting vehicle here is a 1906/7 Comet, the first production car to be made in Montreal, Quebec. Assembled from Clément-Bayard main components, it went out of production after only a year or so. McLaughlin, whose 1911 Model 33 tourer is shown, lasted longer. As carriage builders they aimed to make an all-Canadian car, though it turned out they had to content themselves with Buick chassis fitted with their own beautifully finished bodies. In 1918 they were

taken over by General Motors and many McLaughlin-Buicks found their way to Britain because of preferential tariffs.

Also to be found in Ottawa are other fascinating Canadian originals which are almost unknown to European old car buffs, such as the Tudhope high-wheeler and the Gray-Dort. The former was made in buggy form until 1909 to combat the unmade roads in the Canadian outback. The latter, built in Chatham, Ontario and utilizing a Lycoming four-cylinder engine (not an aero engine!) is said to have been one of Canada's most successful makes and stayed in production from 1915 until 1925.

Present-day enthusiasts will know all about the Bricklin and Manic Canadian-built sports cars but how many are familiar with the Brooks fabric-bodied steam car of the mid-twenties or the fascinating Toronto-built Bartlett with air suspension and solid tires? The prototype Bartlett had retractable spikes which could be made to protrude through the tires and stick into the road to improve grip on icy roads.

Baker Electric built electric runabouts from 1899 until 1914. The batteries are housed under the bonnet of this sporty looking 1908 example

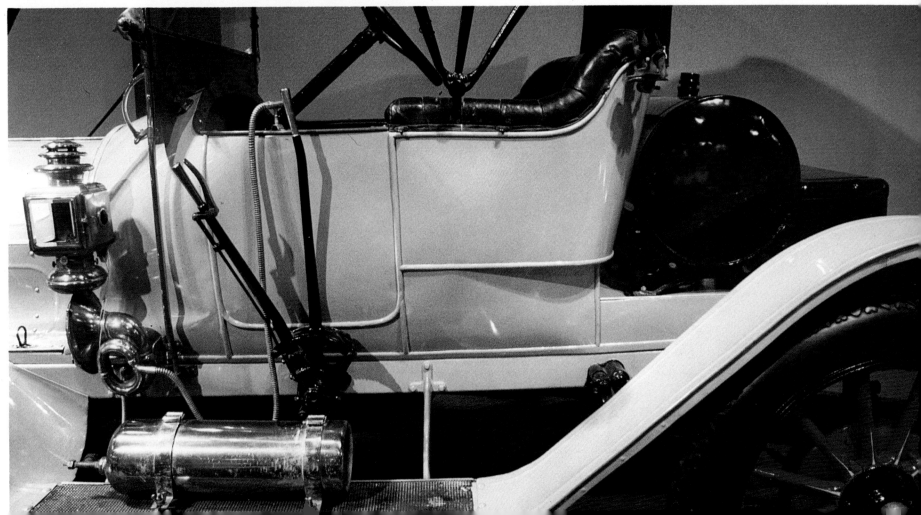

Left: **The 1916 Toronto-built Bartlett Le Roi tourer: air suspension and four-wheel brakes were two of its advanced features. About 125 were built between 1914 and 1917**

Below: **1910 Reo four-cylinder two-seater; Ransom E Olds who produced these attractive cars was the creator of the earlier curved-dash Oldsmobile**

Left: **Despite its venerable appearance the first Tudhope high wheeler was not made until 1906. Highwheelers were in demand because of their ability to traverse the soggy mud roads of the backwoods**

Below: **Brooks of Stratford, Ontario, built about 185 of these four-door, steam powered, fabric-bodied sedans between 1923 and 1926**

Austin
2-seater roadster (1931)
Baker Electric
2-seat phaeton (1908)
Bartlett
pneumatic suspension (1916)
Le Roi C tourer (1916)
Bentley
R-Type saloon (1952)
Bricklin
SV-1 2-seat sports (1975)
Brooks Steam Motors
4-door saloon (1926)
Buick
Riviera sedan (1972)
Le Sabre special sedan (1962)
Gentleman's roadster (1908)
Custom 31 4-door cabriolet (1931)
2-seat convertible (1931)
open runabout (1904)
Cadillac
Fleetwood Eldorado 2-door (1968)
2-door convertible (1947)
4-door tourer (1911)
Case
Six tourer (1921)
Chevrolet
Fleetmaster 10-27 coupe (1947)
Bel-Air Nomad brake (1956)

Chrysler
Imperial LeBaron sedan (1964)
Town and Country 2-seater (1948)
Comet
fabric body (1907)
Delahaye
Desmarais brake (1898)
Dodge
700 microwave locator (1961)
Durant
D40 sedan (1929)
Duryea
2-seater buggy (1908)
Edsel
958B Pacer hard-top (1958)
Falcon
Futura 2-door sedan (1963)
Ford
Model T doctor's coupe (1923)
Model T center-door sedan (1915)
Model T tourer (1926)
Model T tourer (1914)
Model A roadster (1928)
Model A runabout (1903)
stake-body truck (1925)
Gray-Dort
Model 17 tourer (1921)
International Harvester
2-seat wagon (1911)

Jaguar
Mk II saloon (1956)
Mk II saloon (1958)
Kaiser
K-542 Manhattan 2-door sedan (1954)
Le Roy
runabout (1902)
Lincoln
2-door Continental Mk III (1970)
4-door Continental convertible (1962)
Locomobile
2-seater steam carriage (1901)
Lotus
51 Formula Ford (1960)
Manic
GT PAI coupe (1970)
GT PAI coupe (1971)
Marathon Electric
C300 (1975)
Maxwell
roadster (1921)
McLaughlin-Buick
33 tourer (1911)
4-door convertible (1913)
MG
MGB roadster (1980)
Motorette
2-seat 3-wheeler (1911)

Nash
3-door hardtop (1932)
Overland
tourer (1925)
Packard
Super-8 coupe (1937)
sedan (1929)
Clipper sedan (1941)
4-door sedan (1938)
120 sedan (1936)
Peugeot-Lion
2-cylinder tonneau (1906)
Pierce-Arrow
2-door convertible (1934)
Plymouth
4-door demonstrator (1972)
Seth Taylor
steam carriage (1867)
Tudhope MacIntyre
13 hp 2-cylinder (1909)
Vespa
400 coupe (1959)
WS (Ward)
electric delivery van (1920)
Willys-Knight
tourer (1916)
Willys-Overland
90 sedan (1919)

Czechoslovakia

NATIONAL MUSEUM OF TECHNOLOGY

Kostelní 42, 1700 Praha 7. Telephone: (2)-76134.

Location: In the center of Prague, just north of the river.

In common with most European countries, Czechoslovakia has a museum for science and technology with a small but extremely select collection of automobiles. The Tatra collection is complementary to the 'mother' collection in Prague, for both are administered by the state.

In the days when Czechoslovakia was part of the Austro-Hungarian empire, it was a heavily industrialized province; many makes of car and some of the most eminent German automobile engineers originated here. Hans (or Jan) Ledwinka was the one who stayed at home. But expatriates included Ferdinand Porsche, Hans Nibel, (less well known than Porsche but chief engineer of Benz and then Mercedes-Benz) and Edmund Rumpler, who designed the first Nesselsdorfer car, a series of fighter aeroplanes and the first streamlined saloons.

Many of the cars in this collection are sole survivors. The 1899 'Wien' racer which Count von Liebig drove in the first motor race to be held in Vienna is one example; this car is propelled by one of the Benz engines which were the standard propulsive unit for Nesselsdorfer cars during the early period. However the museum's 1897 Nesselsdorfer should have the original Rumpler-designed engine: Ledwinka was responsible only for the gearbox.

Laurin & Klement was the other outstanding Czechoslovak manufacturer: they claim to have used the first high-tension magnetos on their motor cycles which were of the same high quality as their cars. This is evident in the charming 1906 V-twin engined, 8/9 hp two-seat tourer in the museum and in the 1912 and 1924 models bearing the Laurin and Klement badge on their radiators. Laurin and Klement were taken over by the Skoda armaments company in the mid-twenties and cars bearing that name are still built in the old works at Moravská Boreslav.

Praga was another well-known make which initially built a near-copy of the Renault A-type before branching off to produce their own designs, which included the delightful Praga Baby airplane. For sporting enthusiasts one exhibit not to be missed is the Wikov. The manufacturers of these overhead-camshaft sporting light cars believed that commercial success was inextricably linked with sporting wins and their cars took part in every kind of competition for which they were suitable, usually driven by Szejzcki. It is believed that the Wikov Sport in Prague has engine number 331 and is the sole survivor.

Partial list of exhibits

Benz
  Viktoria runabout (1893)
Bugatti
  Type 13 (1912)
Darracq
  voiturette (1902)
Laurin & Klement
  (1924)

Elka
  (1912)
  8/9 hp V-twin 2-seater (1906)
Mercedes-Benz
  W154 Grand Prix single-seater (1938)
Nesselsdorfer
  'Wien' Benz-engined racer (1899)
  voiturette (1897)

Praga
  runabout (1910)
Renault
  (1907)
Tatra
  (1924)
  (1930)

Velox
  10hp single-cylinder (1906)
Wikov
  OHC sports 2-seater (1935)

Below: **The Aero was pre-eminently** *the* **Czech small car. However in 1938 they did make one big model, this 50 hp four-cylinder, front-wheel-drive sporting roadster**

Right: **Bird's-eye view of a rear-engined Tatraplan alongside one of the Tatra front-engined cars, probably a T57**

Right: **Fire engines are great survivors. This is a Skoda Type 154 built in 1929**

Far right: **An RAF FW 35 limousine: motor sport enthusiast Baron Theodor von Liebig founded the Reichenberger Automobil Fabrik in 1907 to build cars of the highest quality**

TATRA TECHNICAL MUSEUM

742 21 Koprivnice, okres Nový Jičin. Telephone: 407-32.

Location: Koprivnice lies east of Prague, off main Brno-Kraków highway E1 close to Pribor and south of Morowská Ostrava. The nearest large towns are Hranice and Frydek-Mistek. The museum is a few minutes' walk from the Hotel Tatra between the main road and the railroad line in the town.

The main hall of the Tatra Technical Museum, stocked with a few of the products of this versatile company

A 1926 Tatra 12 display chassis showing one of Ledwinka's favorite air-cooled boxer motors, in this case a 1056 cc twin

Many of the vehicles testify to the virtuosity of Hans Ledwinka who, like several other talented automotive engineers, came from this part of Europe.

This unique collection sets out to depict the history of Tatra technical innovation going back to the turn of the century when the Nesselsdorfer Wagonfabrik company was formed. In 1923 the name of the old Nesselsdorfer AG was changed to Tatra. It is now a state-owned corporation.

The name of Hans Ledwinka is inextricably linked with Nesselsdorf and Tatra, and the exhibits in this museum form something of a monument to an engineer who is considered by many to be the equal of his better-known compatriot Ferdinand Porsche.

Among the 50 or so exhibits in the modern, airy exhibition hall are five Nesselsdorfer cars including a 1901 Type B wagonette, complete with surrey top. It is propelled by the first of Ledwinka's horizontally-opposed engines: a two-cylinder boxer motor, so called because its two-throw crank causes the pistons

Nesselsdorfer

Type T 4-cylinder ohc fire engine (1921)
Type K fire engine (1911)
Type L 4-cylinder water-cooled bus chassis (1906)
Type U 5.3-liter 6-cylinder ohc racer (1921)
Type T 4-cylinder ohc racer (1921)
Type T 4-cylinder ohc tourer (1922)
Type S 20/30 4-cylinder ohc (1909)
Wagonfabrik horse coach (1907)
Type B 2-cylinder boxer engine (1901)
26/30 chassis (1909)
Type T chassis (1922)

Tatra

605 Delfin racer
603X passenger car prototype (1967)
Dm 4 railcar (1931)
813 8X8 heavy gun-tractor (1966)
138 6X6 Lambarene expedition (1967)
128 V8 air-cooled 3-ton lorry (1955)
111 12-cylinder air-cooled 10-ton lorry (1937)
93 8-cylinder ohv army truck (1937)
prototype motor sledge
72 flat-4 ohv air-cooled command car (1937)
flat-4 air-cooled engine 1½-ton lorry (1935)
27 fire engine (1937)
26/30 air-cooled flat-4 command car (1929)
25 6-cylinder artillery tractor (1933)

603 B 5 flat-8 air-cooled rally car (1967)
600 Rolls-Royce air-cooled saloon (1949)
87 Rolls-Royce V8 air-cooled 5-seater (1945)
77a V8 air-cooled rear engined saloon (1935)
V 570 2-cylinder Volkswagen prototype (1933)
90 prototype 4-cylinder ohc limousine (1935)
70 fire engine (1932)
70c 6-cylinder ohc 6-seat limousine (1932)
75 sport cabriolet with overdrive (1936)
57 flat-4 air-cooled ohv saloon (1936)
52 flat-4 air-cooled 6-seat limousine (1937)
30 flat-4 air-cooled cabriolet (1931)

30 4-cylinder air-cooled 6-seat limousine (1927)
17 6-cylinder swing-axle limousine (1926)
12 fire brigade car (1927)
11 construction vehicle (1925)
11 tourer (1923)
809 aero engine (1936)
3-wheeler chassis
77 chassis (1934)
11 chassis (1923)
Type 10 chassis (1923)
607-2 racer
602 race chassis
607 race chassis
605 mid-engined racer

to 'punch' at each other. His bigger engines of the period, such as the S20/30 of 1909 (also on show), were fitted with overhead camshafts operating inclined valves in hemispherical combustion chambers well before their adoption elsewhere. In the inter-war period Ledwinka's chassis, especially the all-independent tubular ones, were usually judged to handle better than Porsche's Austro-Daimlers and it is interesting to see many of them here without bodywork. They are complemented by an outstanding array of engines from across the years.

The museum also owns the prophetic 1933 V570 Volkswagen prototype which, with its rear-mounted, twin-cylinder, air-cooled boxer engine, demonstrates the Tatra designer's originality, as does his rear-engined Type 77a V8 of 1935 which was the forerunner of the modern Tatra 603. Tatra were equally innovative in the more demanding field of heavy vehicle design and some of the cross-country military trucks and road vehicles in the collection have been listed for their still admirable design engineering.

Above: **Tatra 12 roadster of about 1930**

Right: **Impressive facade of the Tatra Museum at Koprivnice**

Denmark

ÅLHOLM AUTOMOBILE MUSEUM

Ålholm Automobil Museum og Slot, 4880 Nysted, Lolland. Telephone: (03)-87-10-15.

Location: Southern shore of the island of Lolland west of Nysted. Approach from Copenhagen via highway E4 to Orehoved, E64 to Nykøbing and 297 to Nysted.

A fine example of a Porsche-designed Mercedes Model S with cabriolet body built in 1925, the year before the merger with Benz

Ålholm Castle is one of Denmark's most historic buildings, with Viking associations before becoming a royal possession. In the sixteenth century it was the home of the dowager queens of Denmark and then passed into the hands of the Raben family early in the eighteenth century. The castle stands in the center of a large agricultural estate owned and operated by the present Baron Johan Raben-Levetzau and his wife.

The museum is a tribute to the energy of the Baron who started it in 1964 when he discovered the paternal 1911 Rolls-Royce 40/50 Silver Ghost which had

been walled up in a barn since a potential buyer had failed to make a good enough offer. Since that time the collection has grown to more than 200 exhibits covering 1886 to 1939. The vehicles are housed in four modern timber-framed exhibition halls.

Denmark is not a motor manufacturing nation so there are no strictures on the museum to record the national motor industry. Consequently, a catholic approach has been adopted, depicting the evolution of the motor car from its beginnings to the present. From the early days we find a modest selection of

primitive cars. The oldest, and one of the museum's proudest possessions, is an 1886 Daimler-engined horse carriage conversion. An 1897 de Dion tricycle, a 1900 de Dion Bouton and a 1900 Decauville keep it company among many well-restored vehicles from the first decade of the century.

One of the main attractions is the fine selection of early- and mid-1920s American cars. It would be difficult to find elsewhere in Europe examples of a 1903 Ford Model A, a Model N and a Model T under the same roof. There are no fewer than 15 Fords in this show ranging from that early Model A to the 1956 Thunderbird. There is also a minor profusion of Cadillacs ranging from the 1904 single-cylinder through to a 1957 Eldorado. Included in this array is one of the early V8s built in 1917 and a 1935 16-cylinder. And where else would one find a Locomobile 48, America's most luxurious car in 1914, a Packard 3-38, a 1922 Pierce-Arrow or a 1912 Hupmobile 32? At the other extreme is a rope-drive Holsman 1902 highwheeler built for the outback.

However, European cars outnumber American: Rolls-Royce, Mercedes (with and without the -Benz), Delaunay-Belleville, Brasier, Panhard are all represented. So are two examples of the desirable Hispano-Suiza 12-cylinder model, one of them with a most elegant light-blue two-door body, and an equally fascinating Maybach 12-cylinder roadster. There is also one of the huge 40 hp Renaults with a sedanca de ville body and a quite charming openbodied sleeve-valve Minerva from 1921.

While purists might contend that the rival Jysk Museum at Gjern has better restored and more authentic cars, one finds a wider selection at Ålholm. The same purists might object to the atypical bright colors adopted for some of the Ålholm cars and sometimes there is a lack of authenticity in detail. Nevertheless, this is a remarkable collection, especially for the enthusiast or for students of American design. The exhibits are arranged to highlight one marque at a time from the beginning of motoring to 1932. About 90 per cent of them are in running order.

Right: **An unusual 1930 Oakland landaulet poses in snow-covered Danish countryside**

Below: **Ålholm Castle houses some very rare early Americana like this 1910 Maxwell runabout**

AC
Sociable (1909)
Adler
995 cc Trumpf Junior (1937)
2.5 6-cylinder (1938)
Arnott-Lea Francis
1.8-liter (1954)
Auburn
3.4-liter 4-cylinder (1927)
Austin
Mk II Princess Vanden Plas (1963)
Seven (1929)
Seven Chummy (1926)
Ballot
2-liter ohc 2lt (1924)
Bentley
4¼ liter saloon (1936)
Benz
18/45 2 seater sport (1914)
8/20 chassis (1911)
Berliet
5.3-liter brake (1913)
Brasier
1.8-liter phaeton (1906)
BSA
V-twin 3-wheeler (1934)
Bugatti
T.57C cabriolet (1938)
T.46 Kellner saloon (1929)
T.40 tourer (1928)
Buick
8-cylinder 90L limousine (1939)
straight-8 Faux cabriolet (1931)
Six sedan (1928)
Cadillac
V8 Eldorado sedan (1957)
16-cylinder sedanca de ville (1935)
V8 4-door close-coupled saloon (1934)
V8 limousine (1928)
V8 (1917)
Model 30, 20/30 tourer (1913)
Model M single-cylinder phaeton (1906)
Chenard-Walcker
Type U 2-seater tonneau (1912)
Chevrolet
6 cylinder 2GKI cabriolet (1949)
Confederate 2-seater coupe (1932)
Universal coupe (1930)
International 6 sedan (1929)
4-cylinder National phaeton (1928)
4-cylinder National sedan (1928)
4-cylinder roadster (1925)
490 tourer (1916)
Chrysler
Royal C cabriolet (1938)
Citroën
Traction Avant cabriolet (1938)
C4 saloon (1926)
C3 Cloverleaf (1922)
Clément-Bayard
10/12 double tonneau (1912)
Cord
812 Berline (1935)

Daimler
15 saloon (1936)
35 hp landaulet (1930)
Daimler (Canstatt)
2-cylinder carriage conversion (1888)
De Dion Bouton
4-cylinder 1.8 liter saloon (1922)
S 4-cylinder double phaeton (1909)
Model K double tonneau (1903)
D voiturette vis-à-vis (1900)
tricycle (1897)
Decauville
2-cylinder 2-seater Tilbury (1900)
Delage
D6/70 coupe de ville (1937)
Delahaye
135 4-seater cabriolet (1947)
4-cylinder tonneau (1904)
Delaugère et Clayett
4-cylinder 20 hp 2-seater (1904)
Delaunay-Belleville
24 hp open landaulet (1909)
Detroit Electric
2-door coupe (1920)
DKW
Meisterklasse 700 cabriolet (1937)
2-stroke front-wheel drive roadster
(1931)
Dodge
Senior 6 2-seater coupe (1929)
Donnet-Zedel
6-cylinder 2½-liter limousine (1926)
Essex
Six 4-door sedan (1929)
Falcon-Knight
6-cylinder sleeve-valve sedan (1928)
Ferrari
250GTE coupe (1963)
Fiat
520 2-door saloon (1928)
501 saloon (1919)
Ford
Thunderbird (1956)
B Tudor (1932)
Model T tourer (1926)
Model T center-door (1921)
Model T tourer (1909)
Model N 2-seater (1906)
Edsel Corsair (1958)
A cabriolet (1931)
A roadster (1930)
A with gas producer (1930)
A 'Town Car' (1929)
A sedan (1929)
A Tudor sedan (1928)
Model A 2-seater (1903)
Franklin
LL 4-door sedan (1928)
LL tourer (1926)
4-cylinder 2-seater (1904)
Hannibal
USA special

Hanomag
Kommisbrot 2-seater (1926)
Heinkel
Bubblecar (1960)
Hispano-Suiza
Type 68 12-cylinder coupe (1933)
H6B Stelvio 4-seater (1932)
Holsman
2-cylinder belt-drive (1902)
Horch
3.5-liter V8 limousine (1940)
853 4-seater coupe (1937)
Hotchkiss
AM saloon (1923)
Hudson
4-cylinder tourer (1912)
Humber
Super Snipe saloon (1958)
16/60 Snipe limousine (1934)
Hupmobile
2-cylinder 2-seater (1912)
Invisible
V8 (1905)
Jaguar
XK120 open (1950)
Lacroix et Laville
single-cylinder tricycle (1898)
Lagonda
3-wheel forecar (1906)
Lancia
Flaminia coupe (1961)
Artena open tourer (1934)
7th series Lambda (1927)
La Salle
Model 328 Fisher sedan (1929)
Lea Francis
14/70 sports saloon (1948)
Lincoln
V8 limousiné (1925)
Locomobile
48 2-seater + 1 (1914)
Lorraine-Dietrich
15CV 6-cylinder tourer (1924)
Marquette
Six saloon (1930)
Maserati
3500GT (1961)
Maxwell
4-cylinder runabout (1910)
Maybach
Zeppelin DS8 cabriolet (1938)
Mercedes
Model K landaulet (1926)
15/70/100 supercharged 2-seater
(1925)
Mercedes-Benz
200 cabriolet (1935)
130H saloon (1934)
Nürnberg limousine (1928)
Messerschmitt
KR200 bubblecar (1955)
Metz
4-cylinder tourer (1915)

Minerva
32CV tourer (1921)
Morgan
3-wheeler (1914)
Overland
Whippet saloon (1927)
Packard
11C club coupe (1937)
straight-eight limousine (1929)
modified 526 5th series sedan (1928)
Twin-Six tourer (1918)
Single-Six tourer (1913)
Panhard Levassor
4-liter coupe de ville (1908)
Peugeot-Lion
69 single-cylinder (1906)
Pierce-Arrow
twin-valve Six roadster (1922)
Plymouth
Model PE cabriolet (1934)
Model PC sedan (1933)
Model PA sedan (1931)
Model U sedan (1931)
Pontiac
Silver Streak 8-cylinder sedan (1935)
Six sedan (1929)
Six sedan (1929)
Six 2-door sedan (1927)
Rambler
1-cylinder runabout (1902)
Renault
6-cylinder 3.2-liter tourer (1930)
6-cylinder 40CV coupe de ville (1925)
NN tourer (1922)
18 hp coupe de ville (1914)
1 hp tourer (1915)
AX doctor's coupe (1907)
A 2-cylinder (1902)
Rolls-Royce
Phantom III limousine (1935)
Phantom II coupe de ville (1929)
40/50 Ghost landaulet (1923)
40/50 Silver Ghost tourer (1911)
Twenty saloon (1921)
Rover
P4 75 saloon (1956)
Stanley
735 Steamer (tourer) (1917)
Studebaker
Commander 6 limousine (1928)
Speed six (1923)
Studebaker Erskine
6-cylinder sedan (1928)
Stutz
BB torpedo (1928)
Talbot-Darracq
10CV tourer (1924)
Vespa
3-wheel pick-up (1948)
Volkswagen
Schwimmwagen amphibian (1942)

France

HENRI MALARTRE MOTOR MUSEUM

Musée de l'Automobile Henri Malartre, Château de Roche-taillée-sur-Saône (Rhône). Telephone: 16-(7)-822-18-20.

Location: On N433 Neuville road to the north of Lyons approximately 3 miles (5 km) south of Neuville. From the north leave highway at Anse exit and follow signs to Neuville.

Many of the cars of the Malartre collection are displayed inside the Château. This 1904 Corre tonneau with Beaujeu sprung wheels was taken in pieces into this elegant second-floor salon

The Lyons-built 1895
Rochet-Schneider vis-à-vis which
inspired Henri Malartre to start
collecting old cars

The Château de Rochetaillée, which houses the Henri Malartre Museum, is worth visiting in its own right. Its setting, high on the left bank of the mighty Saône to the north of Lyons, makes it one of the most beautifully situated museums in France, if not Europe.

Dating back to feudal times as the castle of the Lords of Villars, it was given to the Chapter of Lyons by King Etienne II in 1151 and became the home of the papal counts of Lyons until the French Revolution, despite being burnt down by the Huguenots in 1562. The spiral main staircase, built in 1182, survives to this day.

Henri Malartre was a scrap merchant; fortunately a discerning one: he was bitten by the collecting bug as young as 19 when he fell in love with a pretty Rochet-Schneider vis-à-vis which had been sent for breaking up. Duly restored, it has taken part in many veteran runs and is one of the stars in the present collection. Fired with enthusiasm, Henri retained many ancient vehicles that came into his hands. They were put on

one side, restored and retained for his collection, now considered to be one of the best-chosen and most sympathetically restored assemblies of old cars in Europe.

Malartre gathered around him as many products of the once thriving motor industry of his home city as he could. As a consequence the castle and collection were acquired by the town of Lyons in 1972. This move gave it the permanence it deserved and allowed the managing body to expand the section devoted to the locally built cars and to improve the standard of maintenance of the vehicles. There is a well-equipped restoration shop staffed by craftsmen on site for this purpose.

A fascinating feature of this museum is that many of the exhibits are in rooms well above ground level which necessitated dismantling the cars and reassembling them.

As usual, it is difficult to single out cars for individual mention from the wealth of truly historic vehicles. The oldest is the Secretand, a one-off wooden vehicle built in 1891. Solely agricultural in concept this wooden three-wheeler, its single front wheel steered by a tiller, is fitted with iron-tired wooden cartwheels and is powered by a quite sophisticated steam engine with a flash boiler. It was built nearby and won the first prize at an industrial exhibition in 1891. Another fascinating old car is the 1894 Panhard Levassor tilbury two-seater with pillion seat of the type which won the Marseilles-Paris race in 1896.

One of the many marques for which Lyons was noted was Rochet, initially in association with Théophile Schneider before the latter went into business on his own. The oldest of these is a Rochet-Schneider of 1895 whose horizontally disposed single-cylinder engine was mounted in the rear and drove the axle by belts and chains. Despite this primitive transmission it was the first car ever to cross the towering Galibier Pass, on the French-Swiss border, in 1891.

Another Rochet-Schneider, the delightful 1908 coupe de ville, is an example of how automobile design progressed in a single decade. It is displayed in the building devoted to the products of the Lyons motor industry. Only one vehicle featured here was not made locally – Adolf Hitler's personal Mercedes parade car, which was too heavy to display elsewhere. A huge tourer mounted on a Mercedes-Benz 770K chassis, it is armoured below the waistline with 16 mm plate and the side screens, windscreen and rear window are made from 52 mm bullet-proof glass. The supercharged engine is specially tuned to haul this weight along at a reasonable speed.

Other fascinating exhibits are the three Sizaires: a Sizaire et Naudin, the advanced all-independently sprung Sizaire Frères and the lofty Sizaire-Berwick. There is a 1904 Aster-engined Corre tourer fitted with remarkable Beaujeu and Vicomtat sprung wheels, which allowed solid tires to be used. The car is appropriately displayed against a background of posters by the makers of the wheels threatening death and destruction to any car owner who is so unwise as to run on pneumatic tires.

The little Noël Benet, built in 1900, proves that there is nothing new under the sun; its single-cylinder engine is set in the front of the car across the frame and drives the front wheels through shafts with constant-velocity joints just like those of a Mini.

As the list shows, the 200 or more vehicles in this notable collection represent a cross-section of the French automobile industry in its heyday.

Quaint but effective: the 1913 Bedelia cyclecar had tandem seats, belt drive and the driver sitting in tandem behind the passenger. It was propelled by a twin-cylinder engine

Audibert et Lavorette
double phaeton (1898)
Bedelia
cyclecar sport (1913)
Noël Benet
4-wheel drive 2-seater (1900)
Berliet
double phaeton (1908)
Léon Bollée
Double Berline (1911)
Brasier
10CV (1908)
Bugatti
49 Gangloff coupe (1930)
Chenard-Walcker
Perfecta (1898)
Citroën
2CV prototype (1934)
5CV Cloverleaf (1922)
Clément-Bayard
2-seater (1913)
Cooper-Climax
4-cylinder Formula 1 (1960)
Corre Aster
tonneau (1904)
Cotterau
2-seat tilbury (1899)
Luc Court
2-seat racer (1901)
Darmant Morgan
Tricar (1918)
DB
Monomil (1954)

De Dion Bouton
doctor's coupe (1900)
6CV populaire (1902)
2-cylinder phaeton (1904)
Delage
D8 torpedo GS (1929)
Delahaye
148L parade car (1950)
Fiat
509S spyder (1926)
Ford
Model T (1910)
Gobron-Brillié
double phaeton (1903)
Gordini
F2 2-liter (1952)
2500 sport prototype (1954)
Hugot
basketwork 2-seater (1897)
Inter
3-wheeler (1954)
Isetta
Velam tricar (1955)
Lancia
Astura Pininfarina (1938)
Lepougeau
steam wagon (1896)
Le Zèbre
2-seat phaeton (1913)
Lorraine-Dietrich
15CV 3½-liter Le Mans (1925)
Lotus-Ford
Super Seven (1964)

McLaren-Ford
M7 Formula 1 (1968)
Maserati
GT coupe (1957)
Mercedes-Benz
300SL gullwing (1955)
770K Hitler's car (1939)
Messerschmitt
KR200 3-wheeler (1955)
Milde
electric 3-wheeler (1900)
Monotrace
single-track 2-seater (1926)
OSCA
V12 barqueta sport (1953)
Ours
3-cylinder double phaeton (1907)
Packard
Caribbean (1955)
Panhard Levassor
Panoramic (1936)
Major coupe (1937)
4-seat tonneau (1899)
4-seat brake (1894)
Peugeot
BB (1913)
double phaeton (1903)
doctor's coupe (1896)
Renault
Vivastella (1933)
AX Marne taxi (1914)
4CVA tonneau (1900)

Rochet Frères
vis-à-vis (1898)
Rochet-Schneider
vis-à-vis 4-seater (1898)
coupe de ville (1908)
vis-à-vis (1895)
Rolland Pilain
2-liter 8-cylinder GP (1923)
Rolls-Royce
25 coupe de ville (1934)
Théophile Schneider
12CV GS Le Mans (1925)
Scotte
steam bus (1892)
Secretand
steam cart (1890)
Sima Violet
Alcyon (1921)
Sizaire-Berwick
SD limousine (1927)
Sizaire et Naudin
12CV runabout (1908)
Sizaire Frères
11CV spyder (1924)
Super Tractavant
tricar (1957)
Talbot Lago
6-cylinder 4½-liter Formula 1 (1949)
Thieulin
racing voiturette (1908)
Voisin
14CV Carène (1932)

Local artisan M. Jules Secretand constructed his mainly wooden steam cart in 1890, and won first prize at the 1891 Industrial Exhibition at Bourg-en-Bresse.

NATIONAL AUTOMOBILE MUSEUM (SCHLUMPF)

Musée Nationale de l'Automobile, 192 avenue de Colmar, 68100 Mulhouse. Telephone: (89)-42-29-17.

Location: On the Colmar road (D20) out of Mulhouse, or from highway A36, following signs to Mulhouse Centre. There are signs to the museum at all the main intersections in Mulhouse.

Opposite: **This 1908 Rochet-Schneider 16CV coupe de ville at Henry Malartre Motor Museum is typical of the high quality cars produced by the Lyonnais manufacturer**

Below: **The classic Ferrari sports racer at 'The Schlumpf': the museum calls it a 500TRC but it looks like a TR57 Testa Rossa**

This massive collection is one of France's newest museums and yet is one of the largest and finest in the world. It will be a very long time before it is known as anything other than 'The Schlumpf' in motoring circles in recognition of the industry and excellent taste of the two men who brought together this outstanding collection of historic automobiles.

The brothers Hans and Fritz Schlumpf, born shortly after the turn of the century, were the sons of a wealthy Swiss textile magnate and made a huge fortune from share dealing and banking. They were so successful that in 1972 Fritz was the sixth-wealthiest man in France.

Fritz started collecting Bugattis in 1956. He was very soon joined by his brother. Their enthusiasm became so obsessive that they would buy whole collections of different makes for the sake of acquiring another Bugatti. One of their coups was to acquire the old Bugatti factory, with its collection of cars and prototypes, from Hispano-Suiza in 1963. A year later they bought the John Shakespeare Collection of 32 Bugattis.

Among the brothers' many assets was a textile factory in Malmerspach on the outskirts of Mulhouse

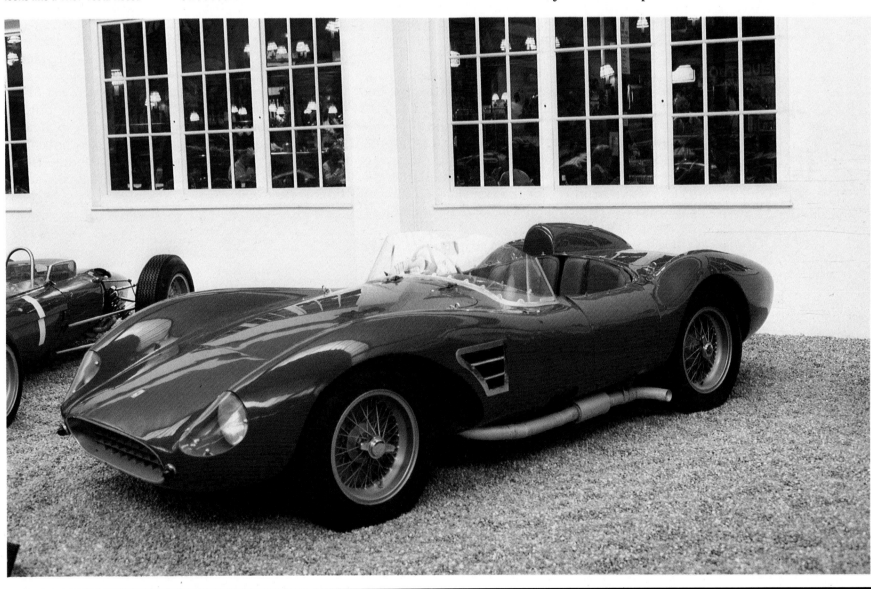

near the French-German border. Here they stored their collection in a huge disused weaving shed whose north-facing windows made it ideal for showing off the cars. The bareness of the great hall, some 24,000 square yards (20,000 square meters) of it, was relieved by mounting 900 ornate cast-iron lanterns, copies of those on the Pont Alexandre III in Paris, on the tops of the iron pillars supporting the roof.

Cheap imports from the Far East cut deep into the European textile industry and, despite financial support from the government, business at Malmerspach declined. The brothers went bankrupt and the workers, poorly paid and working in bad conditions, revolted. The Schlumpf brothers were briefly imprisoned and had to be rescued by a large force of police. Inevitably the collection became the scapegoat. There were accusations that government money had been diverted to it, and the cars and premises came under the control of the textile workers' union.

In a masterly compromise the collection was declared a national monument and moves were made to buy it from the brothers. The result was that the town of Mulhouse, the Département of Haut-Rhin and a number of organizations including the Automobile Club de France and the Committee of the French Salon formed an association to run the collection.

The two brothers have assembled the largest and finest selection of Bugattis in the world. During the fracas, suggestions that the collection might be sold off caused alarm among Bugatti collectors at the prospect of some 123 Bugattis coming onto the market and knocking the bottom out of it. Thankfully the collection survived intact for the edification of Bugatti enthusiasts in particular and of students of automotive design in general.

Bugattis take pride of place because there are so many of them, and they were, furthermore, built in Alsace. They provide a unique opportunity to study the evolution of Bugatti design, from the tiny four-cylinder Type 13 to the fast and practical straight-eight, twin-cam Type 57. The elegant Bugatti Royale Coupe Napoléon overshadows them all by its size and magnificence, but it was not a success either as a commercial proposition or as a prestige car. No royal buyer was found for any of the six examples built and the engine eventually found its niche in railcars. But the Type 57 did make money and there are a number of derivatives to be seen here. There are a great many Type 55s or Type 46s on show, each one a fascinating variation on the main theme.

The oldest of the Bugatti designs is the Hermes-Simplex racer designed by the young Ettore in 1904 for his friend Emil Mathis of Strasbourg. The range ends with the unsuccessful Type 251 Grand Prix Bugatti which was not a true Bugatti: although built at Molsheim it was designed by Giaccino Colombo, the Alfa Romeo designer. In between there are examples of most types and a number of prototypes and partly finished cars from the works.

There is far more to Schlumpf than Bugattis, however. In fact the marque represents only a quarter of the 500 or so vehicles on display. There are mini-collections of Alfa Romeo, de Dion, Ferrari, Maserati and Gordini. Indeed, it is difficult to select just a few examples from so many outstanding cars.

There are 14 Gordinis, built between 1937 and 1955; examples from the first period of Ferrari development, taking in the extremely rare 1948 Tipo 166 Formula 2 car as well as the 1964 250LM, and literally dozens of de Dion Boutons dating from 1898 to 1914. It would be difficult to find more Maybach cars under one roof; Mercedes-Benz is well represented by cars as old as the Mercedes-Simplex of 1905 and as young as the 1955 300SL gullwing. The two most interesting Mercedes-Benz cars are the W125 and W154 Grand Prix cars from the 1930s.

Another charming section is the collection of French light cars from the first three decades when minor manufacturers proliferated: here are examples of lost causes such as the Piccolo, Le Zèbre, Hurtu, Violet-Boget, Barre and others of similar ilk.

The catalog, which includes a complete list of the cars on display, is unfortunately available only in French, although the appendix contains explanatory notes in English. The cars are now in excellent condition, no longer covered in dust as before, thanks to a sympathetic staff and a large, well-equipped restoration workshop.

(Figures in brackets before the date indicate number of examples)

Alfa Romeo
1750/6C (1931)
12C (1938)
Disco Volante (1953)
8C (5) (1932-6)
Amilcar
CGS (1926)
CC (1925)
CO (1926)
Aster
tricycle (1899)
Audi
21/78 hp (1924)
Austro-Daimler
ADR 6 (1931)
Ballot
3/8 LC (1921)
RH3 (1930)
2LTS (1925)
Barre
10 hp (1912)
vis-à-vis (1897)
Baudier
3 hp (1900)
Bentley
Mk4, Mk6 (2) (1937, 1950)
Bentley-Rolls
4½-liter, 8 liter (1929, 1931)
Benz
GR (1918)
Velo (5) (1893, 1897)
Viktoria (2) (1893)
Berliet
A, VL (1911, 1920)
BNC
Course (1926)
Bollée
tricycle (1896)
Brasier
KD (1908)
Bugatti
Type 64 (1939)
Type 56 (1931)
46S (1934)
Type 46 (9) (1930-4)
Type 50 (3) (1936)
Type 57 (9) (1935-9)
Type 57S (4) (1937, 1938)
Type 57SC (5) (1938, 1939)
Type 57C (4) (1938, 1939)
Type 41 Royale (2) (1930, 1933)
Type 101 (4) (1950, 1951)
Type 44 (1927)
Type 32 (1923)
Type 40 (1926-9)
Type 49 (12) (1931-3)
Type 43 (7) (various)
Type 73A (1947)
Type 43A (2) (1929, 1930)
Type 73C (1948)
Type 68B (1942)
Type 38 (2) (1927)
Type 252 (2) (1954, 1955)
Type 52 (2) (1927, 1928)
Type 47 (1930)
251 GP (2) (1955)
Type 51A (2) (1932, 1933)
Type 51 (1931)
Type 17 (1914)
Type 16 (1912)
Type 28 (1921)
Type 23 (1924)
Type 45 (1929)

Type 53 (1931)
Type 37A (1929)
Type 37 (2) (1926, 1928)
Type 50/59B (2) (1938)
Type 35 GP (1925)
Type 35C (2) (1926, 1929)
Type 35 (4) (1925-9)
Type 35B (2) (1927)
Type 35A (5) (1925-9)
Type 55 (8) (1932-5)
Type 13 (6) (1912-21)
Charette
Sicilian
Charron
X (1910)
Cisitalia
D46 (1948)
Citroën
C3 (3) (1922-4)
Clément-Bayard
4M3 (2) (1912, 1913)
Clément-de Dion
phaeton (1899)
Clément-Panhard
VGP (1900)
Daimler
DB18, V8-2.6 and 4.5 (1952-8)
bus (1899)
TE20 (1912)
Daimler UK
DF302 (1954)
Darracq
6.5 hp, torpedo (1901, 1910)
20/28 hp (1907)
Decauville
10 hp (1903)
De Dion Bouton
tricycle (2) (1898, 1899)
G (6), L, Populaire (1901-2)
V (2), AL, EJ2 (1904-14)
BG, BS, BO2, DH (1909-12)
AU, CL, AW, DX, DH (1907-12)
G (2), H, O, S, AB (1901-5)
Delage
F (2) (1908, 1909)
Delahaye
28A, 32 (1908, 1914)
coupe chauffeur (1912)
Delaunay-Belleville
F6, HB6 (1909, 1912)
Dufaux
racer (1904)
Esculape
voiturette (1898)
Farman
A6, NF2 (1923, 1928)
Ferrari
250 Le Mans (1964)
450 America (1954)
250 Mille Miglia (1952)
500 Testa Rossa (1957)
156B F1 (1957)
212 F2 (1950)
500/625 F2 (2) (1952)
166 F2 (1948)
Fiat
509A (1926)
508S (1936)
Fouillaron
tonneau (1906)
Gardner-Serpollet
steam cars (5) (1901-3)

Gladiator
14 hp (1907)
Gordini
21 GCS (1951)
24S (2) (1953)
26S (1954)
23S (1953)
20S (2) (1952, 1953)
17S (1951)
32 (2) (1955, 1956)
16 (2) (1954)
Grégoire
12 hp (1910)
Hermes-Simplex
racer (1904)
Hispano-Suiza
J12 (3) (1932-3)
K6 (2) (1931, 1932)
H6B (1928)
XII Alfonso (2) (1912)
Horch
450, 670, 830 (1930-5)
Hurtu-Aster
23K (1904)
Hurtu-Benz
vis-à-vis (1894)
dos-à-dos (1897)
Isotta-Fraschini
8A (3) (1925-8)
Jacquot
steam car (1878)
Lancia
Lambda (1929)
Epsilon (1912)
Dilambda (1929)
Le Gui
B2 (1911)
Le Zèbre
A, C (1910, 1915)
C (2) (1913, 1914)
A (2) (1910, 1913)
Lorraine-Dietrich
E/C, VHH, FBH (1907-12)
fire engine (1910)
Lotus
18 (1961)
24 (1962)
33 (1963)
MAF
5/14 hp (1914)
Maserati
300S (1955)
250F (2) (1957, 1958)
4CL (1939)
4CS (1933)
4CLT (1948)
8CM (1933)
26B (1930)
Mathis
P (1924)
Maurer
1B (1900)
Maybach
DS7 (2), DS8, SW38 (1929-37)
Menier
brake (1893)
Mercedes
6/25/40 (1922)
Simplex (1905)
39/75 (1907)
14/30 (1909)
400 (1925)
28/95 (1915)

Mercedes-Benz
300SLR (1955)
W125 GP (1937)
38/250SSK (2) (1928, 1929)
SS (1929)
38/250SS (1929)
770K (2) (1938)
300SL gullwing (1955)
540K (3) (1936, 1938)
500K (2) (1936)
320 (1936)
170V (1938)
170H (1937)
W154 (2) (1939)
154 (2) (1939)
600 (1928)
400 (1927)
300S (1955)
300SC (1956)
380 (1933)
320 (1938)
Minerva
AC, AH (1926, 1928)
Monet Goyon
MV (2) (1924, 1925)
Mors
N (1910)
SSS (1923)
OM
665 (1930)
Panhard Levassor
35CV (1926)
X49 (1930)
X49 (1930)
X29 (1917)
CD (1962)
X26 (1915)
X8 & X12 (1911, 1912)
J1 (1904)
Grand Prix (1908)
B (1902)
A1, A2 (1898, 1899)
tonneau (1893)
Pegaso
Z102 (1952)
Peugeot
3 (1891)
8 (1893)
17 (1897)
26 (1899)
99 (1907)
146 (1914)
161 (1921)
172 (1922)
202 (1939)
174 (1927)
176 (1927)
quadricycle (1905)
Bébé (1913-15)
78A (1906)
69 (1905)
56 (1903)
16 (1898)
Peugeot-Lion
VC1 (1909)
Philos
A4M (1914)
Piccolo
7 hp (1907)
5 hp (2) (1906, 1907)
Pic-Pic
20/24 hp (1907)

Pilain
4D, 40 (1910, 1911)
Porsche
908 (1968)
Ravel
9CV (1927)
Renault
C & D (1900, 1901)
EU (2), NM 40CV (1919-24)
NC, I, AG1 (2), AX (1903-11)
Rheda
phaetonnet (1901)
Georges Richard
Pony (3) (1897-1900)
Richard-Brasier
torpedo (1910)
Rippert
(1902)
Rochet-Schneider
torpedo (2) (1911, 1924)
Rolls-Royce
20 hp (2) & 20/25 (1927, 1934)
Phantom III (4) (1936-8)
Phantom II (3) (1930)
Phantom I (1928)
40/50 Ghost (4) (1912-24)
Sage
sport (1906)
Salmson
Val (1926)
Sénéschal
SS (1925)
Simca
Gordini (2) (1937, 1939)
Sizaire et Naudin
voiturette racer (1908)
Soncin
quadricycle (1900)
SS
SS II (1934)
Steyr
220 (1938)
Sunbeam
15.9 hp (1920)
Talbot Lago
26C (2) (1948)
Talbot (London)
95 (1933)
Tatra
8 (1948)
Traineau
horse-drawn
Turicum
D1 (1910)
Vermorel
(1899)
Violet-Boget
A (1910)
Voisin
C7 (1927)
C14 (1930)
C28 (1936)
Zedel
CA, C1 (1908, 1911)

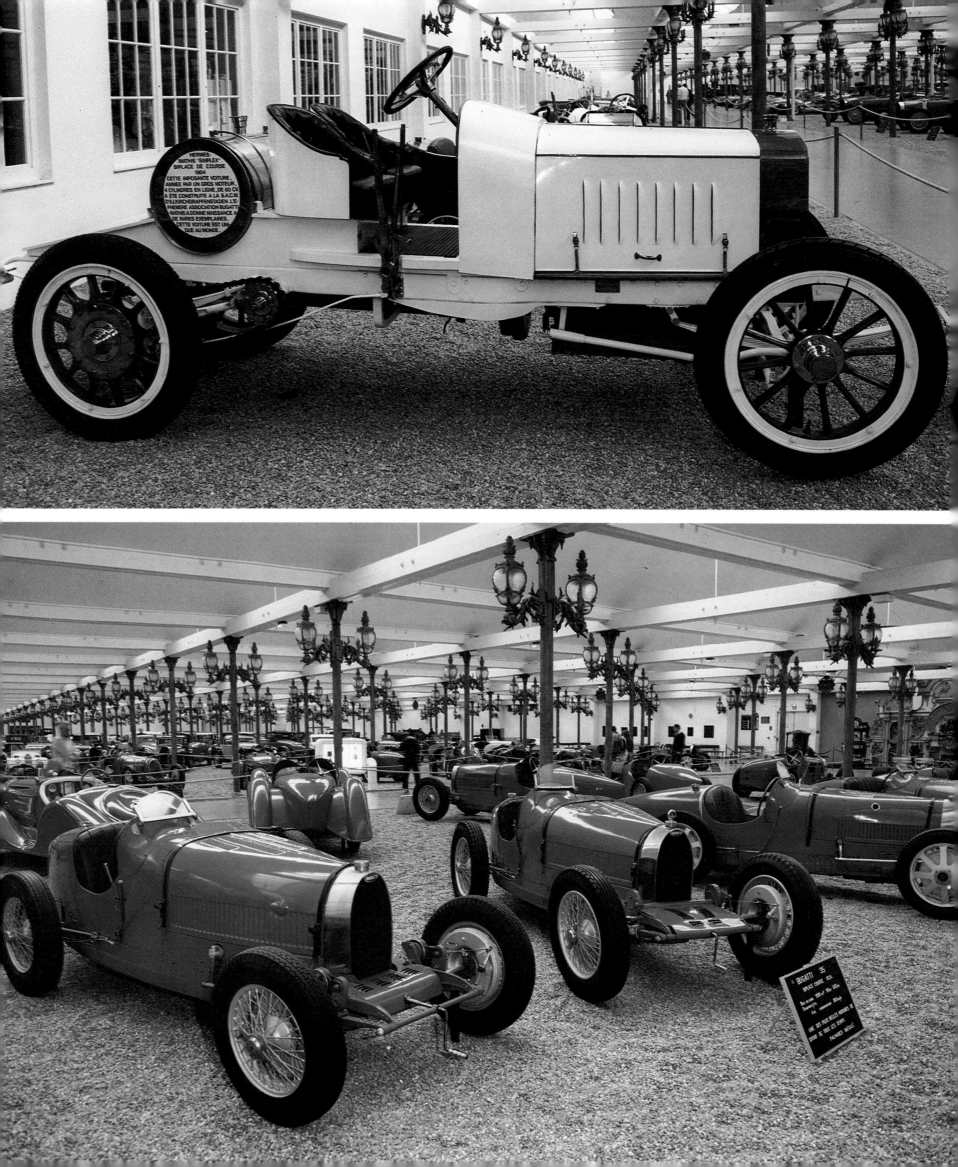

Opposite top: **Ettore Bugatti designed this Hermes-Simplex racer in 1904 for his friend Emil Mathis of Strasburg**

Opposite bottom: **The world's finest collection of Bugattis is assembled at Mulhouse in a sea of French racing blue. The cars in the foreground are the classic Type 35 Grand Prix with which the name will always be associated**

Above: **Display of a roadster body under construction on a replica Type 41 Bugatti Royale chassis. Maybe one day it will be completed**

Right: **1878 Jacquot steamer; a beautifully-built one-off, it is the oldest vehicle in the museum**

NATIONAL MUSEUM OF COMPIEGNE CASTLE

Musée Nationale du Château de Compiègne, Compiègne, 60200 Oise. Telephone: 440-02-02.

Location: 50 miles (82 km) north of Paris on main road N32. Leave highway A1 at Beauvais/Soissons exit from north, or at Senlis when approaching from the south for the attractive drive through Compiègne forest.

Compiègne is a delightful, elegant small town built around a château and set in glorious scenery in the middle of extensive forests. Once a royal hunting lodge, the castle now houses a modest but very important selection of 27 cars, and one of the world's finest collections of state coaches.

The museum is administered by the Louvre in Paris and all the cars there are as rare, genuine and valuable as the treasures in the Musée du Louvre. The collection dates from the mid-1920s, combined from a national car collection and a number of vehicles donated to the Touring Club de France by various celebrities.

France, with a splendid road system initiated by Napoleon, took up self-propelled locomotion with great enthusiasm well before other European countries, and the Compiègne collection's aim is to record this formative period. The cars are unashamedly old with only two built after 1914: a Croisière Noire half-track Citroën from the French trans-Sahara expedition of 1924 and a 1935 Hispano-Suiza coupe. It is difficult to know which takes pride of place – perhaps it should be shared by two almost identical Daimler-engined Panhard Levassors, with the two-seat tilbury

bodies. These were the second and seventh cars to be built by Emile Levassor, the older car being identical to the one in which the great man won the world's first long-distance motor race, from Paris to Marseilles and back, in 1895. It is unique in the collection as it was extensively restored by its makers in the 1920s. Both Panhard Levassors are propelled by German Daimler (now Mercedes-Benz) engines for which Panhard had a manufacturing license.

Another historic machine is the La Jamais Contente, a cigar-shaped electric car built in Paris to enable Camille Jenatzy to compete against Count Chasseloup-Laubat in his Jeantard for the honor of being the first man to exceed 100 km/h (62 mph). Jenatzy won, sprinting over the kilometer at 105.83 km/h (65.76 mph). As Jenatzy and Jeantard were both in the business of making electric cabs the whole episode was a publicity exercise.

Parked along the side of the big hall containing the horsedrawn coaches are two of the creations of Amédée Bollée Senior, the bell-founder of Le Mans who built the first satisfactory French steam-propelled vehicles. The elder of these, La Mancelle,

Left: **The 22nd Renault to be built, an 1899 1½ hp tilbury *à galérie à balustres* was donated by Louis Renault**

Below: **The Count de Dion's first love was the steam car and his engineer Trépardoux built several. This historic 1885 de Dion-Trépardoux steam dog-cart is de Dion car No 2**

Right: **Built in June 1891, a Panhard Levassor tilbury in the Compiègne collection. It was the seventh Panhard to be built and the second to be delivered to a customer**

was built as early as 1878 and is a private steam landau built shortly after L'Obéissante which resides at the Arts et Métiers museum in Paris (see page 56). The other steamer is a vast yellow steam coach (*diligence à vapeur*) built in 1885 as a public service vehicle. Apart from their massive mechanical construction, perpetuated in steam tractors rather than petrol-driven cars, these two vehicles are worthy of close inspection because they both appear to retain their original paint and leather trim – interesting examples of French detail work of a century ago.

The creations of the Comte de Dion's two engineers, Trépardoux and Georges Bouton, are also on display here. Trépardoux was a steam engineer and left the Count when he adopted petrol engines. He was responsible for de Dion Number 2, an 1885 steam dogcart built by Menelle. Bouton's contribution to de Dion's burgeoning fortunes was his high-speed petrol engine, represented here by an 1895 single-cylinder tricycle which, at the time of its construction, was one of the fastest vehicles on the road.

De Dion Bouton engines were sold in considerable numbers to many pioneering French manufacturers, including one Louis Renault. He started building automobiles in 1898 and No. 22, constructed in 1899, is on display, donated in 1929 by Louis himself, by then a multi-millionaire. Next to this veteran stands the ancestor of the modern sedan in the shape of a charming 1900 interior-drive coupe which is at least as tall as it is long.

There are many more historic vehicles – from Amédée Bollée Junior (who made petrol-driven cars), Clément-Bayard, Delahaye, Georges Richard, Krieger and Hotchkiss – which taken together give an almost complete picture of the birth of motoring in France. Only Peugeot and Roger are missing. Incidentally, the display of cycles should not be ignored for among them is one by Georges Michaux, claimed by his compatriots to be the inventor of the pedal.

These two cars are unlikely contemporaries: above is Camille Jenatzy's electric-powered streamliner, Le Jamais Contente, which on 29 April 1899 was the first vehicle to exceed 100km/h and on the left is the tiny 1½ hp de Dion-engined Renault conduite intérieure, built about 1900, which was one of the very earliest coupes

Amédée Bollée Fils
vis-à-vis (1895)
Amédée Bollée Pére
steam bus (1885)
La Mancelle (1878)
Léon Bollée
motor tricycle (1895)
Citroën
Croisière Noire half-track (1924)
Clément-Bayard
2-seat voiturette (1904)

De Dion Bouton
coupe 3/4 (1905)
La Populaire (1902)
vis-à-vis (1901)
quadricycle (1898)
tricycle (1895)
De Dion-Trépardoux
steam dogcart (1885)
Delahaye
brake (Duchesse d'Uzès) (1897)
FN Herstal
voiturette (1901)
Gobron-Brillié
tonneau (1898)

Hispano-Suiza
30/120 coupe (1936)
Hotchkiss
double coupe (1908)
Jenatzy
Jamais Contente (1899)
Krieger
electric coupe (1906)
Panhard Levassor
tilbury 2-seater (1891)
tilbury (1891)

Renault
D1 (1901)
C coupe (1900)
C (1899)
Reyrol-de Dion
Passe Partout (1904)
Georges Richard
voiturette (1897)
Sigma
Guynemeyer torpedo (1914)

NATIONAL TECHNICAL MUSEUM

Musée National des Techniques, Conservatoire National des Arts et Métiers, 292 rue St Martin, 75141 Paris Cedex 03. Telephone: 271-24-14.

Location: Best approached from the north via the Porte d'Aubervilliers and the rue d'Aubervilliers passing along the east side of the Gare de l'Est (East railway station) into the Faubourg St Martin and then into the rue St Martin.

The Musée National des Techniques contains, within the large, dimly lit first hall of this very important institution, one of the smallest automobile sections of all. However, it includes some of the most important landmarks in self-propelled locomotion. One of these is the most famous of all: the Cugnot steam tractor of 1771, a massive timber-framed device with two cylinders driving the single, iron-tired front wheel. This was Cugnot's second attempt at devising a steam tractor for pulling cannon (his first having been in about 1765) and it did work, although with so much weight above the front wheel that it was difficult to steer. Nevertheless, it was briefly demonstrated before running into a wall, destroying the original boiler. The tractor was innovative in using high-pressure steam fed directly into the cylinders in contrast with the atmospheric engines of the period.

The second most important vehicle to be found here is the pioneering steam coach L'Obéissante, built in 1873 by Amédée Bollée, a bell-founder of Le Mans. Apart from its unusual and decorative coachwork this quite practical eight-seater machine, which plied for hire before the motor car, is the first vehicle known to have had the now universal Ackermann steering geometry and independent front suspension.

Tucked away among these monsters from which stemmed a great industry you will find smaller pioneering gems like Serpollet's steam tricycle. Built in co-operation with Armand Peugeot as early as 1890, this device was driven from Paris to Lyons, drawing steam from Serpollet's flash boiler. Another of these steam tricycles is even older, the work of the Comte de Dion and his engineer Trépardoux.

More modern developments are not ignored. It is good to see an example of the elegant H6 Hispano-Suiza, the one real rival to the Rolls-Royce, designed by the brilliant Swiss Marc Birkigt. Tucked away in a section devoted to engines, you will also find one of his 300 hp V8 aero engines which played such a significant part in the air war from 1914 to 1918.

The theme of the museum is to display the French genius for mechanical innovation. One example of this from the early 1920s is a Léon Laisne chassis with tubular steel side members, front-wheel drive and all-independent suspension with the springs housed in the side members.

The engine of the Cugnot steam tractor dating from, incredibly, 1771. The crankshaft had yet to be invented and the connecting rods transferred power to the wheels by racks and ratchets. (Musée Nationale des Techniques de C.N.A.M.-Paris)

Above: **The 1771 Cugnot steam tractor. It worked reasonably well and is generally acknowledged to be the first mechanical vehicle. (Musée Nationale des Techniques de C.N.A.M.-Paris)**

Right: **Léon Serpollet's second steam tricycle, built in 1888, is just one of the ancestors of the automobile to be found at the Musée des arts et métiers in Paris. (Musée Nationale des Techniques de C.N.A.M.-Paris)**

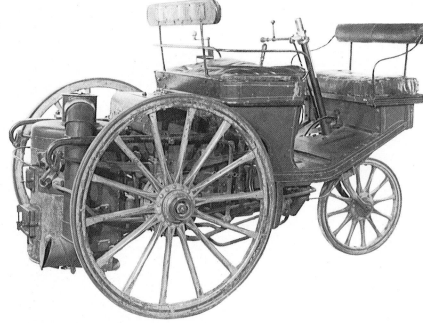

Angeli
    chassis only (1920)
Benz
    dogcart (1898)
Berliet
    2-seat phaeton (1898)
Amédée Bollée
    l'Obéissante steam omnibus (1873)
Brasier
    ¼-scale chassis (1905)
Citroën
    11CV saloon (1955)
    C6 G coupe (1931)
    B-14 (1927)

Cugnot
    second steam gun tractor (1771)
De Dion Bouton
    12CV chassis only (1908)
    vis-à-vis (1899)
Charles Dietz
    model of hot-air 6-wheeler (1816)
    model of steam road tractor (1835)
Ford
    Model T tourer (1908)
Hispano-Suiza
    H6B saloon (1932)

Hotchkiss
    AK chassis (1922)
    chassis only (1903)
Léon Laisne
    independent suspension chassis (1930)
Panhard
    Dynavia prototype (1945)
Panhard Levassor
    M2E (1896)
    tilbury (1898)
Peugeot
    20 hp tourer (1909)
    quadricycle (1893)

Renault
    4CV sectioned car (1948)
Serpollet
    steam tricycle (1888)
Talbot Lago
    Baby, 15CV Wilson gearbox (1951)
Manufacturer unknown
    electric pick-up truck

Above: **A magnificent open drive limousine by Automobiles Peugeot; dated 1909, it is believed to be a Type 105 A/B. (Musée Nationale des Techniques de C.N.A.M.-Paris)**

Below: **Panhard and Levassor had been in business five years when they built this M2 E tilbury two-seater. (Musée Nationale des Techniques de C.N.A.M.-Paris)**

Germany, Democratic Republic (East Germany)

TRANSPORT MUSEUM

Verkehrsmuseum Dresden, Augustus-strasse 1, DDR-8010 Dresden. Telephone: 495-3002.

Location: In the city center.

This historic building in Dresden is the home of the Transport Museum

In the days of a united Germany the part of the country which is now the German Democratic Republic was the home of a number of important car manufacturers. DKW, Audi, Wanderer and Horch were the constituent companies of the Auto-Union combine, whose four-ring symbol is now used by

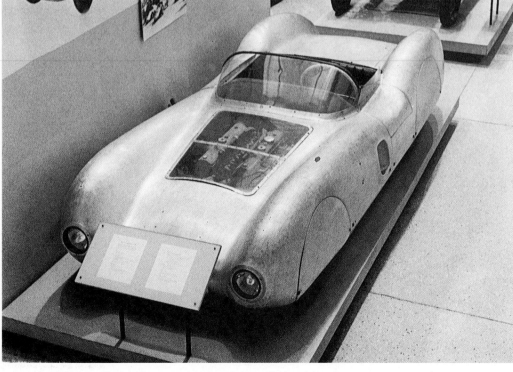

Volkswagen for their Audi range. All four were here, mainly around Zwickau and Schönau. The main BMW car plant was in Eisenach and briefly produced the EMW and AWE cars after World War II: it now produces the Wartburg. There were also less well-known companies such as Phänomen, Hanomag and Simson, the last-named based in the gunmaking center of Suhl.

The Verkehrsmuseum has been able to bring together a representative selection of indigenous vehicles worthy of preservation. These have been very competently restored in the museum's modern workshops. Among them is the first roadworthy Wanderer, the No. 2 prototype 12 hp car of 1902 while the oldest original car is an 1892 Canstatt Daimler-Schroedter shown with one of the ubiquitous 1885 Benz-Motorwagen replicas.

Carl Benz had many associations with the area. The oldest of the museum's nine Benz vehicles is an 1893 6 hp Viktoria and the most modern a charming 1911 14/30 phaeton. A most interesting exhibit is the

Opposite top: **A 1911 14/30 hp Benz phaeton**

Opposite bottom: **An EMW aerodynamic racer built in the Eisenach works where pre-1939 BMW cars were built**

Above right: **The Dresden Museum's Panhard Levassor tilbury dates from 1893 and is one of the earliest survivors of the marque**

Simson-Supra SO, an extremely rare example of this manufacturer's work. In the early 1920s Simson successfully set out to produce a small high-performance sports car, regardless of cost. Power was provided by a four-cylinder, twin-ohc, four-valves-per-cylinder 1950 cc engine which looks modern today. The Supra SO was a less potent version with a single overhead camshaft; it is one of the two or three European survivors.

Incomplete list; 42 cars in all in collection

Audi
70 hp Type M (1928)
AWE
130 hp streamline racer (1954)
Benz
limousine (1910)
tonneau (1902)
Ideal (1901)
Viktoria (1899)
Comfortable (1896)
14/30 hp phaeton (1911)
9 hp dos-à-dos (1899)
6 hp Viktoria (1893)
Patent Motorwagen replica (1885)

Daimler (Cannstatt)
2 hp Daimler-Schroedter (1892)
DKW
2-stroke V4 (1930)
EMW
340-2 sports (1952)
Excelsior (Switzerland)
6CV runabout (1904)
Hanomag
2/10 hp Kommisbrot (1925)
Horch
305 65 hp 8-cylinder (1928)

Mercedes
Knight sleeve-valve engine (1911)
Simplex (1905)
Panhard Levassor
4 hp tilbury (1893)
Phänomen
12 hp Phänomobil 3-wheeler (1924)
Rohr
Type R (1933)
Simson
8/40 hp Supra SO (1925)
Wanderer
12 hp No.2 prototype (1904)

Germany, Federal Republic (West Germany)

AUTOMOBILE AND TECHNICAL MUSEUM

Auto und Technik Museum e.V., D-6920 Sinsheim/Kraichgau. Telephone: 07261-64780.

Location: From highway E12 Heidelberg-Nürnberg, take exit after Heidelberg Weisfoch traveling from the north. Sinsheim is on the north side of the highway and lies on main road N292 towards Heidelberg.

Opposite: **Main hall of the Auto und Technik Museum at Sinsheim**

Above: **A fine example of the Mercedes-Benz 300, in this case a limousine built in 1951**

This very well laid out museum in the Neckar valley to the north of Stuttgart was founded in 1981 as a non-profit-making organization with, at the time of writing (early 1986), some 1000 subscribing members. It very successfully depicts the many uses of the internal combustion engine in cars, trucks and warfare. The exhibits, laid out in groups in open plan, range from Gary Gabelich's Blue Flame land speed record car, the first vehicle to exceed 1000 km/h (621 mph) on the ground, to German World War II tanks and agricultural tractors, trucks and buses.

Blue Flame is the pride of the museum but it is complemented by many other valuable and historic cars. A glance at the list reveals the Ferdinand Porsche-designed Austro-Daimler 3-liter competition car of 1928, an example of which held the Shelsley Walsh Hill Climb record for many years. A rare Bugatti Type 57S sports two-seater is to be found among the choice selection of half a dozen Bugattis, while the Cord 812 supercharged saloon and a number of modern Formula 1 cars also catch one's eye. The latter include the Tyrrell P34D six-wheeler and the Wolf WR2 of 1977 in which Jody Scheckter almost carried off the 1977 Formula 1 World Championship. There are also representative selections of Maybach and Mercedes-Benz cars, some of the latter on loan from the Mercedes Museum.

An old Opel 4-tonner supplied to the German Army in 1915 contrasts with its counterpart from World War II, demonstrating that although commercial vehicle chassis design advanced tremendously between 1915 and 1944, the type of cab called for by the Wehrmacht did not change at all. Among this military hardware, some from the American and Allied sides, but mainly from Germany, is a wide range of jeep-type vehicles, wheeled armored cars, half-tracks and tanks. They are displayed in realistic settings with full-size dummies dressed in the appropriate uniforms and sporting various types of contemporary weapon.

The Sinsheim museum also displays a fascinating selection of static exhibits of engines of various sizes: one of the most interesting of these is a W-18-cylinder Isotta-Fraschini turbocharged engine, designed for high-speed motor boats. Just for good measure the museum also possesses a number of interesting aircraft including what appears to be a replica of a Fokker EIII Eindecker.

A timeless super-car, the 1970 Lamborghini Miura P400S was designed to outshine the Ferrari, and very nearly did

Exhibited cars; others in store

Adler
Trumpf 1.7AV cabriolet (1936)
Alfa Romeo
Giulietta spyder (1959)
Amilcar
CC 2-seater sport (1921)
Austro-Daimler
3-liter race car (1928)
Bentley
3-liter Le Mans (1923)
Benz
Comfortable 3-seater (1897)
Patent Motorwagen replica (1886)
Benz Gaggenau
motor fire ladder (1926)
BMW
V8 limousine (1963)
328 sport (1938)
315/1 sport (1935)
250 Isetta 4-wheeler (1956)
335 cabriolet (1939)
Brasier
11 hp coupe (1908)
Bugatti
57 Ventoux coupe (1938)
57S sport 2-seater (1935)
35C supercharged Grand Prix (1930)
30 8-cylinder 2-liter (1926)
37 Imitation Course (1926)
44 Fiacre 3 liter (1928)
Chevrolet
pick-up truck (1927)
Columbia
electric car (1900)
Cord
812 supercharged saloon (1937)
Daimler
Stahlradwagen replica (1889)
Daimler (UK)
Dingo scout car (1942)
Delahaye
double phaeton 16 hp (1909)

Dodge
US Army command car (1943)
Ferrari
250GT Pininfarina drophead (1958)
330GT (1968)
Dino 246GT (1972)
Fiat
508SC Ballila spyder (1934)
Fittipaldi
F5A Formula 1 (1978)
Ford
US Army armored car (1944)
Model T fire engine (1923)
Model T speedster (1912)
Grout
2-seat steam car (1899)
Hanomag
Kommisbrot (1926)
Hansa
electric truck (1923)
Horch
4 X 4 personnel car (1940)
830BL 4-seat cabriolet (1938)
853A sport cabriolet (1939)
Hotchkiss
Nachschubpanzer (1958)
Jaguar
3.8 E-Type roadster (1961)
Krauss-Maffei
half-track (1937)
Lamborghini
P400S Miura (1970)
Laurin & Klement
50 hp torpedo phaeton (1921)
Lloyd
Alexander TS (1961)
40 LP saloon (1955)
Lotus
Europa twin-cam coupe (1975)
Magirus
motor fire ladder (1921)

Malicet et Blin
3.5 hp vis-à-vis (1897)
Maybach
aero-engine special (1917)
SW38 Spohn cabriolet (1937)
SW38 4-door cabriolet (1938)
SW38 2-seat drophead (1938)
Mercedes
70 Simplex phaeton (1907)
28/95 torpedo (1922)
22/50 hp torpedo (1914)
Mercedes-Benz
K 24/110/160 sports (1928)
230A cabriolet (1938)
500SLC rally car (1980)
C111 Wankel coupe (1970)
500K (W29) (1935)
220A cabriolet (1955)
170S cabriolet (1949)
300 saloon (1951)
770 Grosser (1938)
army cross-country car (1938)
300SL roadster (1958)
320 limousine (1938)
500 Nürnberg tourer (1935)
Mannheim 37 (1933)
Messerschmitt
3-wheel cabin scooter (1955)
MG
PB Midget (1935)
Mors
4 hp chain-drive (1898)
Opel
22/25 torpedo (1914)
Blitz truck (1944)
4-ton army truck (1915)
1.2L 2-door saloon (1932)
50 hp double phaeton (1912)
Packard
light eight limousine (1932)

Peugeot
Bébé (1912)
143 double phaeton (1912)
vis-à-vis (1892)
Piccolo
6 hp voiturette (1905)
Presto
30 hp 4-cylinder phaeton (1924)
Renault Alpine
A 110 (1956)
Rolls-Royce
Wraith 7-seater limousine (1949)
40 50 Phantom II saloon (1934)
20/25 limousine (1935)
40/50 Ghost tourer (1921)
SS
Jaguar 100 (1938)
Jaguar 2.6-liter (1937)
Steyr
RSO/1 tracked truck (1942)
tracked MG carrier (1942)
Stoewer
4 X 4 army scout car (1939)
Tyrrell
P34D 6-wheel Formula 1 (1976)
Volkswagen
amphibian (1942)
Kübelwagen military (1940)
Wanderer
W24 limousine 1.7-liter (1938)
Willys
Jeep (1944)
Wolf
WR2 Formula 1 (1977)

Right: **Mercedes' first production six-cylinder car, the classic 28/95 hp, raced twice in the Targa Florio. This is a 1922 high-speed tourer**

Below: **The star exhibit at Sinsheim is Gary Gabelich's 1001 km/h (621 mph) jet-engined Blue Flame, which broke the World Land Speed Record**

DAIMLER-BENZ MUSEUM

Daimler-Benz AG, Archiv-Geschichte-Museum, 7000 Stuttgart 60 (Untertürkheim). Telephone: 0711-17-2915.

Location: Inside Daimler-Benz factory at Untertürkheim in south-eastern suburbs of Stuttgart. Head for Esslingen on road N10. Alternatively, take bus route D from the bus station (next to main railroad station) in Stuttgart, leaving at 10 a.m.

The story of motoring is almost the story of Daimler-Benz, for the founders of the Daimler and Benz concerns were the pioneers of the automobile in 1886. Rudimentary internal combustion engines had existed even before these two pioneers were born but it was they who saw the potential of the gasoline engine and developed it into a practical power unit for transport. The two concerns merged in 1926 to form Daimler-Benz, producers of Mercedes-Benz cars and trucks; but from the beginning both Daimler, making Mercedes cars, and Benz were at the forefront of automotive development. The museum at Stuttgart-Untertürkheim reveals the history of the two pioneering companies.

For a number of years this has been one of the best museums anywhere in the world simply because the Daimler management in particular had a strong sense of history and for the past 70 years has been carefully preserving cars as reference material. They are beautifully maintained and quite practical road cars.

In 1986, to celebrate the centenary of the motor car, the museum is being given a major face-lift and will be the venue for a number of special events.

A car which set new standards when it was introduced in 1901 was the first Mercedes, the 24 hp, built to the requirements of Emil Jellinek, the Austro-Hungarian consul in Nice, who took the whole production on condition that the cars were named after

In many ways the 1955 Mercedes-Benz 300SL gullwing coupe symbolized the post-1945 revival of Mercedes-Benz. It is the modern counterpart of the emotive 38/250 SSK supercharged cars of the 1920s

his daughter, Mercedes. The mechanically operated inlet valves of its Maybach-designed engine, its gate-change gearbox and pressed-steel chassis frame have caused it to be hailed as the most innovative design of the period.

Naturally, there are samples of the two pioneering vehicles, the 1886 Daimler Motorwagen and the three-wheeled Benz Patent-Motorwagen, the former a conversion of a horse carriage and the latter an automobile designed from scratch. There are so many replicas of the delightful little Benz in the European museums that one suspects a minor industry must exist to make them. The Mercedes name is synonymous with motor racing as a result of their spasmodic but inevitably successful forays into racing and there are examples of most of their Grand Prix cars here. A great rarity is one of the 4½-liter, twin-ohc cars which won the epic 1914 Grand Prix at Lyons, displayed in the same hall as the mighty Porsche-designed, 7.1-liter, 38/250 supercharged two-seaters of the late-1920s, the Hitler-period supercharged 8-cylinder and

12-cylinder single-seaters, which set new bench-marks in racing car design, and the post-war W196 unsupercharged 3-liter racers and their sports car derivatives.

Unsurprisingly, there are many varieties of Mercedes, Benz and Mercedes-Benz touring and sports cars from over the years. The Japanese Emperor's Grosser Mercedes limousine and the Type 600 'Popemobile' merit inspection and invite speculation, while at the other end of the scale, tucked away in a corner, one finds the only example of a rear-engined Mercedes-Benz – the Hans Nibel-designed Type 130 of 1933. Between these extremes there are all types of touring and sports car right up to the present day, making a truly memorable display.

Almost certainly the first Grand Prix car with an overhead camshaft, the 1906 Mercedes-Maybach 125 hp Grand Prix car was also the first six-cylinder Mercedes. It is in running order and a delight to drive

Right: **A 1911 Mercedes 16/40 double phaeton (Jagdwagen)**

Below: **The mighty 1909 Blitzen Benz, World Land Speed Record holder and a legend in American motor racing history. It was faster than any aeroplane until 1920**

Exhibited cars; others in store

Benz
bicycle (1893)
model of Denkmal
race car (1899)
Parsival (1903)
model of 1896 Lieferwagen
model of 1886 Motorwagen
dos-à-dos runabout (1899)
Patent Motorwagen replica (1886)
'Spider' (1902)
Horch-built engine (1895)
2-stroke engine (1885)
landaulet (1909)
FX aero engine (1912)
Blitzen-Benz (1909)
6/18 sports (1921)
Viktoria vis-à-vis (1893)

Daimler
L20 light aircraft (1924)
model of motor boat *Marie* (1888)
L20 Klemm aircraft (1925)
model of 1895 truck
1/5th-scale model of Daimler carriage
Phoenix race car (1899)
Reimenwagen coupe (1898)

model of 1905 post bus
model of 1886 motor carriage
truck (1898)
motor carriage (original) (1886)
'Lanzpreis' boat engine (1912)
boat engine (1890)
motor boat *Marie* (1888)
pumping engine (1892)
narrow gauge locomotive (1890)
Phoenix truck engine (1898)
experimental engine replica (1883)
wire wheel 1.65 hp (1889)
motorized hobby horse (1885)

Mercedes
F7502 aero engine (1924)
Simplex (1906)
22/40 hp phaeton (1910)
Simplex 60 hp tourer (1907)
Type 600 24/100/140 supercharged (1924)
Simplex Reihenmotor (1904)
F 1466/DIII aero engine (1914)
I 41 airship engine (1910)
Targa Florio race car (1924)
1914 Grand Prix 2-seater (1914)

10/40/65 supercharged sports (1923)
16/45 Knight sleeve-valve tourer (1921)

Mercedes-Benz
Type 130 rear-engined saloon (1933)
600 landaulet: Pope's car (1965)
190E 2.3 -16 (1984)
C111/III 3-rotor Wankel (1978)
1972 S-class car (model)
1929 SSKL sports (model)
300SL roadster (1960)
280SE cabriolet (1971)
180 saloon (1955)
770K Grosser (1937)
260 Stuttgart 10/50 (1928)
300SL gullwing coupe (1954)
Japanese Emperor's 770K limousine (1935)
190SL sports (1958)
500K special roadster (1936)
SSK 27/170/225 sports T720 (1928)
W196 Formula 1 race car (1954)
300S A cabriolet (1952)
600D limousine (1959)
Hydrak school model (1958)
170S cabriolet B (1950)

300SL gullwing (1952)
DB721/PTL10 gas turbine (1962)
Nürnberg 460 limousine (1928)
260D Pullman limousine (1936)
300SLR sports-racer (1955)
540K cabriolet (W29) (1936)
370S Mannheim cabriolet (1931)
W196 Formula 1 Grand Prix (1954)
300 Mannheim (1926)
W154 1½-liter Grand Prix (1939)
W30 sports car (1935)
W125 record car (1938)
770 Grosser (1931)
DB603A aero engine (1944)
DB601A aero engine (1937)
DB 600 aero engine (carburetor) (1935)
T80 World-record challenge (1939)
W125/5 single-seat Grand Prix (1937)
W25 single-seat Grand Prix (1934)
38/250S supercharged sports (1927)

Mercedes-Maybach
ohc Grand Prix 2-seater (1906)

Max von Pein, administrator of the superb Mercedes-Benz Archive and Collection, with a Benz Patent Motorwagen

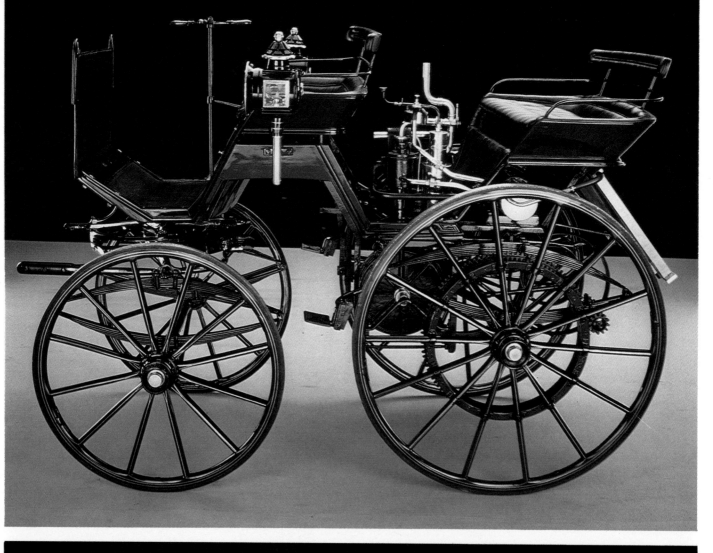

The 1893 Benz Viktoria (below) was the first Benz four-wheeler although the Mannheim concern had been making the three-wheeler since 1886, which is the date of the Daimler Motorwagen (above)

GERMAN MOTOR MUSEUM

Deutsches Auto Museum, Schloss Langenburg, 7183 Langenburg/Württemberg. Telephone: (0-79-05)-241.

Location: From E6/E12 Heilbronn-Nürnberg highway take exit north of Schwäbisch Hall and head for Kupferzell and Braunsbach. Langenburg is on the Braunsbach-Rothenburg road.

Langenburg is a small town in what was once the important kingdom of Württemberg. The castle, or *Schloss*, has been the family seat of the Hohenlohes since the eighteenth century. Parts of the castle are still in use as a residence but much is open to the public; the museum, which was established in 1970, is one of the attractions.

About 80 cars make up the collection; many possess sporting appeal and others are out-and-out racers. There are two outstanding exhibits here – a Mercedes-Benz W25R streamlined record-breaker from 1935, and Rak 2, one of the series of rocket-propelled cars promulgated by Max Valier, Friedrich Sander and Fritz von Opel (grandson of Adam Opel). This bullet-shaped vehicle was propelled by 24 dry-powder rockets containing more than 260 pounds of explosive and is believed to be the first car to be fitted with negative camber wings to keep it on the ground. At the Avus motor circuit, driven by the intrepid Fritz, it reached 125 mph (201 km/h) in a hair-raising run before the media on 23 May 1928. The Mercedes streamliner, fitted with the remarkable 660 bhp DAB V12 engine, was less spectacular but considerably faster, taking flying start records over the mile at 226.4 mph (364 km/h) driven by Rudi Caracciola.

Other high-performance racing cars worthy of mention are the Maserati 450S and 150S sports-racing cars; a pair of 4½-liter Talbot Lagos, one a two-seater Le Mans type and the other a single-seater from the immediate post-World War II period; and one of the single-seat Maserati 1936 6CM 1500 voiturette racers which were so popular with independent racing drivers. Moving into the modern period of racing car design the collection also includes a couple of ground-effect Formula 1 cars in the shape of a Hesketh 308 and a March 751.

The oldest car in the museum is an apparently original 1893 Benz Viktoria with carriage-style coachwork. Many of the continental museums have this model but the 1904 Polymobil Gazelle, a German copy of a curved dash Oldsmobile, seems unique. Other comparative rarities are a 1911 four-cylinder Napier T27 with two-seat racing body, and a pleasant 1913 Sizaire et Naudin two-seater with Sizaire's innovative independent front suspension.

Contrasts at Langenburg: a 1911 Napier in the foreground, and behind it a Porsche 917 sports racer and Fritz von Opel's second rocket car

Adler
15/35 hp tourer (1906)
Alfa Romeo
33/3 sports-racing (1969)
Alvis
4.3-liter sports tourer (1938)
Aston Martin
DB2 drophead coupe (1949)
1½-liter International sports (1930)
Benz
Viktoria carriage (1893)
Comfortable 2-seat carriage (1899)
BMW
600 (1959)
Isetta (1956)
3/20 (1931)
Bugatti
3.3-liter Type 57 (1939)
Buick
D-6-55 roadster (1916)
De Dion Bouton
(1905)
Delahaye
V12 coupe (1937)
Dixi
3/15 hp Austin license (1927)
Ferrari
275GTB coupe (1968)
FMR
Tg500 Tiger (1958)
Ford
Model T (1925)
Hanomag
Kommisbrot 2/10 hp single-cylinder (1927)
Kommisbrot Adac saloon (1924)ˑ

Hesketh
308 Formula 1 single-seater (1974)
Horch
853 straight-eight (1937)
Humber
Humberette runabout (1913)
Jaguar
XK140 (1957)
Mk V saloon (1950)
Lagonda
M45 (1933)
Lancia
Lambda tourer (1927)
Astura Pininfarina drophead (1938)
Lister-Jaguar
sports-racing 2-seater (1956)
Lloyd
400 saloon (1953)
March
751 Formula 1 single-seater (1975)
Maserati
Sebring 3700GT coupe (1965)
150S 4-cylinder 1½-liter sports-racing (1956)
450S sports-racing (1956)
6CM 1½-liter single-seater (1936)
Mercedes-Benz
300D saloon (1959)
300SLR coupe (1955)
W25R 5.7-liter V12 record car (1935)
Messerschmitt
KR500 cabin scooter (1954)
MG
TC roadster (1946)
Napier
4-cylinder 4.1-liter raceabout (1911)

Neander
3-wheeler (1937)
3-wheel experimental (1934)
NSU
Wankel-engined spyder (1964)
HK101 3-track Caterpillar (1941)
Pony motorcycle (1922)
motorcycle (1902)
NSU-Fiat
500 Topolino (1940)
Opel
Rak 2 rocket-propelled (1928)
race car (1913)
Peugeot
quadricycle (1899)
Phänomen
Phänomobil 3-wheeler (1907)
Polymobil
Gazelle 3-seater (1904)
Porsche
917 flat-8 sports-racing (1970)
907 (1968)
904GTS sports-racing (1963)
356B drophead coupe (1961)
356 coupe (1949)
Railton
Terraplane (1937)
Rally ABC
1100 cc sports 2-seater (1928)
Renault
AG-1 runabout (1910)
Riley
Brooklands 2-seater (1939)
Rolls-Royce
Phantom III V12 (1935)

Sizaire et naudin
2.6-liter 2-seater (1913)
Steyr
55 coupe (1938)
Stoewer
D9 tourer (1924)
Talbot Lago
record drophead (1949)
4½-liter Grand Prix (1948)
4½-liter sports-racing (1950)
Vauxhall
20/60 hp sports 2-seater (1930)
Volkswagen
Type 166 Schwimmwagen amphibian (1942)
Winkler
single-track car (1925)
Zündapp
Janus 4-seater (1957)
manufacturer unknown
wooden tricycle (1867)

Twelve years of automotive development: an 1899 Benz Comfortable and a 1911 four-cylinder Napier T27 at Langenburg

NORTH GERMAN MOTOR AND TECHNICAL MUSEUM

Norddeutsches Auto-Motorrad und Technik Museum, 4970 Bad Oeynhausen 11, Weserstrasse 142. Telephone: 05731/ 9960.

Location: Close to Bad Oeynhausen exit from Köln-Hannover highway A2. Weserstrasse runs east-west immediately south of A2.

The North German Motor Museum dates only from April 1973, but in a fairly short time an outstanding collection of 150 cars and 250 motorcycles has been gathered together including, as might be expected, many German rarities. The emphasis is on north German makes of the inter-war years, although most German manufacturers, the famous and the less famous, are represented.

The 1918-39 period in Germany is a fascinating one for the automotive historian because of the multitude of 'minimum' motor cars produced by this ingenious nation to provide some form of mobility at a time of national austerity and financial disaster. The absolute minimum is probably the Mollmobil tandem-seat single-cylinder, two-stroke-engined cyclecar designed by Ing. Gorke. Equally spartan is the Framo, again with a single-cylinder engine and featuring front-wheel drive. The Framo accessory factory was owned by J.S. Rasmussen, the founder of DKW; the little Framo is the true ancestor of the two-stroke front-wheel drive DKWs. Another historic car here is a Rohr Junior made under license from Tatra. Designed

Cockpit of the car which Juan Manuel Fangio drove in the historic 1955 Italian Mille Miglia race

by the great Hans Ledwinka, the Tatra featured a horizontally opposed air-cooled four-cylinder engine and swing-axle rear suspension long before the Volkswagen. Indeed, it may have provided inspiration for Dr Porsche, who was then working for Rohr as a consultant on the design of their big cars.

Included among the many automotive rarities at Bad Oeynhausen are a Brennabor Type L1 built in 1909; an Apollo Type C, one of the very first German small high-performance cars; a big 1925 Maybach Type W5-SG; a 1924 Presto and one of the quaint French Lafittes with a three-cylinder radial engine and friction drive in place of a gearbox.

From the post-1945 period, when, initially, the German economy was struggling hard to recover, come a whole crop of rare economy cars such as the Fulda-Mobil, BMW Isetta, Messerschmitt KR200, and the little Lloyd, nicknamed the 'fugitive's Porsche', built by Carl Borgward. They make an interesting comparison with the luxury cars associated with the Hitler period.

Makes foreign to Germany are also represented, including the predictable Rolls-Royce, in this case a Phantom II, and the equally inevitable Bugatti, a Type 46. With so many cars to house, the exhibits tend to be rather tightly packed, but they are all well restored and, we are told, all in running order.

Exhibits at the North German Museum are tightly packed but easily accessible for viewing

A Team Martini 1971 Porsche 917
Le Mans car. This type started the
long series of Porsche wins in the
24 Hours Race

Adler
2.5-liter streamliner (1937)
Trumpf Junior sports (1936)
Trumpf Junior (1936)
Favorit (1929)
Standard 6A (1928)
10/50 6-cylinder 2.56-liter (1925)
K 5/13 (1913)
5/9 hp (1907)

AGA
C-6/20 (1924)

Alvis
supercharged 4-wheel drive (1928)

Amilcar
CC (1921)

Apollo
C (1912)

Audi
SS 100 (1929)
E 5.7-liter (1912)

Austin
Seven sport (1934)

Bentley
4½-liter (1928)

Benz
16/50 4.2-liter (1921)
8/20 (1912)
Velo (1895)

BMW
F2-69 Formula 2 racer (1968)
2600 V8 (1962)
507 Bauer coupe (1959)
600 twin-cylinder 4-wheel drive (1958)
Isetta bubblecar (1956)
503 3168 cc V8 (1956)
327 (1939)
328 sports (1937)
329 (1936)
315 6-cylinder 1490 cc (1935)

Borgward
Isabella TS (1959)
Isabella coupe (1958)

Brennabor
C (1931)
L1 (1909)

Bugatti
46S (1932)
44 Fiacre (1931)
37 (1929)
Type 40 (1928)

Cadillac
coupe de ville (1961)

Chevrolet
Corvette 6-cylinder (1954)

Chrysler
New Yorker 6773 cc V8 (1961)

Citroën
5CV Cloverleaf (1923)

Columbia
electric (1904)

Cooper
F3 BMC engine (1960)

Cyklon Dreirad
Cyklonette (1913)

Daimler (UK)
Conquest 2½-liter coupe (1954)

De Dion
AC (1905)

Denzel
WD Sport International (1954)

DKW
Front F8 684 cc (1939)
P15 4-wheel drive 2-stroke (1928)

Dodge
WC 51 truck (1943)

Durkopp
P8 2.5-liter (1917)

Elite
12/40 (1919)

EMW
340/2 6-cylinder 2-liter (1952)

Fiat
500 Topolino (1940)
501 (1923)

Ford
Model T (1927)
Model T (1919)

Ford Taunus
Eifel 1172 cc (1939)

Framo
192 cc 4-wheel drive (1932)

Fulda-mobil
197 cc NWF minicar (1955)

Goggomobil
TS250-20 coupe (1965)
T250 247 cc mini-car (1964)

Goliath
Pioneer single-cylinder 198 cc (1931)

Grade
F1 2-stroke single (1921)

Hanomag
1.3 ohv (1938)
3/16 16PS (1929)
2/10 sport (1926)
2/10 Kommisbrot (1925)

Hansa
1700 6-cylinder 1.6-liter (1934)
A sports (1909)

Heinkel
200 3-wheel bubblecar (1957)

Horch
850 coupe 8-cylinder 4.9-liter (1938)
853 8-cylinder 4.9-liter (1937)
400 8-cylinder 4-liter (1930)

International Harvester
buggy (1908)

Georges Irat
MDU 4-wheel drive (1936)

IWK
Amphicar amphibian (1961)

Kleinschnittger
F 125 125 cc mini-car (1952)

Lacroix et Laville
3-wheeler (1900)

Lafitte
Modèle A 3-cylinder radial (1923)

Le Zèbre
Zebra (1913)

Lloyd
Alexander TS (1960)
LP400 386 cc (1956)
LP400 4-wheel drive (1954)
LP300 293 cc 4-wheel drive (1951)

Maico
500 Champion mini-car (1956)

Maserati
Due Posti 4000 coupe (1966)

Mathis
SB 10 hp (1925)

Maybach
DS7 Zeppelin (1930)
W5-SG 6-cylinder 7-liter (1925)

Mercedes
400 15/70/100 supercharged (1925)

Mercedes-Benz
LF311/OM312A fire engine (1960)
L3000S export truck (1942)
300SEL V8 6.3-liter (1970)
600 limousine (1967)
300D diesel (1957)

300SL gullwing (1955)
130 (W23) 1308 cc (1934)
370 Mannheim (W10) (1930)
8/38 6-cylinder 2-liter (1926)
KR200 cabin scooter (1957)

Minerva
DD sleeve-valve engine (1912)

Moll
Mollmobil MO 1 (1923)

Morgan
Supersport MX 2 3-wheeler (1934)

Neumann-Neander-JAP
1000 cc hill climb (1937)

NSU
RO 80 saloon (1970)
Typ 56 Wankel spyder (1967)

Opel
Blitz 1 fire engine (1953)
Blitz ambulance (1952)
Kadett L 993 cc (1964)
Admiral cabriolet (1939)
1.3 Olympia (1936)
P4 1073 cc (1935)
4/20 1018 cc (1931)
4/16 (1927)
8 M 25 (1921)

Panhard Levassor
SS (1913)

Peugeot-Lion
VC (1907)

Phänomen
Phänomobil (1912)

Porsche
356A speedster (1955)

Presto
D 9/30 (1924)
P8 (1918)

Protos
10/30 4-cylinder 2.6-liter (1922)

Renault
C1 (1900)

Rochet-Schneider
14CV chain-drive (1908)

Rohr-Tatra
Junior 6/30P (1933)

Rolls-Royce
Phantom III (1937)
40/50 Phantom II (1935)
20/25 (1932)
20 hp (1925)

Salmson
AL 1088 cc (1923)

Schoche
steam car (1897)

Seck
boxer motor (1898)

Simson
Supra 2 liter (1928)

Stanguellini
Formula Junior (1958)

Steyr
430 (1933)
XX 6-cylinder 2-liter (1929)
Model II 6-cylinder 3.3-liter (1922)

Stoewer
Arkona 6-cylinder 3.6-liter (1939)
R150 4-cylinder 1.5-liter (1934)

Tatra
87/603 V8 2545 cc (1948)

Tempo
Pony 200 van (1939)
200 198 cc 3-wheeler (1936)

Veritas
Nürburgring (1951)
Comet (1949)

Victoria-Spatz
sport-roadster 245 cc (1958)

Volga
gas 24 saloon (1974)

Volkswagen
10/11 Beetle (1949)
166 amphibian (1943)
87 Kübelwagen (1943)

Wanderer
W22 (1933)

Willys-Overland
interchangeable body (1928)

Zündapp
Janus 250 bubblecar (1958)

Engine of a 1904 Gladiator, with the cylinders cast in two blocks of two

Italy

ALFA ROMEO MUSEUM

Museo Storico Alfa Romeo, Alfa Romeo SpA, Castella Postale 1821, 20100 Milan. Telephone: (02)-9-33-91.

Location: Arese is adjacent to the E2 Milano-Stresa highway about 11 miles (18 km) from the center of Milan.

The name of Alfa Romeo is synonymous with motor racing and it is fair to say that this company has had a more continuous association with the sport than even Mercedes-Benz. It is natural, therefore, that the predominant car color in this museum is Italian racing red. It is undoubtedly one of the greatest collections in the world and unique in that it includes – with one exception – only cars built by Alfa Romeo or the old ALFA concern.

The late Luigi Fussi, the Alfa Romeo historian, was one of the men responsible for bringing together this most remarkable collection.

There are Alfa Romeos of all ages on show on the seven mezzanine floors of the modern museum building at Arese.

As the list shows, anyone interested in high-performance petrol engines should visit this museum for here are overhead-camshaft engines dating back to 1914 – since 1925 Alfa Romeo have not made car engines with the camshafts anywhere but in the cylinder head. Only one car is missing: the P1 racer designed by Merosi in which Paul Ugo Sivocci was killed while testing at Monza.

There are examples of all the other pre-1938 Grand Prix cars, including the twin-engined 12-cylinder Tipo A, which boasted two six-cylinder engines, not to mention two gearboxes and propeller shafts feeding power into an axle with two crown wheels and pinions. The engines in this exhibit are not original but most of the remainder is.

Included among the racers are the Merosi-designed Tipo G with Alfa's first double-ohc engine which was not ready in time for the 1914 Grand Prix; the P2 which vanquished Delage, Bugatti and Sunbeam in the 1924 French Grand Prix; Jano's exquisite Monza and Tipo B eight-cylinder supercharged racers; and the all-conquering Tipo 159 which gave Fangio his first World Championship. Nor should the mid-engined 1940 Tipo 512 with its horizontally opposed 12-cylinder boxer engine go unnoticed.

But racing is only the medium which brings the name to the lips of the public. Alfa Romeo's business was passenger car manufacture, albeit passenger cars with the magic touch that only a racing pedigree can bring. Among those at Arese are the old 24 hp which began to establish the Alfa reputation for quality and the 24/30 which confirmed it. After the war came the elegant and reliable RMs and RLs, followed by Vittorio Jano's ohc six-cylinder 6C 1500 which started a European fashion for small sixes. The six-cylinder touring Alfa Romeos, many of them bearing bodies by the great Italian coachbuilders, built in the years leading up to World War II were vital to the well-being of the company, while the Giulietta series of small twin-cam fours brought large-volume production to Alfa Romeo for the first time. Nor should one miss the sports-racing and Grand Prix cars of recent years.

The Alfa Romeo Museum is a graphic reminder that the parent company's attachment to motor racing runs in an unbroken thread from 1912 until the present day – a record which cannot be matched by any other concern. At the same time it contrives to be an exhibition of the finest in Italian coachbuilding and automotive engineering.

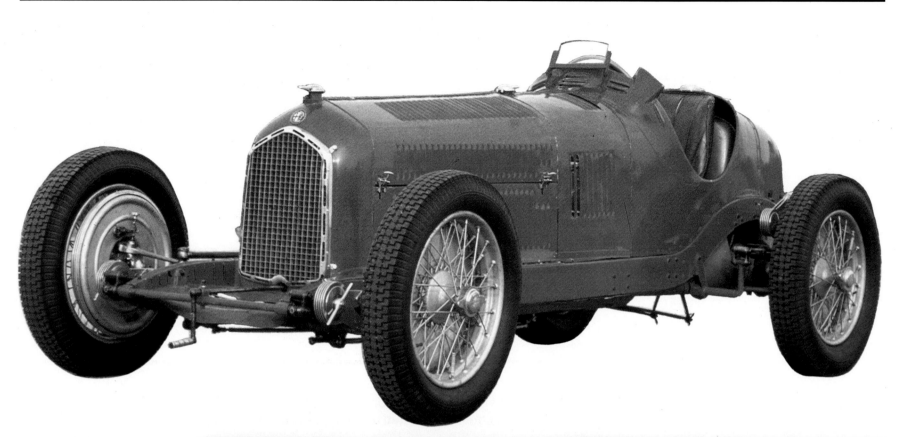

Above: **Regarded by many as the classic racing car of all time, the 2.9-liter twin-supercharged Tipo B Monoposto Alfa Romeo dominated motor racing in the early 1930s**

Right: **It is not recorded whether the Alfa Romeo 15 hp Corsa ever went racing with four people in its exposed bucket seats. It was the first racing Alfa**

Opposite top: **One of the world's most coveted sports cars. This is the Alfa Romeo 8C 2300 Le Mans on the long chassis, which scored a single Le Mans win. Only nine were built, between 1930 and 1933**

Opposite bottom: **The Aga Khan described the Alfa Romeo RL as one of the most excellent cars he had ever driven. Mussolini owned an RLSS like this one, while a racing version won the Targa Florio race**

The display chassis of the twin-supercharged Alfa Romeo Tipo 159 Gran Premio, which dominated Grand Prix racing immediately after World War II. It gave Fangio the World Championship in 1951

Alfa Romeo

Darracq 10 hp 2-seater voiturette (1908)
ALFA 24 hp Castagna torpedo (1910)
ALFA 15 hp torpedo sport (1911)
Tipo G twin-cam gp engine (1914)
40-60 hp 2-seat racer (1914)
40-60 hp aerodynamic saloon (1914)
20/30 hp ES sports tourer (1920)
RL Targa Florio race car (1923)
P2 Grand Prix (1924)
RM sports cabriolet (1924)
RL Targa Florio race car (1924)
RL Super Sport Castagna torpedo (1925)
RL Super Sport Castagna torpedo (1926)
RL Super Sport Mille Miglia (1927)
6C Super Sport spyder (1928)
6C 1500 James Young coupe (1928)
6C 1750 Super Sport spyder (1929)
6C 1750 GT Royal coupe (1930)
6C 1750 spyder Zagato (1930)
8C 2300 Monza racing 2-seater (1931)
Tipo A GP monoposto (1931)
6C 1750 Gran Sport Zagato (1931)
8C 2300 supercharged Le Mans (1931)
8C 2300 Zagato Race spyder (1932)
Tipo B GP monoposto (P3) (1932)

6C 1900 GT saloon (1933)
Tipo B GP aerodynamic (1934)
6C 2300 Castagna 2-seater coupe (1934)
6C 2300 touring 4-door coupe (1934)
Grand Prix Bimotore (1935)
Tipo C 12-cylinder Grand Prix (1936)
8C 2900 Lungo 4-seater coupe (1938)
6C 2300 B Mille Miglia coupe (1938)
6C 2300 short chassis saloon (1938)
Tipo 158 1½-liter Grand Prix (1938)
6C 2500 SS racing spyder (1939)
6C touring Berlinetta (1939)
Tipo 512 rear engine GP (1940)
6C 2500 Super Sport coupe (1947)
6C 2500 Golden Arrow coupe (1947)
1900 Berlina (1950)
6C 2500 Super Sport coupe (1950)
AR 51 La Matta 4X4 jeep (1951)
Tipo 159 1½-liter supercharged GP (1951)
1900 Disco Volante spyder (1952)
6C·3000 CM competition 2-seater (1953)
Giulietta spyder (1954)
Giulietta Sprint coupe (1954)

1900 Super Sprint coupe (1954)
1900 Berlina Super (1954)
1900 Sport spyder (1954)
Giulietta saloon (1955)
2000 Sportiva coupe (1956)
Giulietta TI saloon (1957)
2000 Bertone Sprint coupe (1958)
2000 Berlina (1958)
Giulietta SZ Zagato coupe (1959)
Berlina Tipo 103 prototype (1960)
Giulia Sprint coupe (1962)
2600 Bertone Sprint coupe (1962)
2600 Berlina (1962)
Giulia Sprint Speciale coupe (1963)
Giulia TZ1 Zagato racing coupe (1963)
Giulia GTA Bertone coupe (1965)
Giulia TZ 2 racing coupe (1965)
2600 SZ Zagato coupe (1965)
2600 OSI de luxe saloon (1965)
Giulia Super 1600 saloon (1965)
Scarabeo dream car (1966)
GT Junior 1300 coupe (1966)
Montreal Expo show car (1967)
1750 Berlina (1967)
Carabo dream car (1968)
Tipo 33 2-liter Daytona (1968)

GTA 1300 Junior coupe (1968)
Ital design Iguana coupe show car (1969)
Pininfarina coupe 33 show car (1969)
Tipo 33 2-liter Stradale coupe (1969)
Tipo 33 3-liter Le Mans (1970)
1750 GTAm Bertone competition coupe (1970)
Ital design Caimano show car (1971)
Pininfarina Cuneo show car (1971)
Alfetta spyder-coupe show car (1972)
Alfetta Berlina 1800 (1972)
Pininfarina Eagle spyder-coupe (1975)
Tipo 33 TT12 competition spyder (1975)
Taxi Ital Design show car (1976)
Bertone Navajo show car (1976)
BT46 Formula 1 Brabham chassis (1977)
Tipo 33 SC 12 twin-turbo (1977)
Tipo 33 SC 12 spyder (1977)
Tipo 179C Formula 1 (1979)
Tipo 177C Formula 1 (1979)

CARLO BISCARETTI DI RUFFIA AUTOMOBILE MUSEUM

Museo dell'Automobile Carlo Biscaretti di Ruffia, Corso Unita d'Italia, Torino. Telephone: 677-666/7/8.

Location: South side of Turin, on the left bank of the River Po. Follow Corso Vittorio Emanuele II from front of main railway station to Valentino Park (traffic lights before Ponte Umberto river bridge), then turn right along Corso Massimo D'Azeglio following the river past Piazza Polonia to Corso Unita d'Italia. Bus routes 55 to 60 and trolley bus route 34 lead to the museum.

The foundation of this museum goes back to 1932, when a group of influential Torinese business men, Count Biscaretti di Ruffia among them, decided to perpetuate the history of the automobile, with the emphasis on Italy. Carlo Biscaretti was curator of the resulting collection which was displayed initially at the Municipal Stadium in Turin. It was much easier then than now to find historic vehicles. The result was a choice collection of vehicles which are still in the museum.

From this early beginning, the collection escalated until in 1956 the Agnelli family, co-founders of Fiat with the Biscarettis, and the other Italian manufacturers decided that the collection deserved a more suitable home. Accordingly, the present large modern purpose-built museum was opened in 1957 and Carlo Biscaretti became its first president. When he died two years later the museum was renamed in his honor.

The whole exhibition is beautifully laid out on three levels, on marble floors. The foyer is distinguished by a display of early radiators and several examples of early Italian self-propelled vehicles backed by a bas-relief honoring the men who have been killed motor racing.

Once inside there are various sections demonstrating the development of the motor car in all its aspects. One exhibit in the coachwork section is an old-fashioned landaulet body built with metal panels on a wooden frame; alongside it is a Weymann body consisting of a wooden frame covered with imitation leather. The pioneering Lancia Lambda is also shown with its integral construction of body and chassis. Italy is famous for the artistry of its coachbuilders and there are many examples of their work here, including early examples from Pinin Farina (now Pininfarina) and his brother's firm Stabilimenti Farina.

A number of the historic engines are worthy of inspection, especially the 1892 Daimler V-twin and the beautiful V12 Delage racing engine. The first Fiat engine of 1899 is here, while nearby is the 16 hp Fiat engine with make-and-break electric ignition of 1905, demonstrating the terrific pace of development in the early days of the motor car.

There is a display of racing cars including Alfa Romeo P2, 8C/2300 and the all-conquering Tipo 158, not to mention a selection of Ferrari Formula 1 cars, a W196 Mercedes-Benz and Maserati 26B and 250F Grand Prix models.

The origin of self-propelled locomotion is demonstrated with beautifully constructed models of pioneering self-powered vehicles dating back to 1472, but the earliest real machine is a steam tricycle built by Virginio Bordino in 1852. Professor Count Enrico Bernardi of Padua appears to be one of the first Italian constructors. Two of his vehicles, one built in 1883 and the other in 1893, are on show. An elegant pioneer is the Pecori, a steam tricycle built by the Cavaliere Enrico Pecori at Erba in 1891. Fiat were among the pioneers, their earliest products being built in 1899; a 3.5 hp example constructed in 1899 is the oldest of the many examples on show here.

A favorite exhibit is the immortal Itala with which Prince Scipione Borghese won the Peking to Paris race in 1907. Others worthy of special mention among the 250 exhibits are the giant 1907 Fiat Grand Prix car; the unique Monaco-Trossi, a radial-engined two-stroke Grand Prix car designed by Count Carlo Felice Trossi; Pierro Taruffi's record-breaking Tarf; and the 1899 Prinetti & Stucchi with which the youthful Ettore Bugatti was associated.

The Fiat Centro Historico in the center of the city has a unique collection devoted to their own cars and aero engines which are not represented at the Biscaretti.

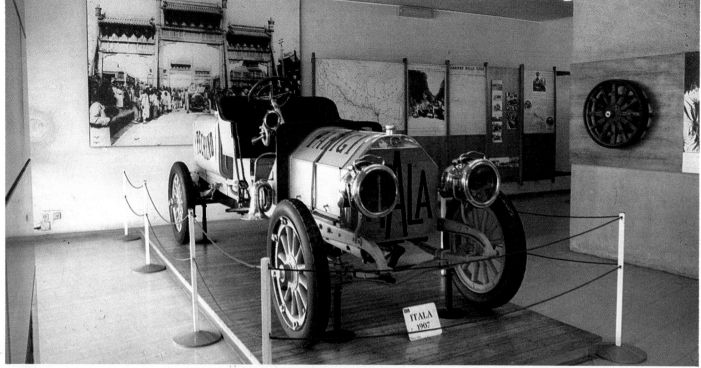

Right: **The 35/45 hp Itala in which Prince Scipione Borghese won the 10,000-mile Peking-Paris Race in 1907**

Below: **A general view of the main exhibition hall in the Biscaretti di Ruffia Museum**

The British-trained Italian engineer Virginio Bordino designed this steam-driven landau in 1853. It was constructed in the Turin Military Arsenal and has a twin-cylinder engine drawing steam from a rear-mounted tube boiler

Adler
  K7 15 hp Morgan taxi (1912)
Alfa Romeo
  6C/3000 Disco Volante (1952)
  Tipo 158 1½-liter GP (1938)
  8C/2300 Touring spyder (1934)
  8C/2300 Touring Milan 2-seater (1933)
  P2 Grand Prix 2-seater (1930)
  6C/1750T (1929)
Ansaldo
  4C 1847 cc sport (1923)
Aquila Italiana
  25/30 hp 6-cylinder (1912)
Austin
  Seven (1932)
Bedelia
  8 hp tandem cyclecar (1911)
Bentley (Derby)
  3½-liter Frenay body (1933)
Benz
  8 hp Ricordi brake (1899)
  3 hp 3-wheel velo (1899)
  Viktoria (1893)
Bernardi
  3½ hp 3-wheel car (1896)
Bianchi
  S4 (1925)
Bollée
  3 hp tricycle (1896)
Bordino
  steam 3-wheeler (1854)
Brixia-Züst
  10 hp (1908)
Bugatti
  Type 52 Bugattina (1927)
  Type 35 Grand Prix (1924)
Ceirano
  5 hp runabout (1901)
Ceirano-Itala
  20/30 hp chassis (1904)
Chiribiri
  Milan model chassis (1924)
Cisitalia
  202 Pininfarina coupe (1948)

Citroën
  11CV front-drive saloon (1934)
  5CV C3 Cloverleaf (1923)
Darracq
  9½ hp runabout (1902)
Decauville
  3½ hp runabout (1898)
De Dion Bouton
  quadricycle 1¾ hp (1899)
  1¼ hp tricycle (1898)
  Model DM chassis (1911)
  Model BG coupe (1907)
  Populaire 2-seater (1903)
  Model G (1901)
Delage
  AB-8 12/14 hp 4-cylinder (1913)
Demeester
  4-cylinder 8 hp (1906)
Diatto
  Model 10 chassis (1920)
Ferrari
  256 Grand Prix chassis (1960)
  4-cylinder 500/F2 (1951)
Fiat
  experimental turbine car (1954)
  500A Topolino (1936)
  1500 6-cylinder chassis (1935)
  508 Ballila saloon (1932)
  509A Weymann saloon (1929)
  520 Super Fiat (1928)
  519S sport (1923)
  501 tourer (1923)
  501S sport (1921)
  Model 2 chassis (1916)
  18BL commercial (1914)
  S57/14B racer (1914)
  Zero tourer (1912)
  '4' 6-seat torpedo (1911)
  18/24 hp tourer (1908)
  18/24 hp (1908)
  35/45 hp chassis (1908)
  130 hp Grand Prix (1907)
  24/32 hp (1906)
  24/32 hp landaulet (1905)

  16/24 hp (1903)
  16/24 hp 2-seater 'racer' (1903)
  12 hp Alessio wagonette (1902)
  8 hp 2-seater (1901)
  3½ hp vis-à-vis (1899)
Florentia
  10 hp runabout (1903)
Ford
  jeep (1941)
  A sedan (1928)
  Model T tourer (1916)
  Model T chassis (1908)
Hispano-Suiza
  K6 6-cylinder (1935)
Hurtu
  3 hp runabout (1898)
Isotta-Fraschini
  Model 8 Castagna body (1920)
  B28/35 hp de luxe (1911)
  AN 20/30 hp (1909)
Itala
  '61' Lavocat et Marsaud (1928)
  Model 61 chassis (1925)
  '11' V12 1050 cc racer (1925)
  25/35 hp (1912)
  35/45 hp 'Palombella' (1909)
  35/45 hp Peking-Paris (1907)
Jaguar
  D-Type Le Mans (1954)
Lancia
  D50 Formula 1 (1955)
  D24 Carrera Panamericana (1953)
  Aprilia saloon (1948)
  Dilambda chassis (1928)
  7th series Weymann saloon (1926)
  6th series tourer (1925)
  Lambda chassis (1923)
  Trikappa 8-cylinder (1922)
  Kappa sport (1919)
  Theta limousine (1914)
Legnano
  A 6/8 hp (1908)
Marchand
  12/16 hp (1904)

Maserati
  250F Formula 1 (1954)
  26B 8-cylinder supercharged GP (1928)
Mercedes-Benz
  W196 single-seater Formula 1 (1954)
  540K roadster (1936)
Minutoli-Millo
  8 hp (1902)
Monaco-Trossi
  8-cylinder radial-engined front-wheel drive
  GP (1935)
Nardi-Monaco
  Chichibio hill-climb car (1932)
Nazarro
  Model 3 chassis (1914)
Oldsmobile
  curved dash runabout (1904)
OM
  Model 665 Superba (1931)
  469S 4-cylinder (1929)
Opel
  5/12 hp 2-seater (1912)
Packard
  Super-Eight (1937)
Panhard Levassor
  X19 Girard & Fils body (1913)
  X 17 SS coupe de ville (1912)
  B1 (1899)
Pecori
  steam tricycle (1891)
Peugeot
  AG Baby (1905)
  2½ hp Saronno (1894)
Pope
  C/60V electric (1907)
Prinetti & Stucchi
  quadricycle (1899)
  4 hp (1899)
Rapid
  16 hp chassis (1908)

Renault
  EU tourer (1916)
  AG Taxi de la Marne (1910)
  AX chassis (1909)
  3½ hp Model C? (1899)
Georges Richard
  3½ hp (1900)
Rolland-Pillain
  RP5 (1918)
Rolls-Royce
  40/50 hp Silver Ghost (1914)
San Giusto
  740 cc chassis (1923)
Sizaire-Naudin
  25 C 12 fire engine (1926)
Stae
  petrol-electric (1909)
Stanley
  Steamer (1898)
Storero
  Model A 25/35 hp (1913)
Tarf 1
  350 cc and 500 cc record breaker (1948)
Temperino
  V-twin utility (1923)
Trossi-Cattaneo
  855 cc sports (1934)
Victrix
  single-cylinder 695 cc (1911)
Vinot & Deguingand
  14/20 hp Buezelin body (1907)
White
  Steamer (1905)

QUATTRORUOTE COLLECTION

La Collezione Quattroruote, 20089 Rozzano (MI), Via A. Grandi, 5/7. Telephone: (02)-824721.

Location: The Rozzano district is due south of the Piazza Duomo in Milan. Take the Via Torino exit from the piazza into Via Meda and following straight on, through the Piazzale Abbiategrasso and under the Tangentiale ring road. Via A. Grandi is the right fork immediately after the ring road.

Quattroruote (Four Wheels) is considered to be one of the best motoring magazines in the world. In keeping with its tradition, it has established a carefully chosen collection of cars to illustrate the entire history of the motor car while paying particular attention to the Italian motor industry. The collection also includes a fine collection of horsedrawn carriages which are of special interest to veteran car enthusiasts because of the similarity of the tonneaus and phaetons to some of the pioneering oldies.

The cars are divided into various categories: ancestors (from the beginnings to 1904), veteran (1905 to 1918), vintage (1919 to 1930), post-vintage (1931 to

1945) and post-war (1946 onwards). The single ancestor is a 1902 de Dion Bouton K1 chassis which admirably illustrates the Panhard drive-system, Georges Bouton's high-speed front-mounted single-cylinder engine running at the then dizzy speed of 1800 rpm and driving the rear axle. Pride of place among Quattroruote's veterans goes to a magnificent Gardner-Serpollet steam phaeton. The Ansaldi-Fiat bears an uncommon name and is mounted, equally unusually, with a limousine type of body by Burr & Co. of New York. The Nazarro Tipo 3 is a great rarity, one of the very few, and is fitted with a raceabout body by Cottino which consists mainly of four bucket

Some of the exhibits devoted to chassis design over the years

seats.

In the vintage section one expects to find a Rolls-Royce of some kind. Quattroruote have two on display: a 40/50 Phantom I landaulet by Hooper and a 40/50 Phantom II interior-drive limousine by the same coachbuilder. Naturally the Lancia Lambda is represented and the two examples illustrate the beginning and the end of the model: a 1st Series and an 8th Series tourer, to show off Vincenzo Lancia's innovatory independent suspension and unitary construction body. Equally fascinating because of its rarity is a 1926 Diatto Tipo 61 saloon built shortly after the departure of Alfieri Maserati to found his own business. Maserati was chief designer in the Diatto racing department. Incidentally, it is interesting that Quattroruote's 6C 1750 Alfa Romeo spyder is bodied by La Sportiva of Milan rather than by the more usual Touring or Zagato coachbuilding houses. Fine cars from the last year in this period are a Hispano-Suiza H6B, a narrow-V8 engined Lancia Dilambda and a luxury Fiat, the six-cylinder 525N.

It may strike the visitor that an Austin Seven would be more at home in the vintage section but the example here is a 1931 model, sitting next to a Fiat Topolino, a design 15 years younger. There are of course some good examples of the smaller Fiats, including an unusual 508 Ballila sports coupe and a six-cylinder 1500 pillarless saloon, which must be one of the few survivors. The other end of the scale is represented by a nice Bugatti Type 57 Gangloff cabriolet and an impressive Mercedes-Benz 540K with the same style of bodywork.

The post-1946 selection is not so strong. The Ducati fabricated-tube chassis is not really the best example of a spaceframe. And one has to assume that the over-styled, Fisher-bodied Cadillacs were chosen to act as a foil to the cleaner lines of the Studebaker Champion and Lark. However a Fiat 600 lends scale to this section. It is to be hoped that, since their most informative catalog was printed, one or two examples of Italian coachbuilding of the immensely fruitful 1950-70 period will have been acquired.

The Quattroruote Collection display area: cars are tightly packed but accessible

Left: **The sporting Bugatti Type 57 and the lordly Phantom III Rolls-Royce were front runners among the European luxury cars of the 1930s**

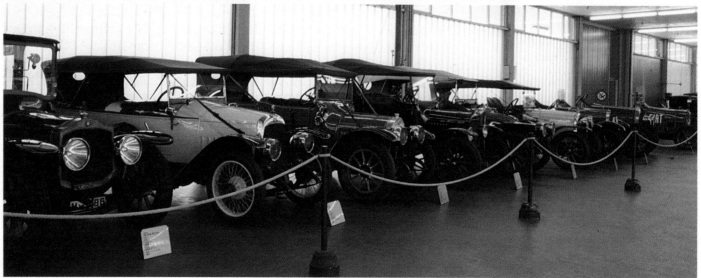

Right: **Vintage means cars built between 1919 and 1930. Quattroruote have a representative selection typifying design progress in that period**

Alfa Romeo
    6C 1750 supercharged spyder (1930)
Ansaldi-Fiat
    Type 2 patent town carriage (1908)
Ansaldo
    4CS 4-seat raceabout (1925)
Austin
    Seven tourer (1931)
Benz
    8/20 torpedo tourer (1914)
Bugatti
    Type 57 Gangloff cabriolet (1939)
Cadillac
    55-6219 limousine (1955)
    55-6237 coupe (1955)
    54-6219 limousine (1954)
Ceirano
    4-seat tourer (1921)
Citroën
    11CV Traction Avant saloon (1939)
De Dion
    EA open-drive limousine (1913)
    K1 chassis only (1902)

Delage
    D1 torpedo (1926)
Diatto
    20A Weymann faux-cabriolet (1924)
Ducatti
    DU4 tubular chassis (1946)
Fiat
    600 saloon (1955)
    500 Topolino (1938)
    1500A pillarless saloon (1936)
    508 pick-up (1934)
    508S Ballila sports coupe (1934)
    508 Ballila 2-seat tourer (1934)
    508 saloon (1932)
    525N 2-seater with dickey (1930)
    521C coupe de ville (1928)
    509A spyder (1927)
    501 Super Sport (1924)
    505 chassis only (1922)
Ford
    Model T tourer (1922)
Gardner-Serpollet
    12/15 hp steam double phaeton (1906)

Hispano-Suiza
    H6B Binder limousine (1930)
Isotta-Fraschini
    Tipo 8A landaulet (1929)
Itala
    Tipo 61 4-door saloon (1925)
Lancia
    Dilambda 227 limousine (1930)
    Lambda 8th series tourer (1928)
    Lambda 1st series 214 tourer (1923)
Mercedes-Benz
    540K cabriolet (1939)
Nazarro
    4-seat raceabout (1913)
OM
    469 S4 tourer (1932)
Panhard Levassor
    BPK 128H 15/35 hp tourer (1926)
Peugeot
    172 BC 2-seat cabriolet (1925)
Renault
    FK tourer (1916)

Rolls-Royce
    20-25 drophead 2-seat coupe (1932)
    Phantom II interior-drive limousine (1929)
    40/50 Phantom I landaulet (1926)
SCAT
    14/1 torpedo 3.6-liter (1914)
Studebaker
    Champion sedan (1950)
Studebaker-Packard
    V8 Lark VIII sedan (1959)
Willys
    MB Jeep (1942)

Netherlands

AUTOTRON DRUNEN

Postbus 51, 5150 AB Drunen, Museumlaan 100. Telephone: 04163-73631.

Location: Drunen is approximately equidistant from Antwerp, Amsterdam and The Hague. It lies on a side road just south of the main highway between s'Hertogenbosch and the small town of Walwijk. It is well signposted.

Attractive farmhouse interior of the Autotron at Drunen, Netherlands, with a Delage Type B tonneau in the foreground

Drunen is a small village near the town of Waalwijk, half-way between Antwerp and Amsterdam. This is the unlikely location of the Autotron – often referred to as the Lips Autotron after its founder – said to be the best motor museum in the Netherlands. With its inventory of about 100 cars, all of them beautifully restored and, with very few exceptions, in running order, it bids fair to be one of the most attractive collections in Europe. Mr Lips is the head of an international company manufacturing ships' propellers and aluminum castings, and the collection reflects his engineering background.

Mr Lips has naturally made sure that the Spijker (Spyker) car is well represented and there are seven of these Dutch cars in this collection. One of these was built in 1904 and so qualifies for the London-Brighton veteran car run, in which it has taken part on a number of occasions. A 1905 double phaeton and the 1911 runabout are two particularly splendid examples of this grand old make. Another interesting example of the marque is a so-called racer dated 1902, although this does seem rather advanced for its stated age. This car has a six-cylinder engine which is claimed, justifiably, to be the first six-cylinder engine put into an automobile, pre-dating Napier by almost a year. This racer is also unusual in having a V radiator instead of the traditional circular one which characterized Spijker's previous locomotive-building activities. Two of the later Spijker C4 types are also on show. One is a two-seater replica of the Tenax which took records at Brooklands in 1920 while the other is an open tourer dating back to 1924. Both of these machines are powered by Maybach six-cylinder engines.

Many of the cars are extremely good examples of their type, others are rare. In the first category come the Hispano-Suiza H6B pointed-tail roadster, the Rolls-Royce 20/25 Barker barrel-body tourer and the 1948 Horsfall-type Spa Aston Martin. These are superb motor cars by any reckoning; the last-named has the added attraction of being an extremely rare example as is the 1937 15/98 Aston Martin Speed Tourer with the pushrod engine. Other rarities include the Buick Type G roadster (1907), Pierce Motorette runabout (1902) and the Toledo Model B steam runabout. The 1901 Toledo runabout brings the museum's inventory of steam-powered vehicles to three, the others being a rare 1906 Stanley open tourer and a 1902 Type F Gardner-Serpollet. A few modern cars are included to give an historical perspective but the emphasis is mainly on old timers and vehicles from the 1920s and 1930s.

The exhibition building, in the style of a Brabant farmhouse, was opened in July 1972.

Below: **The farmhouse-style buildings of Lips Autotron were designed by Anton Pieck**

Opposite below: **Spyker was one of the very first manufacturers to espouse the smooth-running six-cylinder engine. However this 1905 limousine appears to be one of the four-cylinder, 12/16 hp models. It does not appear on the museum list**

Ahrens-Fox
NS-4 fire engine (1928)
Alfa Romeo
Montreal berlinetta (1974)
Alvis
Speed 25 tourer (1937)
Amilcar
M3 cabriolet (1932)
Aston Martin
15/98 speed tourer (1937)
2-liter Spa competition 2-seater (1948)
Barre
Type Y voiturette (1902)
Bentley
R-Type steel saloon (1954)
3-liter Speed Model (1926)
Benz
dogcart (1897)
Patent-Motorwagen replica (1885)
Velo Comfortable (1897)
Borgward
Isabella coupe (1960)
Brush
D-30 runabout (1909)
Bugatti
Type 22 Brescia modified (1926)
Type 57 tourer (1934)
Type 35A Tecla (1926)
Buick
Super 50 power-top (1949)
Type G roadster (1907)
Cadillac
Type K runabout (1906)
Charron
10CV Charronette (1914)
Citroën
DS saloon (1972)
11CV Traction Avant saloon (1939)
5CV C3 Cloverleaf (1923)
B-14 Caddy sports (1926)
Clément-Bayard
4MS torpedo tourer (1913)
Clément-Panhard
light car (1898)

Cord
812 roadster (1937)
DAF
600 saloon (1958)
Daimler
25.3 hp phaeton (1911)
Darracq
light car (1901)
RRX double phaeton (1910)
Darracq-Bollée
tonneau (1899)
De Dion Bouton
quadricycle (1898)
Populaire (1904)
vis-à-vis (1899)
Delage
Type DO sport 2-seater (1921)
Type B tonneau (1906)
Delahaye
phaeton (1897)
Dennis
fire pump (1929)
DKW
3.6 3-cylinder Sonderklasse (1957)
Fiat
Zero torpedo tourer (1912)
508 roadster (1934)
Flanders
Type 20 roadster (1910)
Ford
Model T fire engine (1924)
V8 cabriolet (1937)
A sedan (1928)
Model T tourer (1909)
Model N runabout (1906)
Franklin
Olympic sedan (1933)
Gardner-Serpollet
Type F steamer (1902)
GN
2-seat cyclecar (1921)
Hanomag
Kommisbrot (1925)
Hispano-Suiza
H6B sports 2-seater (1928)

Holsman
Rambler high-wheeler (1902)
Jaguar
E-Type coupe (1961)
Jameson
Merlin-engined Concorde
La Buire
Type A double phaeton (1907)
Lagonda
M45 sports tourer (1933)
Lancia
Aurelia berline (1953)
Lanef-Lacroix
Tri-car (1903)
Le Gui
voiturette racer (1910)
Leyland
FK-7 fire ladder and pump (1937)
Lincoln
359-B Brunn landaulet (1937)
Lombard
Type G-air 2-seater racer (1927)
Lorraine-Dietrich
TFO open-front limousine (1908)
MAE
10 hp roadster (1911)
Magirus
ML fire engine (1931)
Maxwell-Briscoe
Model AB runabout (1910)
Mercedes-Benz
500 Nürnberg limousine (1933)
300SL roadster (1959)
500K cabriolet Type B (1936)
220S cabriolet (1957)
600 limousine (1972)
MG
TA Midget 2-seater (1938)
Millot
phaeton (1899)
Minerva
AB sedanca de ville (1925)
Mors
RX tourer (1912)

NSU
Ro80 Wankel saloon (1969)
Oldsmobile
Holiday 2-door saloon (1956)
curved dash (1901)
Panhard Levassor
2-cylinder tonneau (1902)
35CV double phaeton (1907)
tonneau de course (1896)
Peugeot
Type 68 tonneau (1904)
vis-à-vis (1891)
Pierce
Motorette (1902)
Plymouth
Six sedan (1936)
Renault
4CV saloon (1949)
IR 6-cylinder coupe de ville (1921)
AG Taxi de la Marne (1912)
AX 2-seater (1909)
REO
Model B runabout (1906)
Richard-Brasier
Type O double phaeton (1904)
Rolls-Royce
20/25 Barker barrel tourer (1926)
Twenty Barker coupe (1927)
40/50 hp Ghost open-drive limousine (1912)
Schaudel
8CV tonneau (1902)
Sizaire et Naudin
8CV voiturette (1906)
Spyker
C4 torpedo tourer (1924)
C4 Tenax replica (1920)
18 hp runabout (1911)
36/50 hp 6-cylinder racer (1902)
12/16 hp double phaeton (1905)
35 hp truck (1921)
SS
3½-liter open tourer (1936)
Jaguar 100 (1938)

Stanley
10 hp steam phaeton (1906)
Stimula
voiturette (1907)
Studebaker
Six 2-door sedan (1933)
Sultane
tonneau (1906)
Tatra
600 Tatraplan saloon (1947)
Thirion
fire pump (1903)
Toledo
Model B steam runabout (1901)
Wolseley
Twenty landaulet (1920)
Wolseley-Siddeley
18 hp landaulet (1906)

New Zealand

LEN SOUTHWARD MUSEUM

The Southward Museum Trust (Inc.), Otaihanga Road, Paraparaumu. Telephone: (058)-71-221.

Location: On State Highway 1 north of Paraparaumu.

Len Southward started as a messenger boy in the Wellington Motor Warehouse in 1919. After setting up a motor cycle repair business with a friend the little company was hit by wartime shortages of rear view mirrors and Austin Seven silencers. As a result he began manufacturing the tubes himself and the company he founded is still a main supplier of steel tube to New Zealand industry.

The museum started, as has so often happened, with the acquisition of a Model T Ford. The collection now numbers more than 250 vehicles ranging in age from an 1895 Benz, listed as a voiturette but more likely a Viktoria (the voiturette name was reserved for the three-wheeled Bollées at the time) through a wide selection of cars from every country to Mercedes-Benz gullwing and Maserati 250F. There are many rarities, such as the 1907 Lux dogcart, a 1906 Wolseley tourer, the 1915 Indianapolis Stutz, a Rauch & Lang electric sedan and a Locomobile steam runabout.

The founder's favorite car is the armor-plated Cadillac sedan which belonged to the late Billie Cohen, gangster. On a lighter note he also has a soft spot for Marlene Dietrich's V16 Cadillac, a 1934 super-car and, from the beginning of the century, a 1901 three-cylinder Duryea and a 1910 White steamer.

All the cars and an associated collection of tractors, motor cycles and cycles are housed in the 'Tin Shed'. This is in fact an architect-designed, purpose-built, glass-roofed steel building covering 4400 square yards (4000 square meters) set in green parkland. Opened in 1979 it has its own 474-seat theater with conference facilities and a large restaurant. Naturally, there are fully equipped workshops for vehicle restoration.

Opposite: **A nicely restored 1909 Le Zèbre runabout from Lips Autotron**

Below: **The translucent roof of the Southward 'Tin Shed' provides a diffused light which is ideal for car photography**

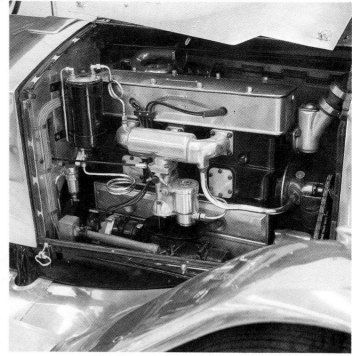

Above: **The engine room of a Vauxhall OE 30/98 sporting tourer. Vauxhalls were popular in the antipodes and many have survived**

Above: **A very rare 1904 Wolseley tourer**

Right: **Southward's copper car is a humorous special with a body constructed completely in copper by Philip Lewis as long ago as 1920. The chassis is a Graham**

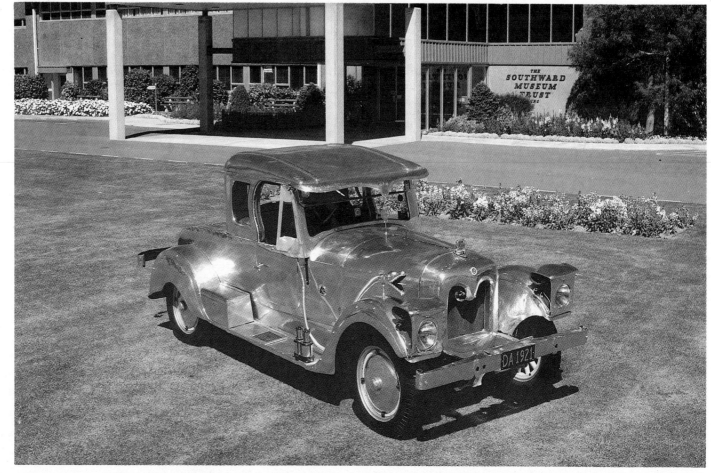

AC
saloon (1951)
Adler
tourer (1910)
Allison-Aero
dragster
Alvis
TD-21 saloon (1960)
Argyll
tourer (1914)
Aston Martin
DB3 engine and chassis (1954)
Auburn
sedan (1936)
Austin
16-4 saloon (1947)
Seven Ruby saloon (1937)
London taxi (1934)
Swallow saloon (1929)
16 hp Six saloon (1929)
Seven tourer (1927)
10 hp chassis (1914)
doctor's coupe (1913)
Auto Car
truck (1918)
Bantam (USA)
saloon (1935)
Begg
F5000 race car
Bentley
8-liter saloon (1930)
Benz
dogcart (1895)
Bianchi
saloon (1923)
BMW
Isetta bubblecar 3-wheeler (1954)
Bugatti
Type 38 chassis (1927)
Buick
fastback (1950)
8 convertible (1940)
sedan (1928)
chassis (1916)
Cadillac
V16 twin cabriolet (1935)
tourer (1911)
single-cylinder runabout (1906)
Chevrolet
caravan (1925)
sedan (1934)
Chrysler
CS 3 liter coupe
Airflow saloon (1933)
roadster (1929)
roadster (1928)
Citroën
2CV saloon (1955)
Traction Avant saloon (193?)
Clément-Talbot
2-seat tourer (1909)
Cooper
Mk VI race car (1952)
Cord
812 saloon (1938)
810 convertible (1937)
Courier
tourer (1923)
Daimler
Royal limousine (1948)
chassis and engine (1910)
saloon (1947)
truck (1926)

Darracq
tourer (1914)
2-seater (1905)
De Dion Bouton
2-seat tourer (1909)
voiturette (1909)
voiturette (1900)
Dodge
coupe (1938)
Six sedan (1928)
4-cylinder sedan (1923)
truck (1920)
Duryea
runabout (1905)
Essex
super-6 sedan (1930)
4-cylinder tourer (1922)
Ferrari
Type 750 Monza (1957)
Flanders
chassis (1914)
FN
roadster (1914)
Ford
Prefect saloon (1948)
Model T roadster (1915)
Model T tourer (1915)
V8 coupe (1936)
Model A tourer (1930)
Model A roadster (1930)
Model T sedan (1926)
Model T tourer (1921)
Model T tourer (1920)
cut-down Model T (1919)
cut-down Model T (1916)
Franklin
limousine (1929)
Glas
Goggomobil sports (1955)
Gobron-Brillié
chassis and engine (1906)
Gwynne
8 hp tourer (1923)
Hillman
Minx (1936)
saloon (1928)
Hispano-Suiza
saloon (1933)
Holsman
high-wheeler (1907)
Hudson
super-6 tourer (1923)
straight-8 sedan (1930)
Humber
Super Snipe saloon (1955)
2-seat tourer (1910)
Hupmobile
runabout
International Harvester
high-wheeler (1909)
Jaguar
Mk V drophead (1948)
Lagonda
V12 drophead coupe (1939)
Lambretta
Bangkok taxi (1956)
Lanchester
saloon (1938)
Lea Francis
tourer (1928)
Locomobile
steam runabout (1901)

Lux (Germany)
dogcart (1897)
Marendaz Special
sports 4-seater (1938)
Marion
tourer (1914)
Maserati
250F single-seater (1956)
8clt single-seat GP (1950)
Maxwell
2-seater (1910)
chassis (1909)
Maybach
SW drophead coupe (1938)
Mercedes
tourer (1914)
Mercedes-Benz
770K tourer (1939)
300 saloon (1955)
300SL gullwing (1955)
Mercury
V8 dragster
Messerschmitt
KR200 3-wheel cabin scooter (1954)
MG
R-Type (1935)
B251 sports (1936)
Minerva
chassis and engine (1927)
tourer (1914)
chassis (1914)
tourer/truck (1914)
Mitchell
tourer (1914)
Morgan
Aero 3-wheeler (1935)
water-cooled 3-wheeler (1921)
Morris
8 hp saloon (1937)
Oxford 2-seater (1926)
Cowley tourer (1925)
NCB
electric van
Napier
tourer (1922)
Nash
sedan (1938)
Nelco
Solocar (1937)
NSU
K101 Caterpillar 3-track (1940)
Oakland
tourer (1921)
Oldsmobile
curved dash runabout (1904)
Overland
tourer/truck (1916)
Owen Magnetic
tourer (1918)
Packard
Eight limousine (1935)
Phoenix (GB)
Quad-car runabout (1906)
Pierce-Arrow
sedan (1934)
Rauch & Lang
electric sedan (1918)
Reliant
3-wheeler
3-wheeler (1952)
Renault
2-seater (1922)

Reo
sedan (1935)
chassis only (1906)
Riley
saloon (1948)
Rolls-Royce
20/25 hp saloon (1929)
40/50 hp Phantom I limousine (1926)
saloon (1923)
40/50 hp Silver Ghost coupe (1921)
40/50 hp chassis (1912)
Rover
saloon (1920)
tourer (1914)
2-seater (1926)
tourer (1922)
tourer (1913)
TT replica (1907)
8 hp 2-seater (1905)
Rugby
sedan (1928)
Saxon
roadster (1915)
Schacht
high-wheel buggy (1907)
Smith Flyer
buckboard (1920)
Standard
V8 saloon (1938)
Standard (GB)
saloon (1929)
Stanley
steam tourer (1920)
Star
tourer (1914)
Buddy Stewart
truck (1925)
Studebaker
saloon (1951)
tourer (1916)
Stutz
sedan (1928)
AA vertical 8 coupe (1927)
special 6 tourer (1921)
Indianapolis race car (1915)
Tatra
saloon (1938)
Trojan
chassis and engine (1926)
Vauxhall
14/40 tourer (1927)
Vinot Deguingand
chassis (1914)
Volkswagen
Beetle saloon (1952)
Schwimmwagen amphibian (1943)
White
steam tourer (1910)
Willys
Jeep (1946)
Willys-Knight
sedan (1931)
Wolseley
Hornet light delivery (1929)
roadster (1920)
Wolseley-Siddeley
tourer (1906)
Woods Mobilette
cyclecar (1915)
Yellow Cab
taxi chassis (1929)
Zim
sedan (1950)

Norway

NORWEGIAN TECHNICAL MUSEUM

Norsk Teknisk Museum, Kjelsåsveien 141, 0491 Oslo 4. Telephone: (02)-22-25-50.

Location: Center of Oslo at the above address.

Not many collections of cars can claim to date from as far back as 1914, the year the Society of Norwegian Engineers founded the Norsk Teknisk Museum. The car collection is part of the transport section of Norway's Museum of Science and Industry and the exhibits range from primitive sledges through to airplanes. However, although the vehicle section is small it is strong in content and the most representative in the country. It features about 40 cars of which half are on view at any one time; about 20 of these are in running order.

The theme is the progress of motor transport in Norway and some of the exhibits are unusual and rare. They include an 1895 Benz Viktoria, which was

the first car to be imported into Norway, and a sleeve-valve Minerva which was owned by King Haakon VII. A prize possession is a rare 1917 Daniels, which is claimed to be the only restored example of this very highly regarded American make in Europe. Another rarity is one of the Löhner-Porsche electric cars which features driving motors mounted in the front hubs to eliminate the mechanical losses inherent in geared transmissions.

An unusual locally produced vehicle is the tandem-seat Bjerring; the tandem configuration was made necessary by the narrow wheel tracks which allowed it to climb mountain paths and to fit into the narrow trench cut by early snowplows. Only six of these

Only about a dozen cars were built by Norsk Automobil Vognfabrik between 1907 and 1911. This two-seat tourer dates from 1909

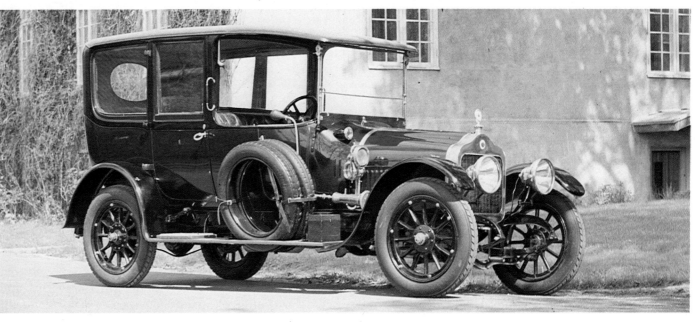

Above: **An unusual 1901 Locomobile wagonette steamer**

Right: **A Norwegian Royal Car: King Haakon VII's 1913 Minerva limousine is preserved in the Oslo museum**

unusual machines seem to have been built, four with air-cooled V4 engines amidships and two with four-cylinder engines at the rear. They were favored by the Norwegian police for patrolling the mountains. The driver sat in the back to put extra weight on the rear wheels and improve traction. A single example of the Norsk, the oldest Norwegian make, is also to be found here, only ten of these cars having been built between 1907 and 1911. The museum's car was constructed in 1909.

Incomplete list; 40 cars in all in collection

Benz
Viktoria (1895)
Bjerring
tandem light car (1920)
Bugatti
Type 30, Weymann racing body (1925)
Cadillac
4-cylinder (1912)
Daniels
unspecified (1917)
Locomobile
Model 48 tourer (1911)
Steamer (1900)
Löhner-Porsche
electric hub-drive (1900)

Maurer-Union
friction-drive twin-cylinder (1908)
Milburn
electric car (1917)
Minerva
King Haakon VII's car (1913)
Norsk
single-cylinder runabout (1909)
Oldsmobile
runabout (1903)
Panhard Levassor
landaulet (1911)
Pierce-Arrow
straight-eight (1930)
Rolls-Royce
40/50 hp Silver Ghost (1916)

Sweden

ALLAN SÖDERSTRÖM AUTOMOBILES

Forenade Bil Import AB, Box 6005, 200 11 Malmö. Telephone: 040-35-00-00.

Location: In the city of Malmö at Ostra Tulgarten 6.

One of the first front-wheel-drive sports cars: the Georges Irat sport two-seater. In models like this, from 1934 and after, buyers had the choice of a Ruby or Citröen engine

This collection of sporting cars is a private one but, apart from the quality of the vehicles displayed, it has the degree of permanence which warrants its inclusion. At the time of writing the cars, which number about 100 (of which 58 are listed), are being rehoused and it is planned to re-open late in 1986.

In choosing the exhibits the emphasis has been on their sporting characteristics and the quality of their design. The family business, Forenade Bil Import, nowadays involves importing Rolls-Royce, BMW and Subaru cars; there are a number of examples of the first two. The Phantom I with a skiff body almost identical to the P1 prototype's is a favorite, while there are two notable BMWs, a 1951 501 prototype and what the owners feel is the one surviving BMW Veritas coupe. Söderström has eschewed imported American cars unless they match up to European standards of design and manufacture. Their outstanding Stutz Black Hawk certainly justifies this policy.

One of the better Swedish collections of Bugattis is

to be found here. Notable examples include the 5-liter eight-cylinder Type 46 coach saloon and a charming Type 44 coach-profile touring coupe with the exaggerated cab line typical of many of Jean Bugatti's designs. The Söderströms are justly proud of their Type 35b Grand Prix car previously owned by Count Salm and raced by Hartmann; there is also an amusing hybrid Type 55/57, a Type 55 with a 57-style 3.3-liter engine and untypical Grand Prix type body. Purists might call this a Type 54/57 because the 55 consisted of a Type 51 engine in a Type 54 chassis. Their Type 13 is also rare and desirable.

The oldest car here is a 1901 Georges Richard with the shaft drive which appeared in that year. The most unusual car is probably the rare Diaz e Grillo from Barcelona, this one being powered by an 1100 cc engine, probably by MAG.

Thanks to the good work of Nils Carlsson, 'Master Nils', the standard of restoration is high and 80 per cent of the cars are roadworthy.

One of the first cars in the Söderström collection is this lovingly restored Talbot-Lago sports two-seater

Alfa Romeo
 6C 2300 Gran Sport spyder (1931)
Amilcar
 CGS 2-seater sports (1925)
Austin
 Seven Nippy 2-seat sports (1934)
Ballot
 3-liter 2/3-seater (1926)
Bentley
 4¼-liter Vanden Plas 4-seater (1936)
 8-liter 3-seat sports (1931)
 S Mulliner Flying Spur coupe (1958)
 4½-liter tourer (1929)
BMW
 1600GT (1967)
 700 twin-cylinder coupe (1962)
 508 saloon (1958)
 507 roadster (1958)
 328 sports roadster (1938)
 315/1 sports roadster (1936)
Borgward
 Isabella coupe (1962)
Brush
 runabout (1910)

Bugatti
 Type 30 (1922)
 Type 55/57 'Grand Sport' (1932, 1935)
 Type 57 cabriolet (1938, 1939)
 Type 57 cabriolet (1938)
 Type 44 coach coupe (1929)
 Type 46 coach limousine (1929)
 Type 35b 8-cylinder Grand Prix (1927)
 Type 38 rebodied 2-seater (1927)
 Type 37 Grand Prix (1927)
 Type 22 Brescia (1923)
 Type 13 2-seater (1910)
Citroën
 C2 5CV 2-seater (1923)
Darracq
 6½ hp single phaeton (1923)
De Dion Bouton
 30 hp raceabout (1907)
Delage
 Type F runabout (1907)
DFP
 2-seat raceabout (1910)
Diaz e Grillo
 2-seat tourer (1916)

FN
 1.3-liter Le Mans (1925)
Fiat
 501 tourer (1924)
Frazer Nash
 Mille Miglia (1953)
Hispano-Suiza
 15.9 hp 2-seat sports (1912)
Hupmobile
 2.8-liter 2-seat tourer (1911)
 2.8-liter raceabout (1911)
Georges Irat
 4-wheel drive roadster (1935)
Jaguar
 XK120 roadster (1950)
Lorraine-Dietrich
 3½-liter sports (1930)
Mercedes-Benz
 300 A cabriolet (1953)
 320 A cabriolet (1938)
MG
 TF roadster (1953)
 TD roadster (1951)
 C-Type Montlhéry Midget (1930)

Morris
 Series MM Minor (1948)
 Cowley tourer (1923)
Pierce-Arrow
 2-seat roadster (1930)
Riley
 1½-liter racer (1935)
 Nine Brooklands (1928)
Rolls-Royce
 40/50 hp Silver Ghost (1925)
 20/25 hp Skiff roadster (1935)
 40/50 hp Phantom I Skiff tourer (1927)
Sizaire et Naudin
 8 hp voiturette (1909)
Stutz
 Black Hawk (1929)
Talbot Lago
 2-seat spyder (1937)

Above: **Söderström's 1925 Amilcar CGS: the most popular model of this sporty French make. Power came from a 1074 cc side valve engine, so the performance hardly lived up to the appearance**

Right: **This 1903 Darracq at Söderström is typical of the small French runabouts which the French industry churned out in their thousands after the turn of the century**

SVEDINO'S CAR AND AIRCRAFT MUSEUM

Svedinos Bil-Flyg Museum, Ugglarp, Kustwagen Halmstad-Falkenberg. Telephone: 0346-43187.

Location: Ugglarp is on the E6 west coast road about 8½ miles (14 km) north of Halmstad. A Canberra bomber parked on the roadside makes it difficult to miss.

This is a most remarkable collection and although somewhat overburdened by the less exciting products of Detroit from the inter-war years, there are cars here that would be hard to find anywhere else. Nevertheless, you may have problems discovering them, for such is Lennart Svedvelt's (Svedino's) passion for acquiring historic machinery that the exhibits are packed tight, cheek-by-jowl and mainly unrestored, in a large hangar-like building.

Most of the rarities are not unforgettable classics; there is not a single Bugatti or Rolls-Royce. But there is a massive 1911 Gräf und Stift phaeton of the type in which the Archduke Ferdinand of Austria was shot at Sarajevo, precipitating World War I. This particular 'Rolls-Royce of Austria' had lingered at the bottom of a lake for 43 years. Rarities from the USA are an Anderson sedan, built in South Carolina in 1923, a 1911 Pierce-Arrow and an unusual artillery-wheeled Auburn. The oldest car here is a wooden wagonette running on steel-tired cart wheels built locally in 1897. This, the Bullerbilen, has its engine offset under the passenger's portion of the park-bench driving seat and drives the live rear axle via a single chain.

One of the great assets of the Svedino museum is its outstanding collection of Volvos, ranging from the OV4 tourer – in which Svedino made a round-the-

The Adler Trumpf sports roadster was one of the most popular of the Hitler-period German sporting roadsters. The mudguards on this Svedino car are non-standard

Left: **This 1918 Pierce-Arrow in Svedino's collection is a great rarity. Notice how, in 1918, the headlamps were faired into the fenders**

Below: **Puch are not so well known for their cars as for their motorcycles. However, this 1912 Puch 14/40 hp has survived 73 Scandinavian winters to remind us of the work of designer Karl Slevogt**

world trip – through all the variations, including the 1936 PV36 Carrioca styled in imitation of the Chrysler Airflow. There is even the former Royal Swedish Volvo convertible, specially built at the Nordberg Coachworks in Stockholm, and now to be found tightly packed among a mass of more plebeian machinery.

Every museum worthy of the name has one: this Swedish 'primitive' is the Bullerin built in 1897 by Jons Olsson. Note the wooden, iron-tired wheels

Adler
2.5-liter six saloon (1938)
Autobahn streamline saloon (1938)
Trumpf sports roadster (1934)
Alfa Romeo
6C 2500 Freccia d'Oro (1951)
Allard
J2X sports 2-seater (1952)
Anderson
Six sedan (1923)
Auburn
roadster (1923)
Austin
Metropolitan cabriolet (1957)
Seven Chummy (1925)
Bardahl Special
American dirt racer (1951)
BMW
501 saloon (1951)
328 cabriolet (1938)
Buick
Six limousine (1929)
tourer (1921)
Bullerbilen
wooden wheeled wagonette (1897)
Cadillac
V8 4-door sedan (1928)
Chevrolet
Six 4-door sedan (1936)
Six sedan (1935)
Six 2-door sedan (1933)
Six roadster (1930)
4-door sedan (1927)
Superior tourer (1925)
Chrysler
sedan (1936)
Six light sedan (1936)
Eight sedan (1931)
Citroën
11CV Traction Avant saloon (1954)
Cord
810 sedan (1936)
Daimler
22 hp phaeton (1908)

De Soto
2-door Airflow coupe (1935)
Airflow saloon (1935)
Dodge
Six sedan (1931)
tourer (1923)
Experimental
2-seater (1950)
Fiat
500 Topolino (1949)
Ford
V8 roadster (1937)
A 4-door sedan (1930)
A roadster (1930)
A pick-up truck (1929)
Model T sedan 2-door (1927)
Model T sedan (1923)
Model T tourer (1923)
Model T tourer (1920)
Model T pick-up (1919)
Model T flat-bed truck (1912)
Model T landaulet (1914)
Model T tourer (1912)
Ford (Germany)
Eifel saloon (1938)
Futurecar
mock-up (1951)
Gräf und Stift
unrestored tourer (1911)
Graham
Six sedan (1928)
Hanomag
1½-liter saloon (1938)
Haynes
model 27 tourer (1918)
Horch
850 cabriolet (1937)
Hupmobile
tourer (1914)
Jaguar
E-Type coupe (1962)
Mk V saloon (1950)
Lancia
sports-racing special (1937)

Lincoln
saloon (1947)
V12 Continental sedan (1942)
fire tender conversion (1926)
Magirus Ulm
fire engine (1922)
Marquette
Six sedan (1930)
Mercedes-Benz
220SE coupe (1959)
170 S/A cabriolet (1950)
320 cabriolet (1939)
320 saloon (1937)
170H RR engine saloon (1936)
MG
2½-liter drophead coupe (1937)
TA Midget (1937)
Minervette
chassis with mudwings (1911)
Morris
Minor Special 2-seater (1929)
Nash
sedan (1938)
Opel
Kadett cabriolet (1939)
Kadett saloon (1937)
saloon (1930)
sports conversion (1920)
Packard
Eight 526 limousine (1929)
Phänomen
Phänomobil 3-wheel tourer (1912)
Piccolo
single phaeton (1905)
Pierce-Arrow
formal limousine (1918)
Plymouth
roadster (1933)
Pontiac
2-door sedan (1927)
Puch
2-door saloon (1912)
Racerbil
single-seat special (1954)

Renault
KJ tourer (1923)
truck conversion (1920)
Model A runabout (1905)
Rovin
mini-car roadster (1948)
Saab
92 saloon (1949)
Scania
truck (1948)
Scania-Vabis
truck (1928)
Seneca
tourer (1920)
Studebaker
Commander saloon (1950)
Tatra
Type 87 6-seat saloon (1938)
Thulin
20 hp tourer (1920)
Tidaholm
country bus (1927)
charabanc (1925)
Volkswagen
2-seat sports special (1958)
Volvo
PV821 (1951)
PV544 (1947)
PV60 saloon (1947)
PV53-56 saloon (1939)
PV51 saloon (1937)
PV36 Carrioca saloon (1936)
PV652 tourer (1936)
PV652 saloon (1935)
Prince Bertil coupe
ambulance (1935)
school bus (1932)
fire ladder wagon (1932)
fire engine (1931)
flatbed truck (1931)
PV652 saloon (1931)
pick-up truck (1928)
OV4 tourer (1928)
PV4 sedan (1928)

Willys
4-door sedan (1929)
Zetos
sport coupe (1958)

Switzerland

SWISS TRANSPORT MUSEUM

Verkehrshaus der Schweiz, Lidostrasse 5, CH6006 Luzern. Telephone: 041-31-44-44.

Location: On the east side of the head of the lake. Take the Gotthard road out of the town and fork right along the lakeside. By bus from the town use route 2.

The Verkehrshaus (transport museum) complex on the lakeside at Lucerne is architecturally one of the best museums in the world and a model of its kind designed specifically to display railroad locomotives, cars, airplanes and space equipment. The sole Swiss planetarium, built by Longines, is also to be found here. The aim of the museum is to preserve historic vehicles and engineering masterpieces and at the same time to contribute to a better understanding of present-day transport problems.

The automobile collection is a significant one because it includes examples from the formative years, before early enthusiasm was overtaken by financial prudence. Many well-engineered cars were being built by a total of about 110 indigenous Swiss constructors. Names like Saurer, Popp, Turicum, Picard & Picqtet, Martini and Dufaux are just some of them.

Every country seems to have a pioneering steam-powered three-wheeler. In Switzerland, engineers who approached this problem were Thury and Nussberger, who built a high-wheeled tricycle with a rear-mounted vertical-tube boiler as early as 1878. This machine is normally in the History and Science Museum in Geneva but is on loan to the Verkehrshaus. However the museum has its own Popp phaeton built in 1898 and examples of the single-

Opposite: Dr Aigner built Ajax cars in Zürich. A feature was the four-cylinder monobloc engine with inlet passages cast into the main casting

Right: The 1919 Pic-Pic, built by Picard et Pictet, was looked on as the Swiss Rolls-Royce. They were one of the few concerns to adopt the Burt McCullum single sleeve-valve principle for their engines

A 1902 Weber double phaeton built by a textile machine manufacturer in Usti. Propelled by a 2½-liter single-cylinder engine, it has an infinitely variable ratio transmission on the lines of the DAF Variomatic

cylinder Berna and Weber cars, not to mention a 1904 Turicum and a splendid example of the straight-eight Dufaux built for the 1905 Gordon-Bennett race. This is ⸜claimed ⸝ to ⸝have ⸍been⸍ the ⸝first ⸍ custom-made straight-eight power unit as distinct from one cobbled up from a pair of four-cylinder engines.

Other notable Swiss cars include a splendid Ajax landaulet and torpedo tourers from Fischer, Martini and Pic-Pic, the latter a fine sporting machine with a body by Gangloff of Geneva reminiscent of those fitted by Vanden Plas to Bentleys.

Adler
  K5/11 (1910)
Ajax
  coupe de ville (1908)
Alvis
  TD21 Graber saloon (1959)
Austin
  Seven tourer (1928)
Benz
  Patent Motorwagen replica (1886)
Berna
  Ideal vis-à-vis (1902)
BMW
  503 (1956)
Chrysler
  straight-8 chassis (1932)
Citroën
  DS21 chassis (1967)
  7S Traction Avant saloon (1934)
  5CV C3 Cloverleaf (1924)
Clément-Bayard
  9 hp tonneau (1904)
Daimler (UK)
  DB18 drophead coupe (1946)
DKW
  Meisterklasse 4-wheel drive (1939)

Dufaux
  Gordon Bennett straight-8 (1905)
Fiat
  508 Ballila (1932)
Fischer
  chassis (1912)
  33CV sleeve-valve tourer (1913)
Ford
  Model T tourer (1922)
Garrett
  steam tractor (1911)
Hispano-Suiza
  K6 saloon (1937)
Lamborghini
  P400 Miura (1968)
Lancia
  Lambda tourer (1929)
Martini
  12/16 chassis (1913)
  12/16 convertible (1913)
Maserati
  3500GT coupe (1960)
Mercedes-Benz
  Type 130 saloon (1934)
  W25 3360 cc single-seater (1934)

Messerschmitt
  KR200 cabin scooter (1956)
NSU
  Ro80 Wankel saloon (1969)
  tracklaying tricar HK101 (1941)
Oldsmobile
  curved dash (1903)
Orion
  flat truck (1903)
Panhard Levassor
  B1 voiturette (1902)
Pic-Pic
  McCullum sleeve-valve (1919)
Popp
  2-cylinder runabout (1898)
Porsche
  356 coupe (1948)
Rapid
  3-wheel 2-seater (1946)
Renault
  AX 2-seater (1908)
Isaac de Rivaz
  working model gas car (1805)
Rolls-Royce
  20 hp cabriolet (1926)

Saurer
  commercial chassis (1956)
  AM11 chassis (1903)
  fire engine (1913)
Thury-Nussberger
  steam tricycle (1878)
Tribelhorn
  electric 3-wheeler (1919)
Turicum
  single-cylinder B1 (1906)
  4-cylinder No.1 (1907)
Volkswagen
  Beetle (1950)
  Beetle chassis (1953)
  Schwimmwagen military amphibian (1942)
Weber
  (1902)

Below: **Most prestigious of the Swiss manufacturers were Charles and Frédéric Dufaux. They built some of the first real straight-eights of which this racer, built for the 1905 Gordon Bennett race, is an example**

Right: **A product of Lorenz Popp, this 1898 Popp Patent motor car has a twin cylinder four-stroke engine**

Union of Soviet Socialist Republics

MOSCOW POLYTECHNICAL MUSEUM

3/4, First entrance, Novaya Square, 101 000.
Location: Novaya Square is in the center of Moscow.

This museum is devoted to science and technology in general in the same way that the Arts et Métiers is in Paris.

The automotive section is a fairly large one containing some 400 items of which 50 are motor vehicles, some of them models, and 40 engines of Russian manufacture. The oldest complete Russian vehicle is a Russo-Baltique built in a railway factory in Riga. Initially these cars were propelled by T-head engines of 4-, 4.8- or 5-liter capacity and were to the designs of a Swiss engineer, M. Potterat. A larger, 7.2-liter, 40/60 hp model to the designs of a German engineer, Valentin, was introduced in 1911. The same designer introduced a series of smaller, side-valve cars which were in production up to the time of the Revolution. A Russo-Baltique won the prize for the car traveling the longest distance in the 1912 Monte Carlo Rally.

The oldest car in this collection is a rare 1898 Stoewer, built in Stettin by the brothers Emil and Bernhard Stoewer. Their earliest four-wheeler was propelled by a twin-cylinder engine of their own design and it is likely that the Polytechnical car is one of these. This veteran is accompanied by an 1899 de Dion Bouton.

Rumor has it that the Rolls-Royce 40/50 hp Ghost limousine which Lenin used during the revolutionary period is housed in this museum. If so one is led to wonder whether this historic machine has been joined by the brace of Silver Shadows owned by the late Leonid Brezhnev?

An 1899 de Dion vis-à-vis from the Moscow Polytechnical Collection speeds through the Russian countryside

The Russian motor industry was not a big one before the revolution. Russo-Baltique produced cars from 1909 to 1915 in a railway works in Riga to designs by Swiss, German and Belgian engineers. One can only guess that this example in the Polytechnical Museum in Moscow might be the 4½-liter car which won the distance category in the 1912 Monte Carlo Rally

United Kingdom

BRITISH MOTOR INDUSTRY HERITAGE TRUST MUSEUM, SYON PARK

Studley Castle, Castle Road, Studley, Warwickshire B80 7AJ. Telephone: 052785-4015.

Location: The headquarters are at Studley Castle between Redditch and Alcester in Warwickshire. The exhibition is in Syon Park, on the A4 near Hounslow in west London and can be reached by bus or underground train. There is good free car-parking.

Starting life as Leyland Historic Vehicles, this collection was established in 1975 to preserve the old vehicles and records of all the companies brought together in the British Leyland Motor Corporation. This might appear to include relatively few marques, but the terms of reference also incorporated the smaller British companies taken over by Leyland group companies. This represents a large portion of the British motor industry and an enormous archive: the Heritage is at present the keeper of more than two million drawings and the records of almost 20 companies, in addition to approximately 240 vehicles on inventory. Apart from making it easy to mount a constantly changing array of exhibits at its Syon Park exhibition hall this large number allows cars to be loaned to other museums and rented out for film and television use.

One commercial activity is to utilize spare capacity in the Leyland factories to manufacture hard-to-obtain spares for private individuals from original factory drawings in the archive. Not only does this contribute towards funds for the Heritage but this much-appreciated service also keeps many well-loved old cars on the road.

The Heritage will be extending its scope with the agreement that it should take in the old vehicles and records of the surviving British companies, including Peugeot-Talbot and the Ford and Vauxhall British operations. As owners of all its cars Heritage will in many ways become a more significant organization than the National Motor Museum at Beaulieu, where many of the cars are on loan.

The vehicles on show at Syon are only a part of the inventory and are changed frequently. Austin built many interesting and exciting vehicles – the tiny twin-cam racing single-seater and the huge six-cylinder racer of 1908 are just two examples. It was the Austin custom to store discarded prototypes in vast cellars beneath the old Austin works at Longbridge where they lay forgotten for decades until the Leyland Historic Vehicle project was mounted: researchers uncovered a fantastic 'Aladdin's cave'.

Leyland also provided vehicles of unique interest for they absorbed Albion, whose 1903 wagonette, and 1909 and 1910 30 hp and 16 hp tourers are of great interest to enthusiasts for Edwardian cars. Leyland's own contribution, commemorating their sole venture into quality car manufacture (we mustn't forget they begat the humble Trojan) is the superb Leyland Eight of 1920. Designed by that great Welsh engineer-driver J.G. Parry-Thomas, it boasts such innovations as leaf valve-springs, servo-brakes and torsion-bar assisted road-springs. Unfortunately it cost considerably more than a Rolls-Royce and found few buyers. The Heritage car was a regular competitor at Brooklands before World War II.

Not all cars are on show

AEC
Rigid Mammoth Major Mk III (1954)
Albion
A3 16 hp tourer (1910)
A6 30 hp tourer (1909)
A2 wagonette (1903)
A1 dogcart (1901)
Alvis
T21 saloon (1965)
Ferret scout car
Saracen personnel carrier
Saladin armoured car
Austin
Metro 1 HLE (1982)
A5 Cambridge saloon (1958)
Datsun-built Seven (1935)
Metro Computervision
Maestro saloon (White) (1982)
Ambassador Vanden Plas saloon (1982)
Allegro 1.5-liter (1982)
Maxi 2 liter 5-door saloon (1981)
Silver Metro (1981)
Metro saloon (1980)
1300 SRV5 (1974)
1800 SRV3 (1974)
Allegro rally car (1973)
Allegro 2-door saloon (1973)
1300 Mk III saloon (1973)
Maxi rally car (1970)
1300 saloon (1968)
1800 Mk II rally car (1968)
Cambridge saloon (1963)
Gipsy fire tender (1962)
A40 Farina saloon (1960)
Healey Sprite (1959)
A55 Cambridge saloon (1958)
A90 Westminster saloon (1955)
A30 Seven 4-door saloon (1955)
A30 Seven 2-door saloon (1955)
A40 Somerset (1954)
K5 fire engine (1953)
A90 Atlantic (1951)
16 saloon (1948)
16 saloon (1946)
Seven Ruby saloon (1938)
Ascot saloon (1937)
18 Iver saloon (1936)
Seven twin-cam single-seater (1936)
Lichfield saloon (1935)
Seven single-seat racer (1934)
12/6 Harley saloon (1932)
Seven Swallow (1931)
Seven 'top hat' saloon (1927)
Seven Chummy tourer (1923)
Twenty tourer (1922)
20 hp Vitesse tourer (1914)
15 hp town carriage (1911)
7 hp open 2-seater (1910)
18/24 Endcliffe tourer (1910)
100 hp Grand Prix (1908)
40 hp York limousine (1907)
30 hp tourer (1907)
Seven Swallow saloon (1927)
Bean
15.9 hp tourer (1923)
Daimler
Double-six saloon (1973)
DK400 limousine (1957)
LC27 ambulance (1954)
2½-liter Consort saloon (1952)
E20 saloon (1937)
LQ20 saloon (1935)
TL30 Worthington bottle car (1921)
23 hp saloon (1911)

12 hp tourer (1911)
TP35 tourer (1907)
TB14 tourer (1903)
Honda
Prelude saloon (1979)
Humber
Snipe Imperial
Jaguar
XJC coupe last-off-line (1978)
XJS saloon (1977)
XJC racing (1975)
V12 E-Type last-off-line (1975)
Group 44 racer (1974)
V12 E-Type coupe (1971)
420G saloon (1970)
XJ6 4.2 liter saloon (1969)
E-Type 4.2 liter lhd (1968)
XJ13 Le Mans prototype (1966)
Mk II saloon (1961)
XK150 fixed-head coupe (1958)
D-Type (1956)
Mk VII saloon (1955)
D-Type Le Mans, ovc 501 (1954)
C-Type Le Mans (1952)
XK120 roadster (1952)
XK120 coupe (1952)
XK120 sports 2-seater (1950)
Mk V saloon (1948)
Lanchester
10 hp Barker saloon (1950)
10 hp saloon (1933)
20 hp tonneau (1904)
12 hp tonneau (1903)
Land-Rover
110 (1982)
V8 station wagon (1980)
V8 station wagon (1977)
4-cylinder (1977)
millionth vehicle (1977)
88 inch tilt (1962)
Number One (1948)
Leyland
straight-8 2-seater (1927)
March
Unipart Formula 3 racer (1978)
MG
EX181 record car (1957)
EX179/219 record car (1964)
EX 135 record car (1938)
MGB GT (1980)
MGB 2-seater (1980)
Midget 1500 (1979)
MGB GT V8 (1976)
MGB GT SSV 1 (1972)
Midget (196?)
TF Midget (1954)
YB saloon (1952)
NB Magnette (1936)
18/80 Mk I sports 4-seater (1931)
old Number One (1925)
Mini
Crompton Electricar (1972)
Moke (1983)
Clubman SRV 4 (1974)
ADO 70 (1970)
Cooper S Monte Carlo rally car (1966)
Cooper S Monte Carlo rally car (1964)
Cooper S Monte Carlo rally car (1963)
Twini-Moke (1962)
Seven Bathgate one-off (1961)
Downton conversion (1959)
Seven saloon (1959)

Morris
Minor fire tender (1955)
Ital estate (1984)
Marina lhd USA-spec (1977)
Marina SRV2 (1974)
Marina coupe 1.3 (1973)
1800S Mk II saloon (1971)
Minor Traveller (1969)
Series VI (1967)
LD van (1962)
Minor tourer (1960)
Series III saloon (1957)
Series MM Minor (1952)
Series MO Oxford (1952)
Series MM Minor saloon (1948)
Commercial ex-WD breakdown (1940)
Eight Series I saloon (1936)
Cowley saloon (1932)
Minor tourer (1929)
10/4 Mower (1927)
Red Flash Brooklands special (1925)
10 cwt light van (1924)
13.9 hp Oxford (1923)
6-cylinder Bullnose (1921)
Oxford Bullnose 2-seater (1913)
bicycle (1894)
Morris Commercial
LC fire engine (1948)
laundry van (1956)
1-ton truck (1924)
Range-Rover
Darien Gap expedition (1971)
Riley
1.5 saloon (1959)
Elf saloon (1970)
4/72 saloon (1967)
2½-liter RMB saloon (1951)
nine Merlin saloon (1937)
10 hp V-twin car (1909)
9 hp V-twin car (1907)
tricar and forecarriage (1905)
Royal tricycle (1899)
Road-Rover
prototype (1955)
Rover
3500S P6B saloon (1977)
3-liter Prime Minister's car (1972)
3-liter coupe (1965)
Rover-BRM Le Mans turbine car (1963)
T.4 turbine saloon (1961)
100 (P4) saloon (1960)
T.3 turbine coupe (1956)
Ten saloon (1938)
Ten 4-door saloon (1937)
Nizam 2-seater 10 hp (1932)
16/50 coupe (1927)
Eight coupe (1922)
12 hp landaulet (1912)
20 hp tourer (1907)
8 hp runabout (1907)
6 hp runabout (1906)
Imperial motor cycle (1915)
Imperial motor cycle (1911)
SS
Jaguar 100 2-seater (1938)
Jaguar 2½ liter saloon (1936)
SSI saloon (1934)
SSI coupe (1933)
SSII coupe (1932)
Standard
Ensign de luxe saloon (1963)
Vanguard Sportsman saloon (1955)
Pennant saloon (1958)
Swallow saloon (1931)

9 hp Teignmouth saloon (1929)
13.9 hp 2-seater (1922)
20 hp cabriolet (1913)
30 hp double phaeton (1907)
Swallow
sidecar
Thornycroft
gun tractor (paraffin) (1919)
30 hp TT car (1908)
40 hp TT car (1907)
40 hp TT car (1905)
20 hp tourer (1904)
steam wagon (1902)
steam wagon (1896)
Triumph
Acclaim saloon (1984)
TR8 lhd fixed-head USA-spec (1980)
TR7 drophead (1981)
TR8 drophead (1980)
Dolomite Sprint saloon (1980)
1500 Spitfire (1980)
TR7 V8 rally car (1978)
Stag hardtop (1977)
2000S estate (1977)
2000 saloon (automatic) (1967)
Herald saloon (1964)
Vitesse saloon (1963)
Mayflower saloon (1952)
Dolomite saloon (1937)
Trojan
2-stroke tourer (1924)
Vanden Plas
4-liter R saloon (1965)
Wolseley
2200 Wedge (1975)
1500 Fleet Mode (1961)
Eight saloon (1939)
Series II saloon de ville (1938)
9 hp Wasp saloon (1934)
Eustace Watkins Hornet special (1932)
E.4 2-seater (1925)
E.3 doctor's coupe (1923)
E.2A Stellite (1919)
10 hp tonneau (1901)
3½ hp voiturette (1899)
tricar, second vehicle (1896)
tricar, first vehicle (1895)

Below: **Forerunner of all Jaguars, the little Austin Swallow was a good looker in its time and its success led to the formation of SS Cars Ltd in Coventry**

Right: **Rover and BRM collaborated to build this Rover-BRM gas turbine car, which successfully completed the 1965 Le Mans race in tenth place driven by Graham Hill and Jackie Stewart**

Left: **Two record-breaking MGs from the Heritage Trust. In the background is Goldie Gardner's Ex. 135, which did an incredible 203 mph with an 1100 cc engine in 1939. Ex. 181, in the foreground, powered by a supercharged twin-cam MGA engine, achieved 255 mph in 1958**

Below: **This group of Heritage Trust cars is fronted by the successful Morris Oxford and Austin Seven models from the two founder companies of BMC**

DONINGTON COLLECTION

Donington Park, Castle Donington, Derby DE7 5RP. Telephone: 0332-810048.

Location: From motorway M1 take exit 24 to East Midlands Airport. Museum is past the airport at junction of airport road and A453 Nottingham-Tamworth road.

In 1933 the Derby & District Motor Club, whose motor cycle races had been held on a narrow circuit in Donington Park near Derby, prevailed on the owner to widen the road and allow them to run motor races. This proved so popular and profitable that the circuit was quickly improved and extended until in 1938 and 1939 it was possible to hold full-scale Grand Prix races.

During World War II Donington Park became a military vehicle depot and the circuit was built over and ruined. Because of its condition it was little used until 1971 when Tom Wheatcroft, a building contractor, bought the remains of the old track and the part of the park containing it in 1971. Since then a completely new Grand Prix circuit has been built, roughly following the lines of the old one.

Wheatcroft's most significant move was to establish the Donington Museum of Single-Seater Racing Cars based on a personal collection he started in 1964 when he bought a single-seater F1 Ferrari of 1952 vintage. More followed and by the time he acquired Donington Park he already owned 40 historic cars.

This is undoubtedly one of the best collections of racing cars in the world with representatives from every significant country. Students of racing car design can study, for example, all the different types of Formula 1 Lotus from the front-engined single-seater to the latest ground-hugging cars. The earliest Cooper Climaxes are here, contrasting with the Cooper Maserati T81 of 1966. There are examples of most of the makes which raced on the pre-1939 circuit, such as the twin-cam supercharged Austin Sevens, the Maserati 8CM of 1933 and an Alfa Romeo P3 monoposto. These make a striking contrast to the modern Formula 1 cars, of which there is a wide selection.

One of the museum's most ambitious projects has been to rebuild one of the 1946 Cisitalia 16-cylinder 1½ liter supercharged Grand Prix cars designed by the Porsche company for Pierro Dusio, the founder of the short-lived Cisitalia organization. Parts of the complex 16-cylinder engine with its tiny pistons and roller-bearing crankshaft are displayed alongside the complete car. This project contributed to Dusio's financial collapse, but the funds were said to have been put to good use by Porsche in founding their own operation in Gmünd, Austria. Donington has a rare

Jim Clark in action at Monaco in the Donington Museum's 1½-liter Lotus-Climax 25, the first monocoque Formula 1 car

Stirling Moss in a Vanwall on his way to a win in the 1958 Moroccan Grand Prix. Vanwall won the Manufacturers' Championship that year

example of a 1960 Porsche 1½ liter single-seater to remind us that Porsche did have the know-how and the resources to build a competitive Formula 1 car if required.

The cars are displayed in a modern well-heated building containing many large photographs and mementos of Grand Prix racing. Several engines are displayed, including a Bugatti railcar unit of the type used in the T41 Royale.

The Tipo 246 was the last successful front-engined Ferrari. This example, now in the Donington collection, is being driven by Mike Hawthorn to a World Drivers' Championship in the 1958 Moroccan Grand Prix

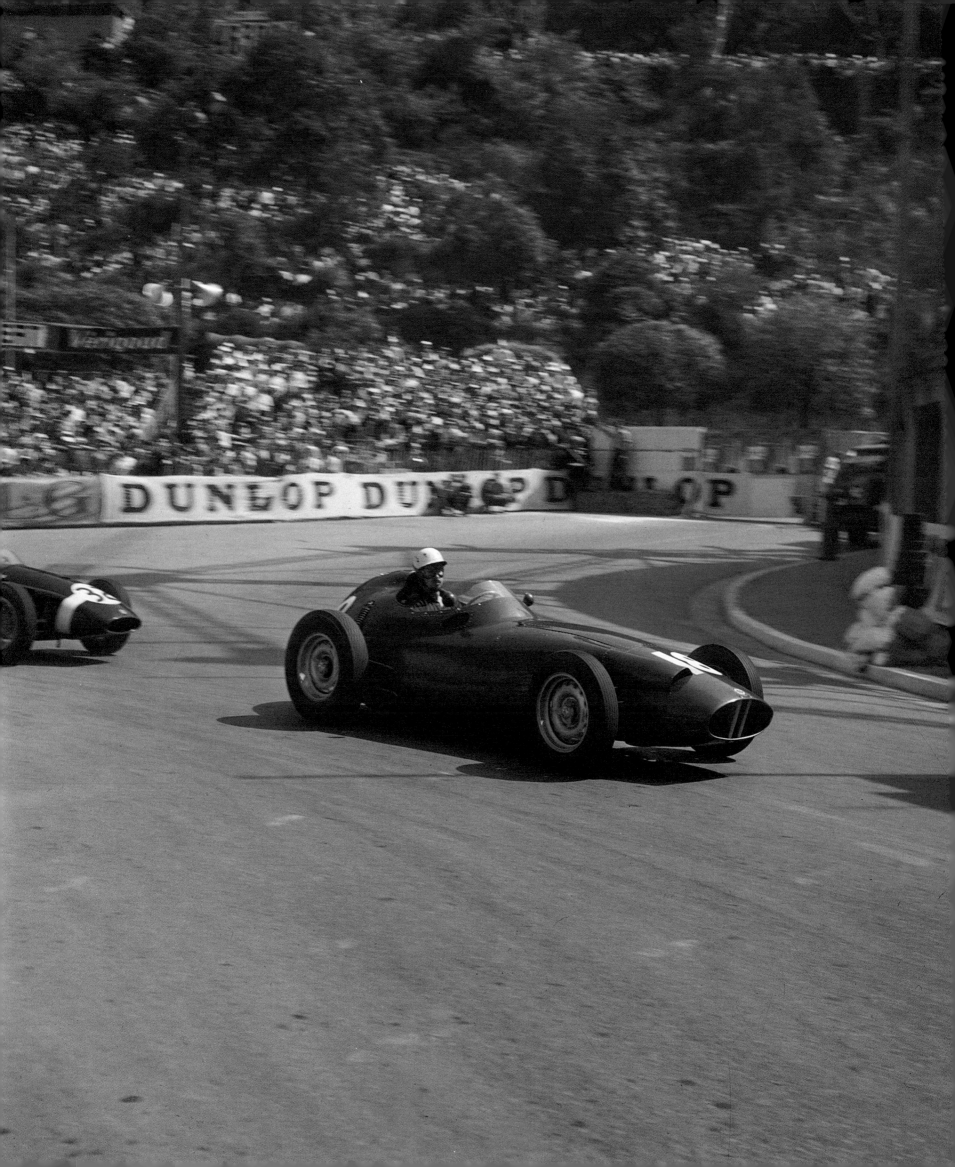

AJB
butterfly-valve engine (1952, 1956)

Alfa Romeo
Bimotore remains (1935)
Tipo B P3 (1932, 1934)

Alta
1½-liter GP (1948)
display engine

Aston Martin
DBR4/250 2½ liter Formula 1 (1959)

ATS
1½-liter V8 Formula 1 (1963)

Austin
twin-cam 750 cc (1935)
side-valve, s/c, single-seater (1936, 1939)
replica pedal car

Auto Union
1½-liter E/D type GP (c1940)

Bellasi-Ford
Formula 1 special, Cosworth DFV (1970)

Bentley
8-liter twin-turbo record (1930)

Brabham-Alfa
BT46 Alfa Romeo engine (1978)
BT45 Alfa Romeo engine (1976, 1978)
BT46B ground suction fan (1978)
BT48 Alfa Romeo engine (1979)

Brabham-Ford
BT52.4 Cosworth engine
BT52.4 Cosworth DEV engine (1980)
BT26/4 Cosworth engine (1969)
BT49 Cosworth engine (1980)
BT44B Cosworth engine (1975)
BT33 Cosworth engine (1970)
BT49C Cosworth engine (1981)

Brabham-Repco
BT25 Repco V8 engine (1968, 1969)

Bristol
Hercules crankshaft
Hercules aero carburetor

BRM
P25 (1959)
H16 display engine (1968)
V16 display engine

Bugatti
Type 51 twin-ohc GP (1931)
Type 41 railcar engine
child's pedal car

Buick
tourer (1927)

Cisitalia
360 16-cylinder Porsche design (1948, 1949)

Connaught
B-Type Formula 1 (1954, 1960)
A-Type Formula 2 (1953)

Cooper
Norton 500 (1951)

Cooper-Bristol
F2 Bristol 2-liter engine (1953)

Cooper-Climax
T51 4-cylinder Coventry-Climax engine (1959)
4-cylinder Coventry-Climax engine (1960, 1963)
T60, Coventry-Climax engine (1962)

Cooper-JAP
1000 (1950)

Cooper-Maserati
T81 formula 1 (1966)

Costin
Protos & wooden monocoque (1967)

Cosworth
DFV V8 F1 3-liter engine (1967)
4-wheel drive F1 (1969)

Cottin Degoouttes
10.6-liter 2-seater (1911)

Coventry-Climax
V8 display engine (1960s)

Delage
1½-liter straight-8 supercharged GP (1926, 1927)

Derby-Maserati
Front-wheel drive single-seater (1935)

Eagle-Climax
T2G (1966)

ENV
preselector gearbox display

Bob Evans
personal car

Ferguson-Climax
P99 4-wheel drive (1961)

Ferrari
312 B1 (1970, 1971)
125 Grand Prix (1949, 1951)
Tipo 500/750 ex-Ascari (1952, 1955)

Frazer Nash
1½-liter Fane single-seater (1935)

Gordini
F2 Simca engine (c1952)

Jaguar
XK cylinder head display

JAP
single-cylinder display engine

LEC
David Purley wrecked car (1977)

Lola-Climax
F1 4-cylinder prototype (1962)

Lotus
25 Coventry-Climax engine 1½-liter (1962)
18 Coventry-Climax engine Formula 1 (1960, 1961)

Lotus-Climax
18, 4-cylinder Coventry-Climax (1960, 1961)

Lotus-Ford
72 4-wheel drive Cosworth engine (1969)
72 Cosworth engine JPS Formula 1 (1970)
64 (1969)
72 Cosworth engine (1973, 1974)
49B Cosworth engine (1968, 1969)
Type 63 Cosworth engine (1969)

Lotus-Pratt & Whitney
56B turbine Indianapolis (1969)

March-BMW
Formula 2 (1975)

March-Ford
701 Formula 1 Cosworth engine (1970)

Maserati
8CM 3-liter engine & crank (c1934)
8CM 3000 Nuvolari car (1934)
4CLT 1½-liter (1948)

Mercedes-Benz
38/250 supercharged 2-seater (1929)

McLaren
MP4 (1984)

McLaren-Ford
M26 Cosworth engine
M23 Cosworth engine (1975, 1977)

Porsche
718 4-cylinder 1½-liter Formula 1 (1960, 1961)
804 8-cylinder 1½-liter Formula 1 (1962)

Rotovic
Ariel-based V12 engine (1965)

Rudge
Ulster motor-cycle

Scarab
Formula 1 single-seater (1959)

Shadow-Matra
DN7 Formula 1 (1975)

Thinwall Special
4½ liter Formula 1 (1952, 1954)
chassis frame (1950, 1951)

Toleman-Hart
TG181 Hart-turbo engine Formula 1 (1981)
TG280 Derek Warwick car (1980)
TG181 Formula 1 (1982)

Tyrrell
006/2 Formula 1 Jackie Stewart car (1973)

Vanwall
front-engine 2½-liter Formula 1 (1955, 1959)
VW14 rear-engine Formula 1 (1961)
display engine (1958)

Vincent-HRD
single-cylinder display engine

Weslake
V12 3-liter Formula 1 engine (1972, 1973)

Wheatcroft
Formula 2 Pilbeam design (c1974)

Williams-Ford
FW08 6-wheel cosworth engine (1981, 1982)
FW86 Cosworth engine (1978, 1979)

Williamson
Roger Williamson's kart

Wolf-Ford
WR1 Cosworth engine (1977)

Wright-Cyclone
carburetor display

Opposite: **Jo Bonnier's P25 BRM, identical to the one now at Donington, in action in the 1959 Monaco Grand Prix**

Right: **The 2.5-liter Scarab, here seen in action in the 1960 Dutch Grand Prix, was financed by Lance Rventlow, son of Barbara Hutton the Woolworth heiress**

MIDLAND MOTOR MUSEUM

Stanmore Hall, Bridgnorth, Shropshire. Telephone: 07462-61761.

Location: on the A588 Bridgnorth-Stourbridge road about 2 miles (3km) outside Bridgnorth.

Above: **In 1934 Riley of Coventry provided inspiration for the SS 100 when they produced their sporting four-cylinder Imp and six-cylinder MPH two-seaters. This is a Riley Imp**

This collection reflects the interest of its founder and owner, T.A. (Bob) Roberts, in fast cars. He started with a Type 43 straight-eight supercharged Bugatti which he still owns and races, and went on from there. Naturally, Bugattis are well represented here, notably Types 23 Brescia, 57S and 57C, but the real excitement lies in the wide spectrum of sports car makes, including many historic cars. Probably the most outstanding is John Cobb's Napier Railton – really a racing car although it can have two seats. This car was the last holder of the outer circuit record at the historic Brooklands track at Weybridge with a speed of 144.3 mph (232 km/h). It is propelled by a 24-liter Napier Lion aero engine and is said to have cost £20,000 in 1935 – equivalent to nearly £500,000 in 1986.

Another star from yesteryear is the supercharged Mercedes-Benz 38/250hp SSK, appropriately registered GP10, once raced by world record holder Sir Malcolm Campbell in the 1929 TT race. This particular Mercedes-Benz sports car was notable for the Stuka-like, soul-searing scream given off when its high-geared supercharger was engaged by pressing extra hard on the accelerator. As a measure of prog-

ress in Mercedes-Benz sports car design the museum also has an example of the 300SL, the 1950s counterpart of the 38/250, featuring a space-frame chassis and gullwing doors.

Builders of high-priced luxury cars of the quality of Rolls-Royce and Hispano-Suiza did not indulge in anything so plebeian as racing in their later years but they always listed higher-speed versions of their cars for sale to sporting owners. It is good to see that the museum has recognized this trend of the 1930s with examples of the Rolls-Royce Phantom II Continental coupe and its arch-rival, the fabulous V12 Hispano-Suiza Type 68.

Sports car development after the end of the vintage period, typified by the Mercedes-Benz and Le Mans Bentley (one car which is missing from the museum's catalog) is represented by the two Type 57 Bugattis and the French Talbots built by Tony Lago. There is a 'cooking' Type 26 Talbot Lago on show and one of its derivatives in the shape of the Type 51 Grand Prix car. This took advantage of the immediate post-World War II Grand Prix formula and won a number of races because its unsupercharged engines consumed less fuel than the 1½ miles per gallon, 1½-liter supercharged Alfa-Romeos it raced against, needing fewer pit stops.

Modern cars on show include examples of all the Jaguar pure racing types powered by the XK120 engine and evolved during the company's Le Mans-winning period. These include a C-Type, the first racing car to be fitted with disk brakes, and the 'long-nose' D-Type driven to victory by Mike Hawthorn and Ivor Bueb in 1955.

Aston Martin carried the British banner in sports car racing when the Jaguar works teams retired from the fray. The museum has a pristine example of one of the works cars, the DB3S which won the Belgian Production Sports Car Race in the hands of Paul Frère. In its time it was driven by Stirling Moss, Reg Parnell, Peter Collins and Roy Salvadori.

Although Henry Ford started his car-building career with racers and at one time held the American outright speed record, the Ford name was not associated with top-line racing for many years until Ford's grandson determined to win the Le Mans 24-hour. He needed to beat Ferrari, which had dominated the race for six years. This he achieved with devastating efficiency and at great expense with the GT40, using a chassis based on the British Lola design. A run of these cars was built in the UK to satisfy the rules for the Le Mans race and an example is listed in the museum catalog.

No sports car collection would be complete without a few Ferraris and there are always some examples of these at Bridgnorth. The 250LM 3.3-liter sports racing coupe, the 4.4-liter Type 365 Daytona made for the American market, a 6-carburetor 275GTB and a lovely example of the Lusso coupe, the most sought-after of all Ferrari sports touring models, can all be seen here.

Bridgnorth contains examples of most sporting marques. There are vintage cars such as the 30/98 Vauxhall, an Alfa Romeo straight eight, a Delahaye 135, and a BMW328 from the 1930s. After World War II come the Healeys from Warwick, in the shape of a Silverstone and the classic 100, a Lotus Elite, and a 230 mph Porsche 917K, the fastest sports car to date.

It is difficult to find a car in the museum which is not capable of being driven at its maximum speed. Many are on loan from owners who may occasionally remove them temporarily for sporting events. But you will always be sure of finding a representative selection of the best sporting cars in this purpose-built, modern museum.

Incidentally, if you like fast machinery the museum also houses a fine collection of racing motor cycles gathered by curator Michael Barker.

Alton Jaguar
  3.8-liter special (1958)
Aston Martin
  DB4GT (1960)
  DB3S (1955)
  2-liter (1938)
Bugatti
  57S coupe (1939)
  57S drophead (1938)
  Type 43 (1927)
  Brescia (1926)
  Type 35B (1927)
Ferrari
  365 GTB4A (1972)
  246 Dino (1972)
  365 GTB4 Daytona (1972)
  275 GTB (1965)
  250LM (1964)
Ford
  GT40 (1965)
Frazer Nash-BMW
  328 sport (1939)
Healey
  Silverstone 2.5-liter (1950)
Hispano-Suiza
  T.68 9½-liter (1931)

Jaguar
  XJ12C racer (1976)
  E-Type 3.8-liter (1963)
  D-Type long-nose (1955)
  C-Type Le Mans (1953)
  XK120 (1951)
Lotus
  Elite 1.2-liter (1962)
Mercedes-Benz
  300SL roadster (1933)
  300SL gullwing (1955)
  38/250SSK TT (1929)
Napier-Railton
  24-liter Brooklands (1933)
Porsche
  917 sports-racing (1970)
Rolls-Royce
  40/50 Phantom II Continental coupe (1933)
  40/50 Phantom II (1930)
Talbot-Lago
  2½-liter America (1959)
  4½-liter Grand Prix (1951)
  Type 26 saloon (1948)

Left: **The driving compartment of GP 10, Sir Malcolm Campbell's impressive 1929 Mercedes-Benz 38/250 SSK sports-racing car**

Top: **The 1938 2-liter BMW 328 two-seater was one of the most effective cars in pre-1939 sports car racing, and established the high performance image of this Bavarian company**

MUSEUM OF BRITISH ROAD TRANSPORT

Cook Street, Coventry, West Midlands. Telephone: 0203-25555, ext. 2315 or 2086.

Location: In the center of Coventry behind the Coventry Theater.

Above: **A 1955 Jaguar D-type Le Mans: this elegant creation of a small team of gifted engineers won three times at Le Mans. In 1957 D-types occupied the first four places**

Coventry was the hub of the British motor industry from its birth at the end of the nineteenth century until 1939. The manufacture of motor cars developed from bicycle making, which Coventry had virtually monopolized thanks to the large pool of skilled labor bequeathed by a healthy weaving industry, watch-making on a big scale and the manufacture of sewing machines. The original cycle makers came out of the sewing machine industry and in a very short time made large fortunes out of what was then a sensational new mode of transport. When petrol engines became available the Coventry manufacturers used them first of all to power cycles and then moved into automobile manufacture.

In 1896 the Daimler Motor Company became the first to be established in Coventry, building cars to the German patents. These first Coventry-built cars were quickly followed by others. In those early days engines were of German or French design and development was restricted for almost six years by entrepreneur Henry J. Lawson, who tried to corner the patent rights of the German and French engine builders. Fortunately he did not succeed and after 1901 the Coventry industry went from strength to strength with dozens of large and small manufacturers. Although Morris at Oxford and Austin at Birmingham produced greater numbers of cars much of their equipment and components came from

Coventry. Coventry had its own firms such as Alvis, Rover, Daimler, Armstrong-Siddeley, Riley, SS Cars and Lea Francis, among others.

The Coventry museum sets out to record this golden era in the city's history. The curator and his assistants have all been brought up in the industry and they have been very selective about the exhibits, which are either Coventry-built vehicles or Coventry-part vehicles, both private and commercial.

There are a number of Daimlers in the museum, but also many other makes to look at. A particularly significant car is the 1910 Maudslay, a luxury tourer with the overhead-camshaft engine pioneered in 1902 by Alex Craig and Cyril C. Maudslay. Another advanced design was the Alvis sports tourer built from 1927 onwards which was one of the world's first production front-wheel drive cars. It is displayed alongside a Riley Kestrel tourer. Riley was a pioneer Coventry car company, the family having been involved in the weaving industry before turning to bicycle manufacture in 1890. It was a go-ahead

company which made detachable wheels and proprietary engines, and was responsible for the first 'three-box' body with the rear-seat passengers sitting ahead of the back axle with their feet in foot wells.

Probably the most prestigious car here is one of the royal Daimlers from King George V's reign. Originally powered by one of the classic sleeve-valve V12 Daimler engines, this beautifully finished limousine was re-engined after the World War II with one of the latest 4½-liter, six-cylinder power units. Its most noticeable feature is its very tall roof, made to enable Queen Mary, who was relatively short, to walk into the car without stooping.

One of the great joys of this museum is the display of light cars of the inter-war years. You are unlikely to find elsewhere a 1923 8 hp Humber Chummy, or a Stoneleigh car, thus named to disguise the fact that it was the cheap end of the Armstrong-Siddeley range. As presented in 1924 it had a V-twin engine using war surplus air-cooled cylinders from the aero engines that Armstrong-Siddeley had made during hostilities.

The SS 100 Jaguar sports two-seater was the company's first genuine 100 mph production car in 1935

A quirk of the design was that the driver sat in the middle with the passengers abreast behind him. Yet another of the oddities is the GWK with variable speed drive, made in Maidstone but propelled by a Coventry-built Coventry Climax engine.

The museum's oldest car is an 1897 Daimler wagonette powered by a V-twin German Daimler engine imported by F.R. Simms, Gottlieb Daimler's British friend who in the 1880s secured patent rights for the Daimler engine for the UK and all the colonies except Canada. The other pre-1900 car in the collection is an 1898 Daimler which was converted to wheel steering in the early 1900s. It was donated to the museum by Jaguar Cars when they took over the Daimler Company and, rebuilt by the museum staff, has taken part in many of the annual London to Brighton car runs.

The museum's premises were opened in 1979 but further developments are promised and it is hoped that the cars can be displayed in settings reminiscent of the period in which each model was built.

Overleaf: **In 1903 Maudslay originated overhead camshafts. They made cars of the highest quality, as proven by this fine 32 hp double phaeton**

Field Marshal Montgomery's Super Snipe staff car originated from the Coventry Humber factory

Alvis
TE21 sports saloon 1alv (1965)
4-wheel drive 4-seater sports (1928)
10/30 tourer (1920)
TA21 saloon (1952)
12/60 (1932)

Armstrong-Siddeley
Whitley saloon (1952)
14 hp saloon (1936)

Austin
A50 saloon (1956)
A40 Somerset van (1954)
A35 saloon (1953)
three-way van (1953)
fire engine (1939)
Seven (1933)

Austin-Healey
BN1 sports 2-seater (1953)

Brabham
BT49 D/18 racer (1982)

BRM
Techcraft (1963)

Chrysler
Centura prototype (1975)

Commer
GS 4 X 4 army truck (1953)
ambulance (1959)

Coventry-Motette
runabout (1897)

Coventry-Premier
3-wheeler (1920)

Coventry-Victor
Venus prototype (1949)

Crouch
Carette 8 hp 3-wheeler (1912)

Crowden
dogcart (1899)

Daimler
Sovereign 2 (XJ6) saloon (1972)
Majestic hearse (1965)
Century (1956)
Conquest saloon (1953)
DB18 saloon (1950)
scout car (1943)
straight-8 saloon (1937)
OPR-3-50 Royal limousine (1935)
M16/20 limousine (1931)
25/85 saloon (1926)
A12 double tonneau (1911)
45 hp double phaeton (1906)
6 hp Marseilles phaeton (1898)
wagonette (1897)

Dennis
fire engine (1937)

Ferguson
R5/2 prototype 4 X 4 (1959)
R4 prototype 4 X 4 (1956)
R5 prototype 4 X 4 (1958)

Freight-Rover
panel van (1982)

Hillman
Hunter (London-Sydney) (1968)
Swallow prototype (1968)
Super Imp (1966)
Minx Mk III (1960)
Radford estate (1956)
Minx saloon (1952)
Aero Minx sports coupe (1935)
Minx saloon (1934)

Hillman-Coatalen
12/15 phaeton (1908)

Humber
Sceptre saloon (1961)
4 X 4 armored car (1953)
Hawk saloon (1952)
Montgomery's staff car (1943)
Super Snipe saloon (1936)
12 hp Vogue (1935)
(1930)
8 Chummy (1923)
12/20 light tourer (1910)
16/24 tourer (1910)

Jaguar
XJ12 Broadspeed saloon (1977)
E-Type (1975)
3.8 Mk II saloon (1963)
Mk VIII saloon (1958)
Mk V saloon (1952)
XK120 fixed-head coupe (1953)
drophead coupe (1948)
Mk V drophead coupe (1951)

Karrier
Gamecock fire engine (1952)

Lanchester
Roadrider saloon (1939)

Land-Rover
safari car (1974)

Lea Francis
14 sports (1952)
Westland coupe (1949)
8.9 hp tourer (1925)

Lotus
Horizon prototype (1982)
Elite (1957)

Maudslay
32 hp double phaeton (1910)
17 hp tourer (1909)

Morris
GPO van (1972)
Mini (1960)
ohv Minor (1955)
Series M saloon (1948)
Series E saloon (1939)
van (1936)
Minor (1932)
Cowley tourer (1922)
Oxford tourer (1913)

Payne & Bates
dos-à-dos 7 hp (1901)

Riley
Kestrel (1935)
Lynx saloon (1934)
12/18 double phaeton (1908)
tricar (1904)

Rover
T4 gas turbine car (1962)
T3 gas turbine car (1956)
gas turbine prototype chassis (c1950)
75 P4 saloon (1954)
75 P3 saloon (1953)
16 saloon (1939)
12 saloon (1934)
16/50 Weymann saloon (1927)
12 hp doctor's coupe (1915)

Rover-BRM
Le Mans sports-racer (1965)

Siddeley-Deasy
18 hp open-drive landaulet (1912)

Singer
Gazelle saloon (1956)
9 sports coupe (1934)
9 hp van (1931)

SS
Jaguar 100 sports 2-seater (1935)
Jaguar 1½-liter (1935)
SS1 fixed-head coupe (1933)
Jaguar 1½-liter saloon (1936)

Standard
Ensign saloon (1960)
Ten (1955)
Vanguard Phase II (1954)
Vanguard Phase I (1949)
Eight saloon (1948)
chassis only (1929)
Flying 14 saloon (1947)
10 saloon (1937)

16 saloon (1935)
Swallow saloon (1930)
Fulham saloon (1929)
24/30 double phaeton (1907)

Stoneleigh
utility tourer (1924)

Sunbeam
Mk III drophead (1954)
Mk II saloon (1953)
Alpine 2-seater (1968)

Sunbeam-Lotus
works rally car (1980)

Swift
cyclecar (1913)
7 hp 2-seat tourer (1910)

Talbot
105 (1934)

Triumph
2.5PI police car (1977)
Dolomite Sprint saloon (1972)
TR6 sports 2-seater (1972)
Vitesse 2-liter (1970)
Spitfire 2-seater (1968)
Herald (sectioned) (1959)
TR2 sports 2-seater (1954)
Mayflower saloon (1952)
2000 saloon (1949)
Gloria sports saloon (1934)

This 1907 Standard 24/30 hp double phaeton was one of the first six-cylinder cars to be built in Coventry

Daimler of Coventry was the first British manufacturer of motor cars and supplied the first Royal car, a 6 hp Marseilles phaeton similar to this 1898 model

NATIONAL MOTOR MUSEUM

Beaulieu Abbey, near Brockenhurst, Hampshire. Telephone: 0590-612345.

Location: Approached from M27 via Lyndhurst.

Edward, Lord Montagu, has made the name of his family home, Beaulieu Abbey, synonymous with motoring history. The Montagu family has been associated with the automobile since the very beginning. His father, John, Lord Montagu, was a pioneer motoring writer and introduced the British royal family to motoring when he gave King Edward VII his first drive in a Daimler. The present Lord Montagu has spent most of his life making the British public aware of the history of the vehicle which has changed the face of the world since the turn of the century.

The National Motor Museum was founded in 1970, using as its basis the Montagu Motor Museum started by Edward Montagu in 1952 in memory of his father. Eight years later, the Motoring Library was founded to cater for a growing demand for motoring information. In 1968 the car collection and library, then valued at more than £500,000, was constituted as a charitable trust to preserve it for the nation. It became the National Motor Museum in 1970 when the British motor industry financed the construction of the present museum building.

This is one of the best-presented museums in the world. Using the latest display techniques, it sets out to tell the history of motoring in all its aspects from 1895 to the present day. It is divided into seven main sections, each leading off the entrance to the museum, the Alcan Hall of Fame. Here you will usually find a display of British-made vehicles of all ages, with the museum's 1909 Rolls-Royce 40/50 Silver Ghost given pride of place. A typical selection from the museum's huge stock would include the old Lord Montagu's 1899 Daimler, an original 1923 Austin Seven, a 1913 Prince Henry Vauxhall, a modern Grand Prix car and the latest model Lagonda.

The museum's latest attraction is Wheels. The visitor is taken in a buggy past a series of beautifully constructed displays with special lighting effects. The presentation starts with the first wheeled vehicles, then illustrates the beginnings of the motor car, the legal difficulties that faced it in the early days, the road conditions and weather problems the pioneers were up against, the social changes it has brought about and the many technical developments right through to the Moon Buggy.

The Wheels experience is an excellent introduction to motoring history. After leaving it, visitors can walk round and see the vehicles in the various halls annexed to the main building. The first of these covers the pioneer and Edwardian period and includes an

1894 Peugeot vis-à-vis in which the occupants sat facing each other, a Knight car from 1895, a 1903 Mercedes 60 racing car, touring Napiers and Rolls-Royces, and some of the Sunbeam racing cars of the years immediately before World War I. Moving into the inter-war period, when motoring became a popular activity and small cars came into their own, we find examples of the Rover 8, the immortal Austin Seven and the smoky two-stroke Trojan, whose engine had only seven moving parts. There is one of the sporting GN cyclecars here alongside a super-charged Bentley, a Phantom I Rolls-Royce tourer, a Hispano-Suiza H6 and one of the gawky but advanced Lancia Lambdas which featured unitary body/chassis construction and independent front suspension long before any other car produced in quantity.

The 1930s brought financial disaster to many firms in the motor industry worldwide and only the healthest survived. In Britain firms such as Morris, Austin, Standard and Rover dominated the scene with their Sevens, Eights and Tens, examples of which can be seen here. Among the luxury cars of that era are a sporting British Talbot 105 saloon and the V12 Lagonda, the last car to come from the drawing board of the great W.O. Bentley.

Another hall features British-built cars which have held the world land speed record; they were the first to break the 200 mph, 300 mph and 400 mph barriers. Several of these record-breaking machines are here, notably the 200 mph, 1000 hp Sunbeam, the beautiful Golden Arrow, and the 1961 four-wheel drive Blue-bird. Richard Noble regained the world speed record for Britain in 1984 with the jet-powered Thrust II which is also displayed at Beaulieu.

Museums are not necessarily only about old cars. More recent vehicles, the so-called classics of the 1950s and 1960s and modern production cars, complete the Beaulieu collection which spans in a logical way the entire history of the automobile in the British Isles.

Left: **Sporting hardware on display at Beaulieu. The John Player Lotus in the middle is flanked by Ian Appleyard's historic XK120 Jaguar and a Type 35 Grand Prix Bugatti**

Opposite: **More racing cars in the main hall of Beaulieu's purpose-built museum building**

Above: **The World Land Speed Record is a British speciality: in the foreground Donald Campbell's 350 hp Sunbeam, behind it the Golden Arrow and in the background Segrave's red 200 mph Sunbeam**

Top right: **Edward Lord Montagu, founder of the National Motor Museum and its main driving force, with the museum's 1909 40/50 hp Rolls-Royce Roi des Belges Ghost**

Right: **Display is a strong point at the National Motor Museum and every attempt is made to show vehicles like these vans in contemporary surroundings**

AC
  11.9 hp tourer (1921)
Albion
  A14 truck (1914)
Alfa Romeo
  unspecified (1948)
  8C-2300 Le Mans 4-seater (1933)
Allard
  dragster 5.8-liter (1961)
  J2 sports (1950)
Alvis
  unspecified (1937)
Argyll
  25 hp (1913)
Aston Martin
  DB5 (1964)
  1½-liter Strasbourg GP (1922)
Atco
  98 cc trainer garden car (1939)
Auburn
  851 speedster (1935)
Austin
  Seven Chummy (1923)
  Swallow saloon (1931)
  Seven Swallow (1932)
  Seven Mini (1959)
  Ten Lichfield saloon (1935)
  Seven (1928)
  Seven Pearl cabriolet (1938)
Austro-Daimler
  ADM/BK tourer (1925)
Bayliss-Thomas
  unspecified (1928)
Bean
  Short-14 (1928)
Bedford
  12/15 cwt van (1936)
Bentley
  4½-liter (1930)
Bentley (Derby)
  4¼-liter (1937)
Benz
  3 hp dogcart (1898)
  120 hp Grand Prix (1908)
Bersey
  electric cab (1897)
Bluebird
  land speed record car (1961)
Bolster
  Bloody Mary special (c1929)
BRM
  Type 15 1½-liter GP (1950)
Brush
  Pony electric milk float (1947)
Bugatti
  Type 35 GP (1924)
Cadillac
  9 hp runabout (1903)
Calcott
  11.9 hp tourer (1923)
Castle Three
  3-wheeler (1921)
Chevrolet
  490 tourer (1919)
Chrysler
  Airflow saloon (1935)
Citroën
  'Kégresse' half-track (1926)
Columbia
  electric runabout (1901)
Cooper
  Mk 3 500 cc single-seater (1949)
Cooper-Climax
  Formula 2 racer (1957)
Cord
  Beverley sedan (1937)

Crossley-Burney
  streamline saloon (1934)
Cubitt
  15.9 hp (1925)
DAF
  746 cc saloon (1965)
Daimler
  15 hp (1910)
  12 hp 4-cylinder (1899)
  22 hp (1903)
  'bottle' display car (1924)
Daimler (Canstatt)
  4 hp (1898)
De Dietrich
  24 hp tonneau (1903)
De Dion Bouton
  6 hp Model O (reg. AA20) (1903)
  Model O (reg. A8790) (1904)
DeLorean
  gullwing coupe (1982)
Dennis
  17.9 hp fire engine and cart (1928)
Ferrari
  312T4 coupe (1982)
Fiat
  3½ hp (1899)
  508S Ballila spyder (1935)
Ford
  Thunderbird (1954)
  Model T van (1914)
  Model T (1914)
  A with trailer (1930)
  GT40 Mk III coupe (1966)
  Consul convertible (1955)
  Anglia saloon (1949)
  Eight chassis (1933)
  Escort saloon (1981)
Gobron-Brillié
  40-60 hp fire engine (1907)
Golden Arrow
  land speed record car (1929)
Grégoire
  unrestored parts (1905)
Healey
  2.4-liter Elliott saloon (1947)
Hispano-Suiza
  37 hp H6 (1929)
  Alfonso XIII (1912)
Humber
  Super Snipe staff car (1941)
  8 hp runabout (1909)
Isetta
  300 bubblecar (1962)
Itala
  120 hp Grand Prix (1907)
Jaguar
  XK150 2-seater (1960)
Jowett
  Long-4 saloon (1927)
  Javelin saloon (1949)
Knight
  tricycle (1904)
  4-wheeler (1895)
Lagonda
  V12 (1939)
Lanchester
  Avon 10 hp coupe (1934)
Lancia
  Lambda 8th series (1928)
  Augusta saloon (1934)
Land-Rover
  Series I (1948)
Leyland
  fire engine (1920)
Lifu
  steam car (1901)

Lincoln
  Continental (1969)
Lotus
  78 JPS 16 John Player GP (1977)
  49 R3 Grand Prix (1967)
M & L
  2-seat trials car (1954)
Maxwell
  25 cwt charabanc (1922)
Mercedes
  60 hp double phaeton (1903)
Mercedes-Benz
  300SL gullwing (1957)
  W196 Grand Prix (1954)
  36/220 sports (1927)
Messerschmitt
  Tiger (1960)
MG
  PA 2-seater sports (1935)
  M-Type 2-seater (1930)
Mini
  Outspan Orange display (1972)
Minissima
  (1972)
Morgan
  Aero 3-wheeler (1927)
Morris
  Minor 850 cc ohv (1931)
  Mini-Cooper S (1964)
  GPO van (1970)
  Minor SV (1949)
  Cowley tourer (1924)
  8 saloon (1938)
Napier
  60 hp (1907)
Newton Bennett
  unspecified (1913)
Opel
  Kadett 1.1-liter (1938)
Peel
  P.50 (1964)
Pennington
  Autocar (1896)
Peugeot
  3½ hp vis-à-vis (1894)
Pope-Tribune
  10 hp runabout (1904)
Progress
  6 hp (1901)
Reliant
  GTS Triplex special (1965)
  Regal 3-wheeler (1954)
Renault
  D voiturette (1899)
  20/30 open-front limousine (1906)
Georges Richard
  10 hp (1903)
Riley
  Falcon saloon (1934)
  Sprite TT chassis (1935)
Rolls-Royce
  40/50 hp Alpine Eagle (1914)
  20/25 hp (1935)
  40/50 hp PI Barker barrel T (1925)
  40/50 hp Roi des Belges (1909)
Rover
  Eight twin coupe (1922)
  6 hp runabout (1909)
Royal Enfield
  quadricycle (1900)
Scamp
  electric (1966)
Sinclair
  C5 3-wheel electric (1985)
Sizaire-Berwick
  20 hp tourer (1914)

Standard
  Vanguard saloon (1951)
  8 chassis (1946)
Star
  chassis only (1928)
Steyr
  unspecified (1942)
Sunbeam
  V12 Cub racer (1924)
  3-liter Coupe de l'Auto (1912)
  1000 hp 200 mph record car (1927)
  350 hp World record (1920)
Talbot (London)
  105 4-door saloon (1934)
Thames
  coach (1913)
Triumph
  Mayflower saloon (1953)
  GT6 chassis only (1970)
Trojan
  PB tourer (1924)
Unic
  12/14 hp taxi (1908)
Vanwall
  Thinwall Special (1951)
Vauxhall
  Prince Henry (1915)
Volga
  saloon (1960)
Volkswagen
  export Beetle (1953)
Williams
  FWo7C-12 Grand Prix (1981)
Willys
  Jeep (1944)
Wolseley
  dogcart (1896)
  25 hp saloon (1937)

United States of America

AUBURN-CORD-DUESENBERG MUSEUM

1600 South Wayne Street, Auburn, Indiana 46706. Telephone: 219 925-1444.

Location: At the intersection of Interstate 69 and State Route 8 in north-eastern Indiana; once in town, museum signs clearly mark the way.

In the very building that more than 50 years ago displayed the latest creations of the Auburn Automobile Company, the Auburn-Cord-Duesenberg Museum now pays tribute to those great classics and to many others as well.

The auto showroom was originally built in 1930 at the site of the Auburn factory. Its ornate architecture reflects the Art Deco motif popular during the jazz era. Imported Italian chandeliers, terrazzo tile floors and ornamental ceiling friezes combine to provide a most fitting atmosphere. The museum is listed on the National Register of Historic Places. Over 80,000 square feet of exhibit space is spread out over the two-story facility.

Today the restored showroom once again displays these celebrated home-grown motor cars. Particularly prized is a 1932 Duesenberg Model J speedster with a custom-built aluminum body designed by the Walter M. Murphy coachbuilding firm. The car was originally bought by Cliff Durant, son of General Motors' founder William Durant, for $15,000. Equipped with a 265 hp engine, it was capable of speeds easily exceeding 100 mph. A one-of-a-kind Cord built for the president of Champion Spark Plugs is also part of the main showroom collection. This gleaming black 1937 coupe has a leather-covered hard top and exposed headlamps rather than the hidden headlamps that Cord made famous, and is an interesting counterpoint to the array of production model Cords on display. A 1932 Auburn V12 sedan imparts an aura that no fine automobile museum can do without, redolent of a high-quality, original-condition car. Less than 10,000 miles were on the clock in this example of Auburn's most prestigious series and, considering that fewer than 1000 V12 sedans were built in 1932, it is remarkable that one should have survived in such splendid condition.

Out of a collection of over 140 automobiles, more than 40 belong to the rich automotive heritage of this rural, mid-western town. Before 1915 several manufacturers, in addition to Auburn Auto, were active in the vicinity. From firms such as McIntyre, Kiblinger, and Zimmerman came vehicles which demonstrate the evolution of the horseless carriage into the motor car. Among the most notable examples of this evolution are a 1904 Auburn and a 1914 Imp cyclecar.

A separate display of Auburn Automobile Company literature includes examples of original advertising, sales brochures and promotional photographs.

Although the museum focuses on locally built legends, the collection is outstanding in other ways. Most of the cars are pre-1940, but the broad sweep of automotive history is nevertheless well represented. Many rare Indiana-built cars such as Stutz, Marmon and Apperson are featured. So are fine examples of Ford, Chevrolet, Packard, Cadillac and Lincoln. From European manufacturers the collection includes Hispano-Suizas and Rolls-Royces – even the Bentley that John Lennon had painted in psychedelic colors.

In September the museum hosts the Auburn-Cord-Duesenberg Festival, the annual meeting of the A-C-D owners' club. Over 200 Auburns, Cords and Duesenbergs come home to Auburn and huge crowds gather to witness the event. Special activities include the Parade of Classics through the streets of Auburn, a huge collector car auction, and shows and sales of antiques, quilts and crafts. Since 1983 the museum has also hosted an annual antique car show in the spring. This show is presented in conjunction with the Classic Car Club of America and also promotes a collector car auction and sale of automotive art.

Left: **In late 1928 Duesenberg introduced the magnificent Model J. This 1931 coupe was custom bodied by the Walter Murphy Company of Pasadena, California**

Below: **A one-of-a-kind experimental auto created in 1936 as a potential low-priced Duesenberg rests in front of the original Auburn showrooms**

Right: **The 1930s showrooms where the Auburn cars, when brand new, used to be displayed for retail. Today the building has been restored as a museum of the Auburn, Cord and Duesenberg marques**

Below: **The Auburn Automobile Company's greatest success was in 1931, a Depression year in which almost every auto company suffered great losses. This 1931 sedan represents the most popular of seven Auburn body styles**

Albany
surrey (1908)
Apperson
tourster (1920)
Aston Martin
DB2 (1953)
Auburn
tonneau (1904)
touring (1907, 1911, 1917)
formal sedan (1912)
roadster (1910, 1919)
Chummy roadster (1916)
sedan (1923, 1931)
sports sedan (1928)
speedster (1929, 1932, 1935)
sedan (V12) (1932)
cabriolet (1933, 1936)
convertible sedan (V12) (1933)
convertible sedan (1933, 1935, 1936)
Austin
Bantam truck (1934)
taxi (1957)
Austin-Healey
Sprite Mk II (1963)
3000 Mk III (1967)
Bentley
8-liter saloon (1931)
saloon (1956)
Bricklin
coupe (1975)
Brush
roadster (1908)
Buehrig
coupe prototype (1979)
Bugatti
Grand Prix Type 37
Buick
touring (1908, 1922)
sedan (1932, 1936)
coupe (1949)
Cadillac
sedan (1925, 1959)
Eldorado brougham (1957)
touring sedan (1939)

Columbia
touring (1923)
Chevrolet
stake truck (1933)
sedan (1933, 1938)
sport coupe (1950)
Corvette (1961, 1978)
Chrysler
Airflow brougham (1937)
Citroën
saloon (1956)
Cord
L-29 experimental model (1932)
L-29 sedan (1929)
812 coupe (1937)
812 Beverley (1937)
custom Beverley sedan (1937)
custom coupe (1937)
convertible coupe (1937)
8/10 replica (1966)
Corvette
coupe (1963, 1974, 1978)
Crosley
convertible (1941)
DeLorean
coupe (1981)
Dodge
coupe (1923)
touring (1925)
Duesenberg
chassis (1926, 1936)
roadster (1926)
dual-cowl phaeton (1929)
coupe (1931)
victoria (1931, 1933)
Gentleman's speedster (1936)
sport tourer (1925)
sedan (1966)
speedster (1932)
Duryea
(1895)
Essex
roadster (1919)
coupe (1929)

Ferrari
coupe (1952, 1966, 1970)
Ford
touring (1913, 1915, 1924)
speedster (1914)
snowmobile (1922)
sedan (1927, 1948)
coupe (1931, 1936)
Thunderbird (1956, 1957)
Thunderbird convertible (1955)
Mustang (1965)
Gasmobile
phaeton (1901)
Graham
Hollywood (1941)
Haynes
Cloverleaf (1918)
Hispano-Suiza
town car (1928)
Hupmobile
(1924, 1936)
Jaguar
saloon (1946)
Kiblinger
runabout (1907, 1908)
Kirsch
paddy wagon (1911)
Krastin
touring (1903)
LaSalle
convertible coupe (1939)
Lincoln
dual-cowl phaeton (1933)
Continental (1959)
Locomobile
steamer (c1900)
limousine (1919)
McIntyre
autobuggy (1908)
Imp cyclecar (1913)
truck (1913)
Mercedes-Benz
500K (1936)

MG
TD roadster (1951)
Nash
sedan (1938)
Overland
touring (1915)
Packard
twin six touring (1918)
convertible victoria (1933)
roadster (1903)
cabriolet (1934)
dual-cowl phaeton (1932)
coupe (1929)
Porsche
356C coupe (1965)
911E Targa (1970)
Rauch & Lang
cabriolet (1916)
Regal
touring (1909)
Rolls-Royce
convertible (1957)
Phantom III limousine (1937)
Studebaker
sedan cruiser (1963)
Stutz
sedan (1926)
Tucker
sedan (1948)
Velie
touring (1918)
Waverly
Stanhope (1899)
Zimmerman
runabout (1908, 1909, 1910)

Cord cars offered a distinctive design, front-wheel drive, and in this 1937 model 812 a supercharged 170 hp engine

THE BEHRING MUSEUM

Corner of Blackhawk Road and Camino Tassajara, Danville, California 94526. Telephone: 415-838-3070.

Location: Danville is east of the San Francisco/Oakland area, just off Interstate 680. From the intersection of Interstates 580 and 680, drive north approximately eight miles to the Sycamore Valley Road exit. Go east 4½ miles (Sycamore Valley Road will become Camino Tassajara) and turn left on Blackhawk Road.

Only one Argonaut automobile was produced before this American manufacturer gave up his attempt at challenging the automotive establishment in 1959

The Behring Museum is a rising star in the world of automobile collections. Since 1982, Kenneth E. Behring and Donald E. Williams have acquired a fabulous collection of automobiles which emphasizes the great automotive designs of the custom coachbuilding era. The entire collection numbers over 200 cars, however, and to provide proper viewing of the exhibits only 100 will be displayed at any one time.

A noticeable emphasis is given to the European lineage of luxury manufacturers with numerous high-quality exhibits seldom seen in public collections. Prestigious manufacturers such as Isotta-Fraschini, Hispano-Suiza, Delahaye, Bugatti, and Delage are just some of the famous European marques included. The engineering art of Europe's finest coachbuilders is demonstrated by the craftsmen of renowned establishments such as Hooper, Saoutchik, Fernandez & Darrin, Vanden Plas and Figoni. Many of the autos feature one-of-a-kind or 'one-off' body styles which are considered individual works of automotive art.

The collection of European cars provides several selections from each decade of the twentieth century. From pre-1910 Panhard and Renault display the

French concept of design. Noticeable changes in the evolution of automotive styling are apparent as the exhibits advance into the following decades. Demonstrating the progression are classic examples such as the 1914 Isotta-Fraschini speedster and the 1913 Fiat roadster, both of Italian origin. The reputation of British automobiles in the 1920s was established by cars such as the 1928 Rolls-Royce experimental design by Barker, the 1924 Daimler cabriolet, and the 1929 Bentley Speed-Six. The avant garde design of the 1930s is displayed in the work of Figoni and Falaschi on the 1937 Bugatti Atalante coupe and the 1938 Delahaye V12 with a coupe body built by Chapron. Fashionable entries from the 1950s include luxury/performance combinations from Aston Martin, Mercedes-Benz and Pegaso.

The selection of American cars is decidedly weighted toward the golden era of 1925-42. This period corresponds to the era of the custom-built car in the United States. The most prestigious, luxurious and expensive automobiles of their day, in fact the most uncompromising in automotive history, are impressively presented. Models such as the 1931 Duesenberg boat-tailed speedster with a body by the

Top: **This 1935 custom convertible coupe was one of several Duesenbergs owned by movie star Clark Gable**

Above: **The 1930 Bucciali is the only known complete and running example of this rare, French-built luxury car with front-wheel drive**

French manufacturer Figoni, and the 1931 V16 Cadillac boat-tailed speedster by Pinin Farina of Italy, provide stunning comparisons. Although both these autos carried European coachwork, most American-built luxury autos offered their most prestigious models with bodies from American coachbuilding firms such as LeBaron, Dietrich, Derham, and Locke. Many of the finest American car makers at this time also built their own bodies which were elegantly equipped. Outstanding examples can be seen in the exhibits such as the V12 Auburn phaeton of 1934, the 1930 Cord phaeton and the 1931 Pierce-Arrow dual cowl phaeton.

Kenneth Behring has established a permanent source of income to provide a sufficient and continual operating budget. Additionally, over 20 years the museum and auto collection will be donated to the University of California which will have access to the collection for the study of automotive design and engineering.

In addition to the 200-car collection, the museum also offers one of the best automotive libraries in the country. The material is particularly valuable in the realm of American automotive styling during the custom coachbuilding era which existed prior to 1933.

Over 100,000 square feet of display area are spread out over two floors.

Above: **The best-remembered Auburn is the supercharged boattail speedster which was built in 1935 and 1936. The original cost of this 1936 model was slightly over $2000**

Right: **The Pegaso was a beautiful but ill-fated attempt to begin automobile production in Spain in the early 1950s**

Aero
Type 50 Tatra convertible (1938)
Alfa Romeo
1750 Zagato roadster (1929)
Argonaut
roadster (1957)
Aston Martin
(1954)
prototype (1967)
Auburn
V12 saloon phaeton (1934)
852 supercharged boat-tailed speedster (1936)
852 supercharged cabriolet convertible (1936)
BMW
M-1
Baker Electric
(1911)
Ballot
2-liter, 3-seater boat-tailed speedster (1924)
Bentley
Speed-Six boat-tail (1929)
Bignan
Type 15000 sport (1923)
Bollée
Léon Bollée tricar No. 891
Bucciali
TAV 8 roadster (1930)
TAV 16 chassis (1930)
Bugatti
Type 57 Atalante coupe (1937)
Type 57-SC roadster (1939)
Type 57-SC, Model 101, roadster (1950)
Cadillac
V16 boat-tailed speedster (1931)
phaeton (1931)
V12 aerodynamic coupe (1935)
V16 convertible coupe (1938)
V16 (1939)
town car (1942)

Chevrolet
Eagle phaeton, 4-door (1933)
roadster (1933)
convertible (1941)
Chrysler
Series 80 Imperial Touralette (1928)
imperial victoria, Series CG, LeBaron (1931)
custom Imperial Eight LeBaron phaeton, Series CL* (1933)
Cord
L-29, phaeton sedan (1930)
supercharged Sportsman's convertible coupe (1937)
Daimler
Big Six tourer (salon cabriolet) (1924)
DK400 'Stardust' touring limousine (1954)
Delage
convertible coupe (1932)
D8SS coupe (1937)
D8S convertible (1939)
Delahaye
Type 145 V-12 coupe (1938)
Type 135 MS convertible (1939)
convertible (1947)
DeLorean
prototype (1981)
Duesenberg
SJ boat-tailed speedster, J-465 (1931)
JN convertible coupe, J-560 (1935)
SJ dual-cowl phaeton (1935)
Fiat
Type 55 roadster (1913)
Ford
Deluxe phaeton, 2-door (1931)
V-8 roadster (1936)
Hispano-Suiza
H6C Tulipwood racer (1924)
H6B Monza sport cabriolet (1923)
K6 coupe chauffeur (1934)
J12 coupe de ville (1934)

Invicta
4½-liter convertible coupe (1934)
Isotta-Fraschini
KM gunboat speedster (1914)
Typo 8A LeBaron boat-tailed roadster (1928)
Typo 8AS roadster (1928)
Jaguar
Mk IV (1949)
Lagonda
convertible (1937)
V12 convertible coupe (1939)
Lanchester
town car
Lancia
Astura convertible (1936)
Astura (1939)
Lincoln
KB dual-windshield phaeton (1933)
Mercedes
dual chain drive phaeton (1906)
Mercedes SS tourer (1929)
540K, cab B convertible (1936)
540K, cab A convertible (1937)
540K special roadster (1937)
G4 armored tourer (1939)
gullwing (1956)
Mercer
Model 30 speedster (1910)
Cobra (1965)
Minerva
town car (1929)
Oldsmobile
curved dash (1901)
Packard
Twin Six town car (1920)
convertible sedan (1930)
town car (1931)
V12 747 convertible victoria (1934)
LeBaron town car (1935)
V12 presidential parade car (1939)
Caribbean (1956)

Panhard
tourer (1906)
Pegaso
coupe, Trujillo (1952)
Pierce-Arrow
Model 42 dual-cowl sport phaeton (1931)
Silver Arrow (1933)
Renault
Type A-1 racing runabout (1907)
Rolls-Royce
Silver Ghost open drive limousine (1915)
Piccadilly roadster (1923)
Phantom I experimental (1928)
Phantom II sedanca AJS town car (1933)
Phantom II roadster (1934)
Phantom III convertible (1936)
Phantom IV sedanca limousine (1952)
Silver Cloud I sedanca (1959)
Phantom V coupe (1961)
Phantom V sedanca, 7-passenger limousine (1965)
Ruxton
4-door sedan (1932)
SS
1 coupe (1933)
1 tourer (1933)
100 roadster (1938)
Talbot Lago
coupe (1938)
Triumph
experimental (1968)

BELLM'S CARS AND MUSIC OF YESTERDAY

5500 North Tamiami Trail, Sarasota, Florida 33580. Telephone: 813-355-6228.

Location: Take US Highway 41 (Tamiami Trail) south from Tampa/St Petersburg until passing the Sarasota-Bradenton airport. Or take Interstate 75 south to exit 40 (University Parkway) west to US 41. The collection is just south of the airport on US 41.

The selection of automobiles displayed in the Bellm collection is a tribute to the diversity and creative spirit which has prevailed throughout automotive history. Over 120 cars, representing every decade of the twentieth century, provide everything from basic transport to unbridled luxury. Successes and failures from the early auto buggies to the most exotic and unconventional cars of the not so distant past are included. The impressive display provides a presentation of auto history both familiar and revealing.

The oldest car exhibited is a 1901 curved dash Oldsmobile – the most popular car in America from 1901 to 1904. Over 1000 were built in 1901, making it the first car in the world to be produced in that quantity. By comparison the 1906 Pope-Toledo seven-passenger touring car here is much larger and more luxurious, naturally produced in smaller quantities for wealthier customers. Both Oldsmobile and Pope began building automobiles before 1900 but whereas Pope expired in 1907, Oldsmobile continues to the present. Another popular model of the pre-1910 selection is the 1904 Rambler. Between 1902 and 1907 Rambler was consistently among the top five producers in the United States.

The Tucker, with its revolutionary rear-mounted engine, was regarded as a success by designers and engineers. However, fewer than 50 were produced, all in 1948

While automobiles like the Oldsmobile and Rambler discovered the potential of low-priced transport, it was the Ford Model T that came to dominate the mass-market approach to car manufacturing and sales. Through 19 years of production beginning in 1908 the Tin Lizzie remained basically unchanged and unchallenged as America's favorite mode of transport. The Bellm collection features several different variations on that famous theme, including 1910 torpedo, 1923 touring, 1924 stake-bed truck and 1925 depot hack.

While the Model T became the symbol of production efficiency throughout the world, the small-scale competitors were realizing it was impossible to compete in price with the mass-produced car. It was also apparent that the assembly line technique was not affordable to those producing limited quantities. Although auto registrations rose considerably in the 1920s, it was also a period which brought the demise of a great number of manufacturers.

The 1916 Saxon touring was one unsuccessful attempt at competing in the low-price field. After the industry-wide sales slump in 1920-1, Saxon never fully recovered and eventually disappeared in 1923. The Star, represented here by a 1925 touring model, was another casualty of the low-priced field and passed away in 1928 after a brief six-year lifespan. Other exhibits from now-defunct manufacturers include a 1918 Templar roadster and a 1926 Moon sedan. Templar was out of business by 1924 while Moon survived until 1929. From the final year of Lincoln production before the company was bought by Ford, a 1921 Lincoln pick-up truck is exhibited. The V8-powered pick-up truck was a limited production model used by Lincoln dealers as a service vehicle.

Several companies that survived the 1920s stumbled in the following decade as the American auto industry became increasingly dominated by the Big Three. Pierce-Arrow and Auburn, both companies with long and illustrious histories that ended in the 1930s, created some vivid memories with their stylish motor cars. Two unique styling concepts from

Franklin automobiles attained a lofty reputation based on their high standards and their use of air-cooled engines, as typified in this 1930 model

major corporations, the 1936 De Soto Airflow and the 1937 Lincoln Zephyr, are also displayed. Each provides a striking demonstration of the effects of streamlining on the design of mid-1930s automobiles.

The Bellm collection is particularly strong in American cars of the 1950s and early 1960s. During this time manufacturers sought to make motoring glamorous again. Since the previous decade had been dominated by the war effort, automotive styling had been greatly reduced in importance. The key to winning the sales race was considered to lie in increasing horsepower while adding a flamboyant styling.

To demonstrate the overall design concepts common to the American car at this time, the Bellm collection displays an expansive variety of models. The year 1957 is represented by Buick, Cadillac, Lincoln and Ford vehicles. The least expensive and most interesting is the Ford Fairlane 500 Skyliner which features the unusual retractable hardtop, a concept originally meant for the Lincoln. The divergent paths taken by Corvette and Thunderbird are

illustrated by the Corvettes of 1955 and 1962, and the Thunderbirds of 1956 and 1962. Another contrast in styles is obvious with the first-year Plymouth Barracuda and the Ford Mustang of 1964. Among the most expensive models from Detroit in the 1960s are the Chrysler Imperials and limousine models by Lincoln and Cadillac. For the sake of comparison, Rolls-Royce and Bentley motor cars from this era are also displayed.

Right: **Mercer motor cars were built between 1909 and 1925 in Mercer County, New Jersey. Bellm's 1922 touring model is a rare survivor from this once great manufacturer**

Below: **The Lincoln Zephyr was powered by a V12 engine and was distinctive for its departure from conventional styling. The most popular model was the four-door sedan, of which this is the 1937 version**

Incomplete list

American Bantam
convertible (1939)
Auburn
boat-tail speedster (1933)
Austin
Princess (1951)
convertible (1930)
Bantam (1939)
Avanti
(1963)
Bentley
(1959)
Bricklin
(1975)
Brush
roadster (1907)
Buick
Model F (1908)
special sedan (1938)
sedan (1957)
Cadillac
(1909)
Eldorado convertible (1960)
sedan (1957)
limousine (1964)
Carter Car
touring (1912)
Chevrolet
Impala convertible (1963)
pick-up truck (1959)
Chrysler
Imperial (1960, 1962)
Corvair
stepside truck (1963)
convertible (1963)
hardtop (1960)

Corvette
convertible (1955)
removable hard top (1962)
T-top (1972)
Daimler
(1952)
DeLorean
(1981)
De Soto
Airflow sedan (1936)
Firedome sedan (1956)
Dodge Brothers
touring (1922)
Charger sport coupe (1967)
Dorris
coupe (1916)
Edsel
Citation (1958)
EMF
roadster (1909)
Flanders
roadster (1912)
Franklin
(1919)
roadster (1930)
Ford
Model T Torpedo (1910)
Model T touring (1923)
Model T truck (1924)
Model T depot hack (1925)
Mustang convertible (1964)
Fairlane retractable hard
top (1957)
Horch
sedan (1939)
International Harvester

truck (1911)
Jaguar
Mk VIII sedan (1961)
Kaiser
sedan (1954)
Henry J (1950)
Lincoln
Zephyr sedan (1937)
Mk I convertible (1948)
pick-up truck (1921)
limousine (1966)
Mk II (1957)
Premier (1959)
4-door convertible (1966)
Luverne
truck (1916)
McIntyre
(1906)
Marion
(1905)
Moon
sedan (1926)
Nash
Ambassador custom (1955)
Metropolitan (1954)
Oldsmobile
(1905)
curved dash (1903)
Overland
touring (1914)
Pierce-Arrow
convertible coupe (1925)
touring (1923)
sedan (1923)
Plymouth
Barracuda (1964)

PMC
highwheeler (1908)
Pontiac
convertible (1966)
Pope-Toledo
touring (1906)
Rambler
rear entrance tonneau (1904)
Reo
R5 touring (1912)
Rolls-Royce
(1955, 1961)
Silver Ghost limousine (1921)
Saxon
touring (1916)
Schacht
(1905)
Scimitar
(1959)
Simplex
touring (1917)
Star
touring (1925)
Studebaker
Commander (1950)
Turismo Hawk (1963)
Stutz
Blackhawk sedan (1971)
Templar
roadster (1918)
Thunderbird
removable hard top (1956)
retractable hard top (1962)
Tucker
sedan (1948)

VW
Series 1500 (1961)
Waverly
electric (1900)
Willys Knight
touring (1918)
jeepster (1950)
Woods
Mobilette (1914)

Above: **The Reo automobile took its name from the initials of Ransom E Olds, who formerly built the early success known as the curved dash Oldsmobile. Olds began building Reo automobiles in 1904; this touring model is from 1907**

Right: **The 1904 Rambler was one of the most popular cars of its era. Its two-cylinder engine produced 16 hp and the rear seat, known as a tonneau, was removable**

CRAWFORD AUTO-AVIATION MUSEUM

10825 East Boulevard, Cleveland, Ohio 44106. Telephone: 216-721-5722.

Location: East of downtown Cleveland in the suburb of University Circle. From Interstate 90, take the Liberty Boulevard exit and proceed to East Boulevard at East 105th Street.

The Crawford Auto-Aviation Museum exhibits more than 150 antique and classic automobiles, motor cycles and aircraft, highlighting the technological and stylistic development of transportation. The creation of this collection is the responsibility of Frederick C. Crawford, the Honorary Chairman of the Board of TRW Inc. which, since 1901, has supplied parts for vehicles made around the world.

The history of the Crawford Museum began with the conclusion of the Great Lakes Exposition in 1937. Frederick Crawford bought a 1910 Duryea phaeton from one of the exhibitors and several other autos which had been on display. Other autos were quickly added and in 1943 Crawford's growing collection was presented to the public as the Thompson Collection named for the Thompson Products company which later became TRW. In later years the collection was known as the Thompson Auto Album and Aviation Museum, then the TRW Collection. This was presented to the Western Reserve Historical Society in 1963 and, through the combined efforts of Frederick C. Crawford and the society, the present museum building was erected and opened in 1965.

Of particular note in this collection are the Cleve-

land-built automobiles which played an important role in the motor-manufacturing industry from the turn of the century until the Depression years of the early 1930s. Between 1898 and 1931 it spawned over 80 separate automotive marques over 25 of which are displayed here.

During the late nineteenth and early twentieth centuries, the electric vehicle was considered a serious alternative to petrol-engined transport. The Crawford Museum displays an excellent selection of electric cars including the Baker, Rauch & Lang and Raulang Electrics, which were all built in Cleveland. Generally speaking electric cars were marketed as a woman's car. Most were elegantly appointed and free from crank starting, as well as being quiet and clean. The major drawback was a limited range of travel before recharging was necessary and so they were most often used as an 'around town' car. Baker Electric merged with Rauch & Lang Electric in 1914 and in the following year Owen Magnetic became part of the merger. The company went on to produce electric vehicles until 1930, well beyond the peak of electric car popularity. Other examples of electrics in the Crawford collection include a 1916 Owen Magnetic,

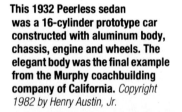

This 1932 Peerless sedan was a 16-cylinder prototype car constructed with aluminum body, chassis, engine and wheels. The elegant body was the final example from the Murphy coachbuilding company of California. *Copyright 1982 by Henry Austin, Jr.*

a 1917 Rauch & Lang and a 1918 Detroit Electric.

During this era another alternative to petrol-driven vehicles was the steamer. One of the most successful steam-powered cars was produced by the White Sewing Machine Company of Cleveland. Among those on display is a 1902 White Stanhope model from the first year of production by that company. Other White steamers to be seen here include limousine, touring and runabout models which indicate the development of this type before World War I.

Another Cleveland-built car, the Winton, was a well-known name in the pioneering days of the gasoline-powered automobile. Winton cars were on the roads as early as 1896 and manufacturing continued until 1923. The collection features seven Wintons including a 1903 two-cylinder model known as the Red Devil and an 1899 one-cylinder roadster.

Beyond the shores of Lake Erie the Crawford Museum features a fine selection of automobiles from around the world. Noteworthy European exhibits from the turn of the century include the 1895 Panhard Levassor, the 1897/98 Benz and the 1902 Darracq. The period between 1910 and 1920 is represented by a splendid collection of sports-touring automobiles among them such items as a 1920 Mercer raceabout, 1916 Pierce-Arrow, 1919 Packard twin-six and a 1914 Peerless. The latter is another of the products of Cleveland and was for many years one of America's most costly prestige motor cars. Peerless remained in production from 1901 to 1932.

The great European makes of the 1920s can be seen here: Hispano-Suiza, Isotta-Fraschini and Rolls-Royce. The Rolls-Royce contingent includes three examples from the 1920s and four from the 1930s. The Crawford Museum also offers a glimpse at European cars of the 1950s and 1960s with representatives from Mercedes-Benz, Daimler, Ferrari, Jaguar and Lotus. The newest car in the collection is a 1981 Aston Martin Lagonda.

Every August since 1970 the museum has hosted a car show in conjunction with the Veteran Motor Car Club of America. Hundreds of beautiful privately owned automobiles ranging from the brass era to the showroom racers before 1970 are exhibited. The two-day show is evenly divided between pre- and post-World War II motorcars. The older cars are displayed on Saturday and the 1946-69 autos are shown on Sunday.

Every two years the museum also sponsors a Concours d'Elegance which commemorates the automobile industry's technological achievements in Cleveland. Over 100 cars take part and are judged by experts looking for quality and authenticity as well as elegance and design.

This 1930 dual-cowl phaeton demonstrates the Packard concept of dignified motoring. *Copyright 1982 by Henry Austin, Jr.*

Over $5000 was required to buy the powerful and luxurious Simplex motor car of 1909. *Copyright 1977 by Henry Austin, Jr.*

Right: One of the most prestigious steam-powered automobiles of the pre-1914 era was produced by the White Sewing Machine Company of Cleveland, Ohio. This 1909 model demonstrates the company's emphasis on size and stature. *Copyright 1978 by Henry Austin, Jr.*

Abbott-Detroit
speedster (6-44) (1916)
Alco
Berline limousine (Six) (1913)
American Gas
runabout (A) (1902)
American-La France
custom combination firetruck (Type 40) (1919)
American Underslung
6-passenger touring (Type 666) (1914)
AMX
coupe prototype (1966)
Apperson
7-passenger touring (1918)
Aston Martin
Lagonda 4-door sedan (1981)
Auburn
cabriolet (8-95) (1930)
Model 851 convertible coupe (1935)
Austro-Daimler
3-passenger Cloverleaf roadster (1913)
Autocar
rear-entrance tonneau (1903)
runabout (Type XV) (1907)
Avenger
coupe (GT12) (1968)
Baker Electric
runabout (1902)
Newport (1904)
Imperial (1906)
roadster (1913)
Bentley
4-door sedan (1934)
drophead coupe (3½-liter) (1935)
Benz
Comfortable (velocipede) (1897/98)
(Duc) (1900)
Bobsey
sports racer (SR-7) (1975)
Brush
runabout (BC) (1909)
Bugatti
touring (Type 44) (1930)
Buick
touring (35) (1912)
town brougham (29) (Series 115) (1928)
convertible coupe (56-C Super) (1941)
Cadillac
runabout (S) (1908)
5-passenger touring (1913)
7-passenger touring (Type 51) (1915)
town sedan (353) (1930)
sport phaeton (355B) (1932)
sedan (Sixty Special) (1941)
brougham (Eldorado) (1957)
convertible (Eldorado; GMC Blue Boy) (1971)
convertible (Eldorado; GMC Yellow Bird) (1975)
convertible (Eldorado) (1976)
Chandler
7-passenger touring (Chandler Six) (1916)
Comrade roadster (33A) (1926)
Chevrolet
Standard sedan (Independence Series AE) (1931)
¾-ton pick-up truck (Master) (1937)
convertible coupe (Corvette 2934) (1956)
sport coupe (Corvette 837) (1963)
Chitty-Bang-Bang II
sport tourer (Custom) (1921)
Chrysler
Airflow brougham (CU) (1934)
Airflow 6-passenger sedan (Imperial C-

2) (1935)
4-door sedan (Windsor Town & Country) (1948)
Cleveland
roadster (40) (1920)
touring car (1920)
Columbia
surrey (Mark XIX) (1901)
Concord Car
2-seater (111DW) (1980)
Continental
hardtop coupe (Mk II) (1956)
Cord
phaeton convertible sedan (812) (1937)
Crawford
touring (12-30) (1912)
Daimler
coupe (DB18 Special Sport) (1951)
convertible coupe (DB18 Special Sport) (1951)
roadster (SP.250) (1962)
Darracq
2-seat tonneau (1902)
DeLorean
coupe (DMC-12) (1981)
De Soto
2-door Sportsman (Adventurer) (1958)
Detroit Electric
brougham (1918)
brougham (75) (1918)
Dodge Brothers
touring (1922)
Duplex
¾-ton delivery truck (A) (1909)
Duryea
Electra (1910)
Elmore
touring (30) (1908)
Faywick Flyer
touring (1908)
Ferrari
Testa Rossa (replica) (1960)
Le Mans (replica) (1965)
spyder (275GT/S) (1966)
spyder (365 California) (1967)
Dino (246GT) (1970)
spyder (308GTSi) (1982)
Firestone-Columbus
motor buggy (1908)
Flanders
Suburban (20) (1910)
Flint
touring (B-40) (1925)
Ford
touring (Model K)
runabout (Model S) (1908)
touring (Model T) (1909)
touring (Model T) (1914)
touring (Canadian Model T) (1914)
coupelet (Model T) (1915)
center-door sedan (Model T) (1916)
coupe (Model T) (1924)
station wagon (Model A) (1929)
Tudor sedan (Model A) (1929)
deluxe coupe (40) (1934)
Tudor touring sedan (1936)
convertible club coupe (Deluxe) (1940)
convertible (98A Custom) (1949)
4 X 4 all-terrain (M151A1) (1951)
convertible coupe (Thunderbird 40A) (1955)
Galaxy '500' (1964)
Model 87, Thunderbird (1964)
coupe (GT40) (replica) (1966)
Franklin
5-passenger light tonneau (F) (1905)

4-door sedan (1928)
Freeway II
3-wheel (motorcycle) (1980)
Gardner-Serpollet
steam carriage (1899)
Harrods
delivery truck (1938)
Hispano-Suiza
Salamanca (H6B) (1923)
drophead coupe (Type 49 Barcelona) (1926)
Hoffman
4-passenger touring (general utility) (1903)
Hupmobile
runabout (A) (1909)
touring (D) (1911)
Imperial
limousine (Crown) (1958)
International
commercial car (MW) (1912)
Isotta-Fraschini
brougham (Type 8-A) (1927)
Jaguar
roadster (XK120) (1954)
saloon (3.4-liter) (1959)
saloon (420 G) (1967)
roadster (XKE Series 3) (1973)
Jewel
Stanhope (E) (1907)
Jordan
Speedboy phaeton (G) (1929)
Krieger
landaulet (1906)
Lancia
tourer (Lambda 4th series) (1924)
limousine (Astura AV series) (1936)
Lincoln
7-passenger touring (L-101) (1921)
sport sedan (K) (1936)
panel brougham (1940)
convertible (1966)
presidential limousine (1967)
coupe (Continental Mark III) (1971)
Locomobile
Sportif (Type 48, Series 5) (1919)
Lotus
Le Mans (Lotus II) (1956)
Europa coupe (converted to electric) (1968)
Maserati
Gran Turismo (Ghibli) (1968)
Mercedes
Grand Prix chassis with V8 Hispano-Suiza aircraft engine (1912)
Mercedes-Benz
cabriolet A(500K) (1934)
open tourer (770K) (1940)
coupe with sliding roof (220) (1951)
convertible sedan (300) (1952)
gullwing coupe (300SL) (1956)
roadster with coupe roof (280SL) (1971)
Mercer
raceabout (Series 5) (1920)
Messerschmitt
3-wheeler (1954)
MG
Midget (TD) (1950)
Midget roadster (1963)
Milburn
brougham (22) (1917)
Minerva
7-passenger town sedan (1929)
Mitchell
7-passenger touring (S) (1910)
McLaren
Formula 5000 (M-10-B) (1969)

Oakland
touring (40) (1912)
Oldsmobile
runabout with dos-à-dos seat (R) (1902)
runabout (1904)
station wagon (replica)
Orient
buckboard (1904)
Owen Magnetic
7-passenger touring (0-36) (1916)
Packard
runabout (C) (1901)
phaeton (Thirty) (1911)
doctor's coupe (1-38 or 1338) (1913)
sport runabout (Twin Six) (1919)
roadster (243) (1926)
roadster (640) (1929)
dual-cowl sport phaeton (745 Deluxe) (1930)
coupe (1407) (1936)
convertible coupe (1937)
Palmer-Singer
touring (6-40) (1911)
Panhard Levassor
2-place cab (1895)
Peerless
Roi des Belges touring (9) (1905)
7-passenger touring (60-Six) (1914)
touring sedan (Prototype) (1932)
Pierce
knockabout (Motorette) (1902)
Pierce-Arrow
runabout (36) (1912)
custom raceabout (66 A-4) (1916)
convertible coupe (Custom) (1929)
Pope-Hartford
5-passenger touring (31) (1913)
Prunel
2-seat tonneau (F) (1902)
Rauch & Lang
coach (J6) (1917)
Red Bug
buckboard (c1923)
Renault
touring (14-20) (1912)
Rollin
coupe deluxe (G) (1924)
touring (G) (1925)
Rolls-Royce
Piccadilly roadster (Silver Ghost) (1924)
4-passenger saloon (1927)
dual-cowl phaeton (Phantom I, or New Phantom) (1929)
town car (20/25 hp) (1930)
dual-windshield phaeton (Phantom II) (1930)
sedanca coupe (20/25 hp) (1933)
limousine (Phantom III) (1937)
Sunshine sport saloon (25/30 hp) (1937)
2-door saloon (Silver Shadow) (1967)
Rover
sedan (1961)
Royal Tourist
rear-entrance tonneau (O) (1904)
touring (F) (1905)
SS
sports 2-seater (100 Jaguar) (1937)
Sandusky
1½-ton stake truck (C) (1912)
Sears
motor buggy (H) (1909)
Silver Eagle
race car (1970)
Simplex
double roadster (1909)
Stanley
Gentleman's Speedy Roadster (1905)

Stearns
touring (15-30) (1910)
Stearns-Knight
4-passenger Cloverleaf roadster (L-4) (1917)
5-passenger sedan (Six) (1925)
Stevens-Duryea
7-passenger touring (Y) (1910)
Studebaker-Garford
2-door landaulet (H) (1907)
touring (G-7) (1910)
Studebaker
2-door hardtop (Avanti) (1964)
Stutz
torpedo roadster (Series E) (1914)
Templar
roadster (A-445) (1922)
Thomas Flyer
touring (F) (1908)
Toledo
Stanhope (A) (1901)
Tri Moto
3-wheeler (1900)
Vauxhall
tourer (30/98) (1925)
Volkswagen
2-door sedan (1946)
Westinghouse
convertible (Mk II) (1967)
White
Stanhope (B) (1902)
touring (D) (1904)
limousine (F) (1906)
runabout (H) (1907)
runabout (K) (1908)
touring (O) (1909)
fire truck (1913)
truck (1913)
town car (16 Valve 4) (1917)
Yellowstone park bus (15-45) (1925)
Willys
¼-ton 4 X 4 'Jeep' (MB) (1944)
Winton
motor carriage (1898)
phaeton (1899)
phaeton (1899)
Gordon Bennett racer (Bullet No. 2) (1903)
touring (1903)
touring (M) (1907)
touring (1921)
Woods Mobilette
roadster (5) (1914)
X600 by John Weitz
aluminum-bodied sports car (prototype)

BRIGGS CUNNINGHAM AUTOMOTIVE MUSEUM

250 East Baker Street, Costa Mesa, California 92626. Telephone: 714-546-7660.

Location: in the south Los Angeles suburb of Costa Mesa. From the San Diego Freeway (Interstate 405), take the Bristol Street South exit. At the intersection of Bristol and Baker Street, turn left and proceed under the Newport Freeway bridge. Enter the museum parking area at the corner of Baker Street and Redhill Avenue.

The Ford GT-40 was a low, sleek coupe that won several European competitions in 1964-66. In 1967 it was followed by the tougher GT-40 Mark IV

Opposite: **The first Winton automobile was produced in 1896, and before 1900 the company was among the most productive of the early American manufacturers. This one-cylinder, tiller-steered model at the Crawford Auto-Aviation Museum is from 1899.**

Copyright 1982 by Henry Austin, Jr.

The Briggs Cunningham collection is a select combination of pure racing machinery and personal sporting cars. More so than any other collection, these cars characterize the definition of auto enthusiast. Each car represents a special engineering genius, automotive know-how, artistic flair, innovation and craftsmanship. It is immediately apparent that these are cars that were built for more than mere transport. In most cases they represent the best cars money could buy for either the road or the track. Many are engineering masterpieces – the creators of automobile legends which competed in the greatest races and established reputations on the highways. The collection is an exceptional showcase of the technical and aesthetic advancements throughout automotive history.

Briggs Cunningham's collecting began in the mid-1940s when he bought a 1912 Mercer raceabout, a great American sports car of its day. A 300 cubic inch, four-cylinder engine made 80 mph possible and its handsome design with shining brass fittings suited its athletic prowess. The raceabout set the tone for what would become the Cunningham collection.

While Mercer was perhaps America's finest sports car at that time, the car that achieved similar recognition in Europe was the 1912 Hispano-Suiza Alfonso XIII, named in honor of the ruling Spanish king. Hispano-Suiza, a Spanish-Swiss joint enterprise, established a solid reputation with the Alfonso XIII model and went on to produce highly regarded performance luxury cars for those who could afford the privilege. A 1932 custom-bodied dual-cowl phaeton with a V12 engine is also exhibited.

The Cunningham Museum is unique among American collections because of its emphasis on fine quality European cars. There are no fewer than seven Bentley models on display. During the period when W. O. Bentley designed and built the cars (1919-31), the marque developed a great racing tradition in Europe. Five times between 1923 and 1930 the Bentleys came home first at the Le Mans 24 Hour endurance race. The 3-liter model exhibited is very similar

Duesenberg racing cars were among the most successful racers of the 1920s. This supercharged model was driven to second place in the 1929 Indianapolis 500

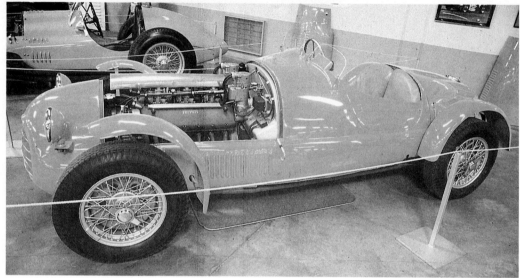

This 1948 Ferrari, powered by a V12 engine, was the first Ferrari brought into the US and only the eighth car manufactured by the Italian company

to the racing versions in chassis and engine design. The body, however, was custom-built by the Vanden Plas coachbuilding concern in Belgium. It features a fabric-covered body and a rare wooden deck on the boat-tail rear. Another notable Bentley is a 1930 6.5-liter competition model known as the Speed Six. The Speed Six models were the top cars at Le Mans in 1929 and 1930. Because of the company's financial instability Rolls-Royce took over production of Bentleys in 1931 and the Bentley image was altered from sports racing to a less expensive alternative to the Rolls-Royce. Nevertheless, it remained a superior quality motorcar. The 1939 example, a two-door saloon coupe with custom body by James Young, has been recognized as an outstanding design.

Other superb European automobiles include a 1914 Rolls-Royce 'Colonial' Silver Ghost (one of only 173 built), a 1914 Mercedes-Benz Grand Prix racing car and, the most distinguished auto in the collection, the 1927 Bugatti Royale. The Royale is one of the largest and most expensive cars ever made. The straight-eight engine displaces 778 cubic inches and the wheelbase measures 170 inches. In 1927 the approximate cost of the most famous Bugatti was $35,000, and today the estimated value is over $3 million. Including a prototype vehicle, only seven Royales were built.

The American-built motor cars in the collection exhibit a similar tendency towards performance and luxury. Most notable are the Duesenbergs. Easily the most powerful passenger cars of their era, the standard Model J developed 265 hp while the supercharged version supplied a phenomenal 320 hp. The Duesenberg legend is well documented at the Cunningham Museum. Not only is there an example of their famous racing machine but also two of their fabulous passenger cars – a dual-cowl phaeton and a short-wheelbase roadster.

Although Duesenberg offered unsurpassed performance, several other American manufacturers produced cars on the highest levels of luxury and engineering sophistication. The Cunningham collec-

Approximately 500 Mercer raceabouts were built between 1911 and 1914. A combination of handsome design and powerful engine made the raceabout one of the premier sports cars of its era

tion contains the Cadillac and Marmon V16s as well as Packard, Lincoln and Auburn V12s, each considered a world-class auto.

There is a selection of post-World War II sports-racing cars including those built and raced by Briggs Cunningham at Le Mans during the 1950s. Several other competitive racing cars in the collection were owned and raced by the famous sportsman, including a 1948 Ferrari, a 1961 Maserati and a 1964 Porsche Carrera sports-racing coupe.

The Cunningham Museum's inventory has over 100 cars on display. Each is driven regularly and kept mechanically sound as well as in good external condition. An additional display features close-up views of more than 20 prominent engines, and a selection of automotive art adds further interest.

The C4R racing car was built and driven by Briggs Cunningham. Powered by a V8 Chrysler hemi engine, the C4R was placed fourth at Le Mans in 1952

One of only six Bugatti Royales in existence is this two-door coupe with custom body by Kellner. Briggs Cunningham bought this Royale in 1950 from Ettore Bugatti's daughter

AC
cobra (1966)
Alfa Romeo
Mille Miglia (1934)
American Underslung
traveler (1911)
Austin
mini-Cooper 'S' (1967)
Ballot
race car (1919)
Grand Prix race car (1920)
Bentley
3-liter Speed Model (1926)
6½-liter Speed Six (1930)
4½-liter sports touring (1931)
8-liter sports touring (1931)
TT race car (1933)
4½-liter Overdrive model (1939)
Continental R Type (1952)
BMW
sports roadster (1938)
Bugatti
Type 52 (1926)
Royale (1927)
Supersport (1933)
Bu-Merc
sports racer (1939)
Cadillac
roadster (V16) (1930)
Le Mans race car (1950)
CERV
1 Corvette experimental model (1960)
II Corvette experimental model (1963)
Chevrolet
Rail dragster (1959)
Cistalia
Type 202 (1950)
Citroën
SM (1977)
Cunningham
boat-tail speedster (1917)
sports racer Le Monstre (1950)
sports racer Model C-1 (1951)
sports racer Model C-3 (1952)
sports racer Model C-4R (1952)

sports racer Model C-4RK (1952)
sports racer Model C-5R (1953)
sports racer Model C-6R (1954)
Delage
Grand Prix race car (1927)
Duesenberg
race car (1928/34)
dual-cowl phaeton (1930)
sports roadster (1935)
Eagle
Formula 1 racer (1967)
Indianapolis racer (1975)
Ferrari
250 spyder (1957)
250 Lusso (1964)
Model 166 Corsa (1948)
750 Monza sports racing (1954)
365 GT 2.2 (1969)
Dino (1972)
Ford
roadster (1929)
GT-40 racer (1966)
Frontenac
T racer (c1926)
racer (1932)
Hispano-Suiza
Alfonso XIII sports roadster (1912)
Model H6C chassis (1928)
dual-cowl phaeton (V-12) (1932)
Jaguar
sports racing C Type (1953)
sports racing D Type (1955)
sports racing E Type (1962)
Junior
midget racer (1940)
Lagonda
drophead coupe (V12) (1939)
Lamborghini
P-400 Miura (1968)
Lancia
Lambda tourer (1923)
Lincoln
dual-cowl phaeton (V-12) (1932)
Locomobile
sports tourer (1925)

Lola
Indianapolis race car (1972)
MacNamara
Indianapolis racer (1971)
Marmon
convertible sedan (V-16) (1931)
Maserati
4 CS sports racing (1934)
250 race car (1957)
Birdcage sports racing (1961)
Mercedes
Grand Prix racer (1914)
Targa Florio (1924)
Mercedes-Benz
gullwing coupe (1955)
SSK roadster (1929)
300 SEL sedan (1968)
Mercer
raceabout (1912)
MG
K-3 Magnette sports racer (1933)
Offenhauser
midget racer (1937)
Kurtis-Kraft midget racer (1946/8)
midget racer (1938)
Osca
sports racer (1954)
Packard
modified roadster (1929)
phaeton (V12) (1933)
Peugeot
3-liter race car (1913)
Pierce-Arrow
roadster (1915)
Porsche
GTS Carrera sports racer (1964)
Rauch & Lang
electric (1911)
Regal Underslung
coupe (1913)
Renault
(1927)
Rolls-Royce
colonial tourer (1914)
Phantom II limousine (1936)

Phantom II Continental (1931)
Phantom III (V12) (1937)
Scarab
Formula 1 racer (1959)
sports racing (1957)
Simplex
sports roadster replica (1914)
SS
100 (1938)
Stutz
4-passenger speedster (1929)
Sunbeam
3-liter (1929)
Talbot Lago
race car T 26 E (1952)
Vauxhall
sports tourer (1927)
Wills Sainte Claire
roadster (1922)

The Model T Ford was unquestionably the car that extended car ownership far beyond the rich and privileged. From its introduction in late 1908, the Model T remained in production for nearly 19 years during which time 15 million 'Tin Lizzies' rolled off the assembly lines. This is a 1909 model

HENRY FORD MUSEUM AND GREENFIELD VILLAGE

20900 Oakwood Boulevard, Dearborn, Michigan 48121. Telephone: 313-271-1620.

Location: The Henry Ford Museum and Greenfield Village is on Oakwood Boulevard between Rotunda Drive and Michigan Avenue in Dearborn. Signs mark the way from either Interstate 94 or the Southfield Freeway (Highway 39).

Without a doubt, no one man made a greater impact on the American automotive scene than Henry Ford. From his implementation of mass-production techniques, automobiles became the number one business in the United States and Ford became a name recognized around the world. As a matter of record, in 1914 over 500,000 cars were sold in the US. Two years later Ford sold that many Model Ts alone. It seemed everyone wanted a car and Ford had devised a plan to sell each of them one. By making transport affordable he became a folk hero to the nation he was putting on wheels and the most talked-about man in the country.

Ford decided to pay tribute to what he considered to be the work ethic of pre-industrial America and in 1927 he proposed to build an 'industrial museum'. The Henry Ford Museum and Greenfield Village first opened to the public in 1933 and vividly demonstrates how quickly life in America had changed as a result of industrialization. His collection of Americana is simply astonishing in its scope. Within this re-creation of American history lies an automotive repository worthy of recognition in its own right, which

is indeed one of the great collections of the world. It includes one of the oldest motor vehicles known to exist – an 1865 Roper steam carriage which Henry Ford acquired in 1930. It is the fourth of ten self-propelled road vehicles built by Roper from the early 1860s to 1895. From the pioneering days of gasoline-powered vehicles is an 1893 model of the three-wheeled Benz 'Velocipede'. The first motor vehicle offered for sale to the American public in quantity was the Duryea Motor Wagon of 1896. The Ford Museum has the only one in existence.

Other autos from the first decade of production include a 1903 curved dash Oldsmobile – the world's first mass-produced car with over 20,000 built between 1901 and 1905. 'Old Pacific' is the nickname of a Packard which was driven from coast to coast in 62 days during the summer of 1903 and is now on display. In a strange twist of fate the Selden Auto Buggy, built to support the patent claims of George Selden, found a home with Henry Ford. From 1903 to 1911 a number of US and some European manufacturers paid royalties to Selden for every car they produced. Ford not only refused to pay a royalty but also proved in court that the patent was invalid.

Ford history is, of course, prominently exhibited. Among the examples is the first car built by Henry Ford. He initially tested the vehicle in 1896 and referred to it as the Quadricycle. The first of several racing cars which Henry Ford drove to attract financial backing in 1901 is also on display. Of the same vintage is the famous Ford 999. In this huge four-cylinder car Henry Ford set a new speed record of 92 mph during 1904. Ford's first car offered for public sale, a 1903 Model A, is also displayed. It featured a two-cylinder engine, a detachable rear seat compartment and a steering wheel instead of a tiller.

By introducing the high-volume, low-priced automobile at a time when demand was practically boundless, Ford created the most appreciated car of all time. When introduced in 1908 the Model T's price ranged between $825 and $1000 and during the course of production, prices were lowered by over 50 per cent. Before giving way to the Model A in 1928 over 15 million 'Tin Lizzies' were sold. Because of the overwhelming success of the Model T the automotive

industry in the US was bolstered considerably and the American lifestyle was transformed.

Approximately 180 automobiles, arranged in chronological order, make up the Ford Museum collection. Naturally, the spotlight shines on the history of Ford cars. With about 20 per cent of the automobiles Ford products, the collection is notably diverse. Much consideration has been given to the first 20 years of automative development, yet there are exceptional automobiles representing every decade through to the 1960s.

In addition to the automotive displays, the 12-acre Henry Ford Museum complex features a wide assortment of bicycles, motor cycles, aeroplanes and trains. Certainly the entire transportation collection ranks among the best anywhere.

Each year in September an Old Car Festival is held in Greenfield Village featuring hundreds of pre-1930 automobiles. A similar event occurs each August in which cars of the 1930s, 1940s, and 1950s are assembled for show.

An excellent array of non-Ford automobiles in the Ford Museum collection includes this rare 1923 Chevrolet with experimental 'copper-cooled' engine

The Selden Auto Buggy was the basis for a patent which at one time required most US auto manufacturers to pay royalties on every car they produced

In 1896 Henry Ford built this, his first car, which he referred to as the Quadricycle. Seven years later Ford founded the Ford Motor Company and with it he became the major force in the auto industry for the following two decades

Overleaf: **In 1901 Henry Ford built and drove this racing machine to a new speed record of 92 mph while driving on a frozen lake. Famous racing driver Barney Oldfield also set several speed records with this racer**

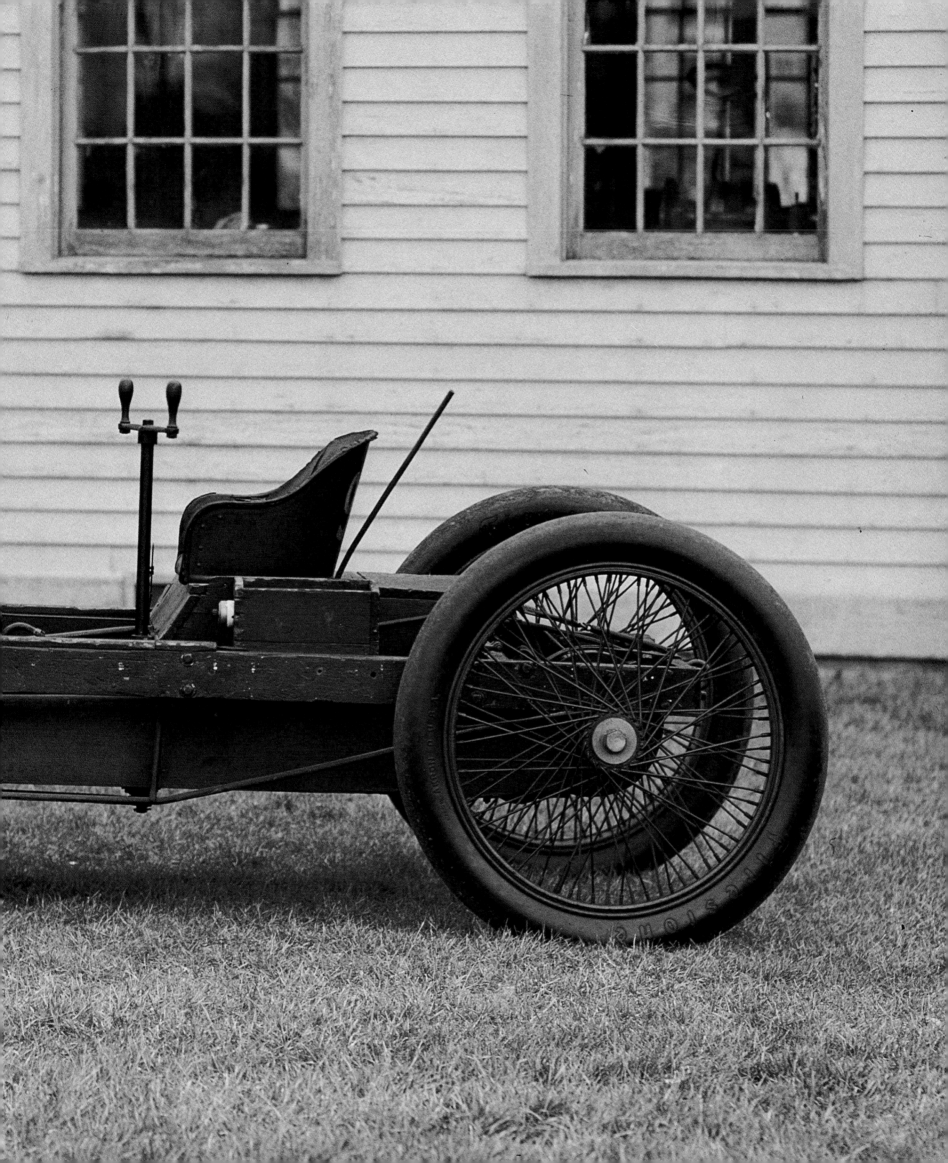

Not all on exhibit

Alcoa Aluminum Pierce-Arrow
sedan (1925)
American Austin
roadster (1930)
Apperson
touring (1916)
Auburn
convertible sedan (1930)
Auto-Red-Bug
buckboard (1928)
Autocar
runabout (1898)
Baker Electric
runabout (1901)
victoria (c1912)
Bantam
roadster (1937)
Benz
2-passenger velocipede (1893)
Comfortable 3-passenger (1896-99)
Parsifal 5-passenger tonneau (1903)
1/5 working model (1885)
Brewster
town landaulet (1915)
Brush
runabout (1911)
Bugatti
Royale Type 41, convertible (1930)
Buick
touring (1908)
roadster (1914)
Cadillac
runabout (1903)
V-8, 7-passenger touring (1915)
Chalmers-Detroit
Model E speed roadster (1909)
Chevrolet
Royal Mail roadster (1915)
V.8 touring (1918)
Copper Cooled coupe (1923)
4-door International sedan (1929)
Corvette V8 (1955)
convertible (1956)
Corvair sedan (1960)
Chrysler
Imperial dual-cowl Sportif (1927)
custom Imperial landau sedan (1932)
4-door sedan Airflow (1930)
Derham Parade Car (1940)
turbine (1964)
Columbia Electric
victoria (1901)
Cord
convertible phaeton sedan 5-passenger (1937)
Crosley
Hotshot roadster (1951)
Daimler
victoria (1897)
De Dion Bouton
motorette (1900)
Detroit Electric
Model 47 brougham (1914)
coupe (1922)
Doble
steam phaeton (1925)
Dodge Brothers
touring (1918)
Duesenberg
2-door convertible victoria (1931)
Duryea
motor wagon (1896)
3-wheel trap (1899)
Edison Electric
runabout (c1889)

Edsel
4-door hardtop Citation (1958)
Elmore
touring Model 30 (1908)
Essex
coach (1924)
Federal
truck (1910)
Ferrari
Testa Rossa (1958)
Ford
Quadricycle (1st Ford) (1896)
runabout (2nd Ford) (1898)
Quadricycle (replica) (c1963)
racer (1st) (1901)
runabout (1901)
racer 999 (1902)
runabout (1902)
Model A runabout (1903)
Model C 5-passenger (1904)
Model C tonneau (1904)
Model B touring (1905)
Model F touring (1905)
Model K touring (1907)
Model R runabout (1907)
racer 666 (1907)
Model S 3-passenger roadster (1908)
T touring (1909)
Kulick T racer (1910)
Smith Form-A-Truck (1911)
T touring (1912)
T touring (1913)
cyclecar (1914)
T touring (Burroughs) (1914)
T taxi (Fisher body) (1917)
T center-door sedan (1919)
special coupe (H. Ford's) (1919)
TT Farm truck (1925)
T cutaway chassis (1926)
T touring (15-millionth) (1927)
A touring (1st) (1928)
A coupe (H. Ford's) (1929)
A roadster (1929)
A station wagon (1929)
A town sedan (1929)
A pick-up (1929)
A phaeton (1930)
AA farm truck (1930)
V8 cabriolet (1932)
Miller special (race car) (1935)
V8 touring sedan (1935)
V8 tudor sedan (1937)
V8 deluxe cabriolet (1939)
V8 4-door sedan super deluxe (1942)
V8 tudor sedan (serial 1) (1949)
V8 pace car (convertible) (1953)
Thunderbird (1956)
Mustang I (1962)
Mustang (1965)
Mark IV Le Mans race car (1967)
Escort (serial 1) (1981)
Franklin
runabout (1905)
Airman sedan (1928)
Fruehauf
trailer (1914)
GMC
Model 16 stake truck (1918)
Graham Brothers
house car (1928)
Haynes-Apperson
surrey (1897)
Holsman
runabout (1903)

Hudson
limousine (Derham) (1951)
Hupmobile
3-passenger coupe (1911)
Ideal
Stage Coach housetrailer (1935)
International Harvester
roadster (1910)
AW truck (1911)
farm truck (1912)
Kaiser
traveler (1949)
Kelsey
motorette 3-wheel roadster (1910)
Lane Steamer
touring (1910)
La Salle
roadster (1927)
opera coupe (1937)
Lincoln
camp truck (1922)
touring (1923)
convertible victoria coupe (1929)
Zephyr V12 sedan (1936)
Brunn touring cabriolet (1937)
presidential 'Sunshine' Special (1939)
Continental cabriolet (1941)
presidential 'Bubble Top' (1950)
X-100 experimental (1953)
Continental Mk II (1956)
Continental presidential X-100 (1961)
Lotus/Ford
Indianapolis car (1965)
March/Cosworth
Indianapolis car (1984)
Marmon
Model 34, 4-passenger roadster (1921)
Maxwell
Model AB runabout (1911)
Mercedes-Benz
300 SL-R racer (1955)
Mercer
22-72 sport touring (1916)
Mercury
8 town sedan (1939)
Nash
Quad truck (1918)
touring (1918)
sedan (1926)
Northern
runabout (1904)
Oakland
runabout (1911)
Oldsmobile
runabout (1903)
Overland
runabout (1904)
Owen Magnetic
7-passenger touring (1915)
Packard
'Old Pacific' (1903)
Model L touring (1904)
Twin-Six camp truck (1915)
Twin-Six touring (1916)
roadster Model 6-26 (1929)
V12 convertible victoria (1939)
Peerless Brewster
victoria (1911)
Pierce-Arrow
roadster (1904)
Plymouth
coupe (1933)
DeLuxe 4-door touring sedan (1939)
Pope-Hartford
tonneau (1904)

Pope-Tribune
Model A runabout (1904)
Rambler
5-passenger tonneau (1904)
7-passenger limousine (1912)
Rapid Bus
open omnibus (1906)
Rauch & Lang
electric towncar (1912)
Reo
Model G 4-passenger runabout (1909)
Riker
electric 3-wheeler (1896)
electric truck (1898)
torpedo racer (1901)
Rolls-Royce
limousine (1926)
Roper
steam carriage (1865)
Saxon
Model 14 roadster (1916)
Scripps-Booth
'Rocket' cyclecar (1913)
Sears
motor buggy (1909)
Selden
patent motor buggy (1907)
Stanley
Steamer runabout (1903, 1910)
Star
station wagon (1923)
Stevens-Duryea
Model U limousine (1908)
Stoddard-Dayton
sport touring (1912)
Studebaker
(EMF) touring (1913)
Starlight coupe (1951)
Avanti (1963)
Stutz
Bearcat roadster (1923)
Thomas Flyer
touring (1906)
Tucker
torpedo 4-door (1948)
Volkswagen
sedan (1949)
Waverly
electric surrey (1903)
Welch
touring (1907)
White
Stanhope steam carriage (1902)
Steam Model G 7-passenger touring (1907)
camp truck (1921)
Wills Sainte Claire
roadster (1926)
Willys-Knight
touring (1924)
Winton
4-passenger surrey (1900)
limousine (1915)
Woods
dual-power Model 44 coupe (1916)
mobilette (1917)

GILMORE-CLASSIC CAR CLUB MUSEUM

6865 Hickory Road, Hickory Corners, Michigan 49060. Telephone: 616-671-5089.

Location: 15 miles northeast of Kalamazoo. From Interstate 94, take Exit 80 (Sprinkle Road) and travel north 5 miles. Turn right on Gull Road (M-43) and proceed 5 miles into Richland. Turn left at the traffic signal and drive north 6 miles. At the intersection of Hickory Road turn right and enter the museum grounds.

The Gilmore-Classic Car Club Museum is the singular result of combining an outstanding private collection with the founding of a national museum featuring the cars recognized by the Classic Car Club of America (CCCA).

David Gilmore, a former chairman of the board of the Upjohn Pharmaceutical Company, created the Gilmore Car Museum as a showcase for his sumptuous collection of classic, antique and special-interest autos. In 1966 it was opened to the public. The CCCA became interested in establishing its own museum in 1982 and two years later opened an exhibit area on the grounds of what then became the Gilmore-Classic Car Club Museums. The CCCA was founded to honor the finest automobiles of the classic era (1925-42). During this unique period superior-quality cars reflected an extraordinary combination of art, engineering and craftsmanship. Since Gilmore's personal collection was heavily influenced towards the classics, the marriage was a natural.

Gilmore bought the site in the early 1960s and a number of distinctive old wooden barns from nearby farms which were dismantled, restored and re-erected on the 90 acres which now make up the museum grounds. Six of these barns house the 130 or more vehicles at the museums.

Prominently displayed is a significant selection of Packards. Before World War II Packard established an impeccable reputation for reliability, quality and precision. Certainly the most widely admired and cherished Packards are the smooth and silky V12 models. The Gilmore-CCCA Museums display two, including one from 1939, when the last of the coupe bodies were equipped with the V12 chassis. Also displayed is the sporty and luxurious four-door convertible sedan of 1940 – one of the final efforts of an era made famous by superlative 12- and 16-cylinder luxury cars. The origins of Packard prestige are demonstrated by high quality motorcars from 1905 to 1908. During the period separating these two models, Packard sales rose by more than 300 per cent.

At the National Automobile Show in 1930 Cadillac unveiled the world's first 16-cylinder production car. For the next ten years the V16 would be Cadillac's ultimate statement in luxury. The 1937 convertible sedan on exhibit has been cared for by the Gilmore family since it was new. Two dual-cowl phaetons from the Roaring Twenties indicate the Cadillac image of elegant, open air tourers, and a 1903 roadster represents the first Cadillac production year.

A precious supply of Rolls-Royces illustrates the British version of the quality crafted car. Exhibits from 1910 through to 1938 provide interesting parallels to the American classics. On one end of the chronological scale is a 1910 Silver Ghost – the car that made Rolls-Royce synonymous with reliability, elegance and wealth. Also exhibited is the extravagant Phantom III Park Ward limousine of 1938 and several models from the second two decades of the twentieth century.

The classics represent the vanguard of automotive evolution during the most uncompromising period of the automobile's development. They were larger, more beautiful and more powerful than anything else on the road. Their importance becomes apparent when viewed next to their mass-market contemporaries. Many were fitted with bodies which were built by custom coachbuilding firms catering to the most discriminating buyers.

Among the recognized classics on display are rare European models such as a 1925 Minerva fixed-head coupe with custom body by Vanden Plas, a 1927 Bugatti Type 43A roadster, and a 1939 Daimler sedanca coupe custom-bodied by Gurney Nutting. The American industry is well represented by such prestigious vehicles as a 1929 Duesenberg with dual-cowl phaeton body by LeBaron, a 1925 Pierce-Arrow roadster, and a 1940 Lincoln Continental convertible victoria. Augmenting the selection of classic luxury cars is an excellent variety of antique automobiles and post-World War II sports cars.

During the first weekend in August the annual Red Barn Spectacular attracts hundreds of antique, classic, and special-interest autos for an outdoor exhibition. An automotive swap-meet and arts-and-crafts show are further attractions.

With few exceptions, this outstanding collection may be seen from May to October.

Above: **To avoid the heavy tariff on imported automobiles Rolls-Royce established an auto factory in the US in 1920. It was in Springfield, Massachusetts, and this 1929 Ascot phaeton is an elegant example of the 'Springfield Rolls'**

Right: **General Motors bought the Fleetwood Body Company in 1925 and operated it as their custom coachbuilding subsidiary primarily for the most luxurious Cadillac models. An example of Fleetwood's craftsmanship is this 1937 Cadillac V16 Imperial convertible sedan**

Opposite: **A 1938 Rolls-Royce and a 1911 Lozier pose in front of the restored antique barns which house the Gilmore-Classic Car Club of America Museum**

Before 1914 numerous companies competed for the quality car market in America. This 1911 Lozier was a greatly respected model

The custom-bodied Dietrich convertible victoria was probably the most widely admired automotive status symbol in America in the 1930s

Incomplete list

AC
Bristol (1957)
Alfa Romeo
Veloce (1956)
spyder (1956, 1967)
American-La France
fire engine (1899)
Bugatti
Type 43A roadster (1927)
Cadillac
roadster (1903)
dual-cowl phaeton (1925, 1929)
V16 convertible sedan (1937)

Eldorado hardtop (1956)
Barritiz (1957)
limousine (1959, 1964)
Citroën
SM (1972)
Daimler
(1939)
Duesenberg
dual-cowl phaeton (1929)
LaSalle
sedan (1931)
Lincoln
Continental convertible (1940)

Lozier
sports tourer (1911)
Minerva
coupe (1925)
Packard
Model 15 (1905)
runabout (1908)
phaeton (1930)
convertible victoria (1936)
speedster sedan (1937)
Darin convertible (1939, 1940)
V12 convertible sedan (1940)
V12 coupe (1939)
160 sedan (1941)

Pierce-Arrow
roadster (1925)
limousine (1931)
Rolls-Royce
Silver Ghost touring (1910)
London Edinburgh tourer (1913)
'Baby Rolls' 20/25 (1925)
Springfield Phantom I (1929)
Springfield Phantom I
Ascot phaeton (1930)
Phantom II Sedanca (1930)
Phantom II coupe (1933)
Phantom III limousine (1938)

The chauffeur-driven Bugatti Royale coupe de ville is one of the largest cars ever built. It weighs over 7000 pounds and is nearly 20 feet long. The cost of the Royale in 1932 was $42,000

HARRAH'S AUTOMOBILE COLLECTION

Box 10, Reno, Nevada 89504. Telephone: 702-355-3500.

Location: From the Harrah's Hotel/Casino in downtown Reno, take Glendale Avenue (an extension of East Second Street) for 3½ miles.

Browsing through the vast reaches of the Harrah's Automobile Collection is like having the pages of an automotive encyclopedia materialize before your eyes. It is one of the most inclusive and, at the same time, exclusive collections to be seen. Seemingly every car imaginable can be found here. Many are one-off models, and all are in exemplary condition. Most have been restored by the highly regarded in-house restoration shop under the scrutiny of perfectionist Bill Harrah. Nevertheless, there still remain a few unpolished gems.

William F. Harrah is the man who has given his name to this collection, the like of which will never be duplicated by another individual. Although Harrah died in 1978, the collection continues to reflect his enthusiasm for the motor car and his feelings that these rare cars should be seen and admired.

Harrah began collecting in 1948, two years after opening his first casino in Reno, Nevada. His interest in pre-World War I cars at that time led him to the home of a 1911 Ford and 1911 Maxwell. Quickly the collection outgrew the garage space and warehouses became necessary. That was only the beginning. By 1959 Harrah had acquired approximately 50 cars, mostly through dealings for one or two cars at a time. But in 1961 he made his first big purchase consisting of 30 cars from the J. B. Nethercutt collection (now the Merle Norman Classic Beauty Collection). Other collections were later bought, but the majority of cars were acquired singly.

When the automobile collection was first opened to the public in 1962 there were slightly more than 300 cars on display. Yet even at that time the total number of cars owned by Harrah had surpassed 600. In the next 15 years the collection continued growing at an extraordinary pace. At its peak the collection included approximately 1500 cars.

After Bill Harrah's death the acquisition of automobiles stopped. Within a year Holiday Inns bought the Harrah's casinos and hotels, as well as the automobile collection. One year later it was announced that the world's biggest car collection was for sale. The governor of Nevada formed a committee to 'structure a transaction' with Holiday Inns, intending to acquire 'the essence of the collection'. Harrah's stated that they 'would be willing to assist in the effort to establish a public foundation which would have as its goal the preservation of the most significant vehicles of the collection'.

By early 1986 the number of cars on display had been reduced to approximately 550. Two separate auctions had eliminated 700 cars from the inventory and in the process set record prices for both Duesenberg and Packard as well as many other marques. A final auction will whittle down the remainder to the target of 300 cars. It is the intention to build a multi-million dollar museum in Reno so that the core of the collection will remain intact.

The plans for the new William F. Harrah Automobile Museum call for an exhibition hall of 192,000 square feet, displaying over 300 cars on two levels. The facility will also include an automotive research

Above: **Franklin automobiles featured air-cooled engines, unlike most of their contemporaries. This touring model from 1930 was known as the Pursuit and featured a 95 hp six-cylinder engine**

Below and opposite: **This 1933 Duesenberg Model SJ supercharged speedster was bought by Bill Harrah in 1962 with only 1432 miles on the odometer and has never been restored**

library and restoration/preparation area. Completion is expected in 1988.

In the meantime the collection will continue to be exhibited in the original 13-building complex in the Reno suburb of Sparks. The facility includes the showrooms, professional restoration shops, administrative offices and an extensive automotive research library. The cars are displayed in three large warehouses – at one time packed side-by-side and fender-to-fender. The reduction in numbers greatly improved viewing conditions and, despite a near 75 per cent reduction, an excellent chronology of automotive history can be seen.

Many of the cars are extremely rare production models and others are believed to be the only models still in existence. One of the most famous cars in the collection is the 1907 Thomas Flyer which won the famous New York to Paris automobile race of 1908. It has been restored to the condition in which it fin-ished the race. Famous manufacturers such as Duesenberg, Bugatti, Packard, Mercedes-Benz and Pierce-Arrow are represented by several of their best models.

Befitting the Harrah's image, 'star' cars are featured in special displays throughout the collection. There is the 1949 Mercury driven by James Dean in 'Rebel Without a Cause'. John Wayne admirers will covet his 1953 Corvette, and jazz age aficionados have Al Jolson's custom-built 1933 V16 Cadillac to admire. Lana Turner's 1941 Chrysler, Frank Sinatra's 1961 Ghia, Sammy Davis Jr's 1971 Duesenberg and John F. Kennedy's 1962 Lincoln Continental are also displayed.

Even though the workshop has not restored a car for the collection since 1978 the staff continues to provide this service for outside customers.

(No list of exhibits available during early 1986)

Right: **Avant garde auto design is executed by the French coachbuilding firm Saoutchik on this 1949 Delahaye coupe de ville. Originally designed for the 1949 Paris Auto Show, the price of this motor car reached $20,000**

One of the most remarkable endurance competitions of all time, the New York to Paris auto race of 1908, was won by this 1907 Thomas Flyer. The journey was completed in 171 days

Morgan began production of high-performance three-wheeled vehicles in 1910. This 1934 version is powered by a V-type two-cylinder air-cooled engine

IMPERIAL PALACE AUTO COLLECTION

3535 Las Vegas Boulevard South, Las Vegas, Nevada 89109. Telephone: 702-731-3311.

Location: The Imperial Palace is at the corner of Flamingo Road and Las Vegas Boulevard (The Strip), within several minutes' drive of Interstate 15. The auto collection is housed on the fifth floor of the hotel's parking facility.

One of the most rapidly growing collections in the United States is the Imperial Palace Auto Collection which belongs to Ralph Engelstad, the owner of the hotel/casino complex where the cars are displayed. Since 1981, when the collection opened to the public, Engelstad has been extremely active in buying, selling and trading rare and unusual automobiles. Although the number of cars exhibited constantly hovers around 200, about 300 more vehicles in varying condition are kept in warehouses with certain models designated for treatment in Engelstad's restoration shop.

The collection consists of a wide variety of mainly American automobiles, although several prominent

European models are also included. Nevertheless, the heart of the collection is devoted to American classics with numerous examples of prestigious marques such as Duesenberg, Packard, Cadillac and Pierce-Arrow. An unusual feature is a selection of motor cars which have become memorable for their famous or infamous owners.

One such car is a 1930 Cadillac 16-cylinder sedan once owned by the gangster Al Capone. In addition to the rare V16 engine, this Cadillac had such non-standard options as bullet-proof glass, armor plating, portholes to accommodate the barrels of machine guns, and an exhaust system which could set up a smoke screen. An even greater degree of infamy has

Opposite top: **The Imperial Palace Collection displays over 200 antique, classic and special interest automobiles in the midst of one of America's most popular tourist destinations – Las Vegas, Nevada**

Above: **The 1914 Detroit Electric is an example of the high quality electric car which became noted as a ladies' automobile because of its quiet and smooth operation**

Left: **The Thomas Flyer of 1905 was a large and powerful automobile which sold for over $3000**

Left: **The 1908 Unic demonstrates the tall and boxy design of the enclosed car during the era when fully enclosed bodies were custom built and comparatively expensive**

Opposite: **The Model J Duesenberg was introduced in December 1928 and continued as a limited edition luxury automobile until 1937. During that time, fewer than 500 were built and sold around the world. This is a 1934 model**

been gained by the custom-built 1939 Mercedes-Benz ordered by Adolf Hitler. The entire car is bullet-proofed and armor-plated. Each door weighs 900 pounds and the entire car weighs slightly less than six tons. More honorable are several custom-built limousines which have transported presidents and heads of state.

Among the pre-1920 automobiles are the products of Duryea, Haynes-Apperson and Franklin. Also from this era are a selection of steam-powered and electric cars, as well as a stately 1910 Rolls-Royce limousine which at that time cost over $15,000. From the 1940s and 1950s the collection contains several uncommon names such as Tucker and Muntz – cars then outside the mainstream of the auto industry. Unusual styling features can be viewed in exhibits like the Graham 'Sharknose' and the best known failure of all time, the Edsel.

Since 1982 the Imperial Palace has been hosting an annual 'Antique Auto Run' – in October a scenic adventure tour open only to cars of pre-1938 vintage.

The participants (approximately 500 cars) depart the Imperial Palace and cruise down the Las Vegas Strip parade-style to begin the event.

Incomplete list

Alfa Romeo
(1939)
American-La France
speedster (1918)
Buick
touring (1905)
town car (1932)
Cadillac
dual-windshield V16 phaeton (1931, 1930)
V16 sedan (1938)
Carter Car
(1907)
Chrysler
New Yorker (1954)
convertible limousine (1952)
Columbia
(1905)
Crosley
race car (1950)
Delage
limousine (1928)
DeLorean
(1981)
Detroit Electric
(1914, 1916)

Duesenberg
convertible coupe (1929)
dual-cowl phaeton (1934)
town car (1933)
duPont
victoria (1930)
Duryea
wagon (1897)
Edsel
Pacer convertible (1958)
Firestone
Columbus (1908)
Ford
Model A rear-entrance tonneau (1903)
Model N (1906)
Model T pie wagon (1913)
Mustang (1966)
Fordson
tractor (1923)
Franklin
landaulet (1907)
Gatts
(1905)
Graham
sedan (1939)
Haynes Apperson
(1899, 1903)
Holsman
highwheeler (1908)

Horch
(1931)
Hupmobile
(1932)
International Harvester
highwheeler (1907)
Jimison
(1902)
Kissel
roadster (1925)
Knox
Waterless touring (1904)
La Nef
(1898)
Lenawee
(1903)
Lincoln
(1925, 1937)
town car (1940)
limousine (1962)
Locomobile
(1913)
Mercedes-Benz
Model 770K (1939)
Mobile
Steamer (1900)
Murray
(1902)
Muntz
Jet (1951)

Nash
Metropolitan (1959)
Oldsmobile
curved dash (1904)
Packard
(1934)
Pierce
bus (1905)
Pierce-Arrow
(1922)
Pope Waverly
electric (1906)
Reo
(1912)
Rolls-Royce
(1933)
Silver Ghost limousine (1910)
Safaricar
custombuilt hunting vehicle (1977)
Stanley
Steamer (1911, 1913, 1921)
Unic
sedan (1908)
Waltham Orient
buckboard (1906)
Willys-Knight
(1929)
Yellow Cab
(1923)

"THE BRICKYARD"

INDIANAPOLIS MOTOR SPEEDWAY HALL OF FAME MUSEUM

Location: The speedway is northwest of downtown Indianapolis. It can be reached from Interstate 465 on the west side of town by taking Exit 16A and driving southeast on Crawfordsville Road.

Above: **The museum also exhibits a number of racing engines, including this Cosworth, as well as special exhibits featuring helmets, trophies and various engine components**

The annual Indianapolis 500 race (held on the last Sunday in May) has been one of the most spectacular and eagerly anticipated sporting events in the world for more than 75 years. The combination of tradition and intense competitiveness makes it the pinnacle of open-cockpit racing.

Fortunately, tradition is well enshrined here. The bounty of lore and legacy is well preserved and ready to be relived in the Indianapolis Motor Speedway Hall of Fame Museum.

Naturally, the focus is on the Indianapolis-style racing cars. More than 25 winners of the 500 are on display. Beginning with the Marmon Wasp, winner of the inaugural race in 1911, the collection includes several examples from every decade up to the present. These exhibits represent an exclusive look at the evolution of state-of-the-art race-car design.

Four of the cars were two-time winners: the Doyle Maserati driven by Wilbur Shaw in 1939 and 1940, the Blue Crown Spark Plug special driven by Mauri Rose in 1947 and 1948, the fuel-injected special driven by Bill Vukovich in 1953 and 1954, and the Belond special driven by Sam Hanks in 1957 and Jimmy Bryan in 1958. Also among the most success-ful cars is the Lola Ford which was driven to the auto

Preceding pages: **The first 500-mile race at the Indianapolis Motor Speedway was won by the Marmon Wasp in 1911 at an average speed of 74.59 mph**

racing Triple Crown by winning at Indianapolis, and later adding the Pocono 500 and the California 500 during the 1978 season.

Several examples of the famed Miller racing cars are displayed. Harry Miller and his associates are considered by many to be the best ever Speedway de-signers. The Miller cars dominated the race during most of the 1920s and early 1930s. They set many pre-cedents with engineering innovations and also gained recognition for their high standards of metal craftsmanship.

In addition to the racing machinery, the museum displays approximately 30 vintage, antique and classic cars. From this group comes a sizable selec-tion of cars built in Indiana during the early 1900s. Marques such as Duesenberg, Stutz, and Marmon represent Indianapolis manufacturers with close ties to the speedway. The Duesenberg brothers, Fred and Augie, built a reputation by virtue of their victories at the track in the mid-1920s. A detuned version of their successful straight-eight racing engine also powered their high-performance luxury car, the Model J. Other outstanding Indianapolis-built cars in the collection include an 1895 Reeves horseless carriage, a pres-tigious 1914 American Underslung and an extremely rare 1917 Pathfinder V12 touring car.

The entire collection totals over 125 racing cars and a like number of passenger cars. However, exhi-biting techniques allow only about 60 vehicles to be displayed at a time. Each car is easily viewed from all sides in this layout. The exhibits are spread out over two marble-floored levels.

Additional displays consist of racing memorabilia and accessories which trace the evolution of such items as helmets, spark plugs, carburetors and other engine components. An impressive array of trophies belonging to one of the all-time great drivers, Rudolf Caracciola, is also exhibited. Caracciola was a good friend of Tony Hulman, owner of the Speedway from 1945 to 1977. The latter made many improvements to ensure the continued success of the 500. He also init-iated the Hall of Fame Museum which was first opened in 1956 and expanded in 1976 to its present size and prominence.

After 'the 500' each May, the Speedway hosts num-erous car club gatherings and shows throughout the summer. One of the biggest of these events is the Annual Grand Classic, which attracts over a hundred of the world's finest cars built between World Wars I and II. This, and another large show for autos designated as Milestone Cars (post-World War II), are scheduled each July. Another grand event is the annual Hoosier Auto Show and Swap Meet, scheduled for the third weekend in September each year.

More than 25 Indianapolis 500 winning cars are featured among the 60-plus cars exhibited in this collection

Incomplete list

Indianapolis 500 Winners:
Marmon
    wasp (1911)
National
    (1912)
Delage
    (1914)
Duesenberg
    (1922)
Miller
    (1928, 1932)
Boyle Special-Maserati
    (1939-40)
Blue Crown
    special   front-wheel-drive   Offenhauser
    (1947-48)
Kurtis
    fuel-injected special (1953-54)

Offenhauser Belond
    special (1957-58)
McLaren
    (1972)
Penzoil
    special (1980)

Antiques and classics:
American Underslung
    (1913)
Chevrolet
    corvette (1957)
Cord
    L-29 cabriolet (1932)
    812 phaeton (1937)
Crosley
    convertible (1951)
Davis
    touring (1922)
Haynes
    touring (1909)

Haynes-Apperson
    roadster (1900, 1906)
Interstate
    dirt track racer (1916)
Lexington
    touring (1920)
    sedan (1922)
Maxwell
    roadster (1909)
Monroe
    (1916)
National Electric
    (1899)
Overland
    touring (1910)
    roadster (1912)
Packard
    Patrician (1956)
Pathfinder
    V12 touring (1917)

Premier
    (1903)
Reeves
    (1895)
Richmond
    touring (1908)
Roosevelt
    coupe (1929)

Right: The winner of the 1952 Indy 500 was this Agajarian Special. Troy Ruttman, at 22, became the youngest driver ever to win this race

Below: The Miller racing cars were the dominant force in Idianapolis races from the late 1920s to the mid-1930s. Driver Louie Meyer brought this Miller home first in the 1928 race

MERLE NORMAN CLASSIC BEAUTY COLLECTION

15180 Bledsoe Street, Sylmar, California 91342. Telephone: 818-367-1085.

Location: From downtown Los Angeles, take the Harbor Freeway (11) north to the Golden State Freeway (Interstate 5). Continue north on the Golden State Freeway until the Roxford Street exit. Turn right on Roxford Street, then right on San Fernando Road, and finally left on Bledsoe Street. The collection is housed in the tallest building on Bledsoe Street.

Each of the automobiles presented here absolutely embodies the magnificence of the motor car. The very essence of dazzling elegance, creative art and overwhelming beauty is displayed with the style and grace this collection deserves. Undeniably, the combination of exhibits and their setting presents a unique and vivid definition of functional fine art.

The Classic Beauty Collection is owned by the Merle Norman Cosmetics Company. However, the person responsible for assembling the automotive collection is J. B. Nethercutt, chairman of the board and co-founder of the company. One of the world's most renowned automotive collectors, Nethercutt has been acquiring cars since his first purchase, a 1936 Duesenberg, in the mid-1950s. Since 1972 this exquisite selection of automobiles has been appropriately exhibited in a salon-type setting designed to recapture the grandeur of the auto shows of the classic era.

The main exhibit area is called the Grand Salon Showroom. Immediately the opulence of a past era unfolds as you pass through the huge solid bronze entry doors. Inside the green and black marble floor reflects the images of about 35 legendary motor cars.

The Grand Salon showroom has been designed to recreate the look of the most opulent automobile showrooms of the 1920s

The most prized possession among the gems of the collection is the stunning 1933 Duesenberg sedan which was built as a show car for the 1933 Chicago World's Fair. Due to its original price, the car has always carried the sobriquet 'Twenty Grand Duesenberg'. The one-of-a-kind close-coupled sedan body was built by the Rollston Company of New York; the supercharged engine and chassis alone cost $9500. The Twenty Grand is the epitome of the classic-status automobile.

In addition to Duesenberg, the most predominant marques are Rolls-Royce, Cadillac and Packard. The Rolls-Royce collection begins with a 1913 Silver Ghost town carriage and includes all six of the magnificent Phantom series cars. Also present are the Silver Wraith, the Silver Cloud and the Silver Shadow. The Cadillac section is dominated by the fabulous V16 models. From 1930 to 1940 the 16-cylinder car established new levels of status in the luxury market. The most lavish models were built before 1932, when the Depression forced changes throughout the car industry. The Classic Beauty Collection includes three distinct styles of the 1930 Cadillac V16 including a sedan, a dual-cowl phaeton, and a town car originally owned by the famous film director Cecil B. DeMille. Throughout its limited production the V16 created a vogue image which served Cadillac well. Although considered a rare treasure the Classic Beauty Collection has gathered eight exemplary models.

During the classic car era (1925-42), no other American car was able to match the reputation of Packard. Unquestionably the eight-cylinder version was the most popular of the 'quality' cars. At the top of the line, however, was a distinguished V12 model which frequently incorporated bodies designed and built by the famous custom coachbuilders. Naturally, Packards are prominent in this collection and several V12 models with custom designs by Dietrich and LeBaron are included.

Further examples of the apex of automotive art are provided by the top European manufacturers, such as Minerva, Hispano-Suiza, Isotta-Fraschini and Mercedes-Benz. Elegant creations from other prestigious American manufacturers include a V16 Marmon and V12 models by Pierce-Arrow, Lincoln and Auburn. The pre-classic era is well represented, too, and provides an interesting contrast of styles between one decade and the next.

In addition to displaying approximately 60 beautifully restored automobiles (the entire collection numbers 173 and all cars are exhibited in rotation), the Classic Beauty Collection displays over 1100 radiator mascots. Many of these hood ornaments came to symbolize the marques which created them such as the 'Spirit of Ecstasy' which is synonymous with Rolls-Royce. A portion of this collection includes the gorgeous crystal ornaments crafted by the artist René Lalique. The mascot collection is exhibited on a mezzanine area which provides a stunning overview of the Grand Salon Showroom.

Tours of the Merle Norman Classic Beauty Collection are offered free of charge from Tuesday to Saturday; reservations are necessary, however.

A strong and smooth 160 hp twelve-cylinder engine powers this 1934 Packard convertible sedan. The US coachbuilding firm of Dietrich was responsible for the body

Incomplete list

Alco
touring (1912)
American Underslung
touring (1914)
Auburn
cabriolet (V12) (1932)
Austro-Daimler
Alpine sedan (1932)
Bentley
coupe de ville (1951)
Bugatti
Brescia (1926)
Grand Prix (1933)
Cadillac
dual-cowl phaeton (V16) (1930)
town car (V16) (1930)
imperial cabriolet (V16) (1930)
convertible coupe (V12) (1931)
phaeton (V16) (1932)
coupe (V8) (1932)
imperial limousine (V16) (1933)
convertible victoria (V16) (1935)
convertible coupe (V8) (1938)
convertible sedan (V16) (1938)
5-passenger coupe (V16) (1940)
Chrysler
convertible sedan (1932)
Newport (1941)
Cord
L-29 town car (1930)
phaeton (1937)
Cunningham
limousine (1919, 1931)
Daimler
touring saloon (V12) (1928)
formal sedan (V12) (1931)
De Dion Bouton
roadster (1912)
DeLorean
coupe (1983)
Doble
steamer coupe (1930)

Duesenberg
touring (1925)
sedan (1933)
dual-cowl phaeton (1934)
convertible coupe (1936)
Durant Star
coupe (1927)
Ferrari
convertible coupe (1967)
Ford
Model T touring (1911)
Model A sport coupe (1930)
roadster (1936)
Franklin
limousine (1911)
runabout (1912)
sedan (1924)
club brougham (V12) (1933)
Hispano-Suiza
coupe de ville (V12) (1933)
Isotta – Fraschini
all-weather landaulet cabriolet (1928)
Kissel
speedster (1929)
Lagonda
convertible coupe (V12) (1939)
Lincoln
phaeton (1921)
coupe (V12) (1932)
2-window Berline (V12) (1937)
touring coupe (V12) (1938)
continental coupe (V12) (1947)
Locomobile
victoria sedan (1925)
Matheson
touring (1911)
McFarlan
twin-valve Knickerbocker cabriolet (1923)
Marmon
sedan (1930)
sedan (V16) (1932)

Mercedes-Benz
touring (1913)
cabriolet (1938)
gullwing coupe (1956)
Napier
touring (1910)
MG
TC roadster (1948)
Minerva
convertible town cabriolet (1928)
limousine de ville (1930)
Oldsmobile
Limited limousine (1911)
Packard
touring (1904)
formal sedan (V12) (1939)
sedan (V12) (1920)
imperial sport landaulet (1930)
sport sedan (1931)
convertible coupe (V12) (1932)
convertible sedan (V12) (1934)
sport phaeton (V12) (1934)
touring sedan (V12) (1937)
club sedan (V12) (1937)
sport sedan (1941)
Peerless
touring (1903)
Pierce-Arrow
touring (1907, 1915, 1918, 1919)
sedan (V12) (1932)
touring (V12) (1933)
limousine (V12) (1937)
Pope-Hartford
touring (1911)
Premier
roadster (1912)
Renault
all-weather town cabriolet (1923)
Reo
Royale sedan (1933)
Rolls-Royce
town carriage (1913)

Marlborough town car (Phantom I) (1930)
town car (Phantom II) (1930, 1932)
Croydon convertible (Phantom II) (1932)
V12 sedanca de ville (Phantom III) (1937)
saloon (Phantom IV) (1956)
touring limousine (Phantom V) (1966)
limousine (Phantom VI) (1972)
saloon (Silver Wraith) (1955)
limousine (Silver Wraith) (1958)
saloon (Silver Cloud III) (1963)
saloon (Silver Shadow) (1967)
Simplex
touring (1916)
Stevens-Duryea
touring (1915)
Stutz
sedan (1931)
Tucker
sedan (1948)
Voisin
victoria (1923)
Volkswagen
sedan (1946)

Rudolph Valentino was the original owner of this custom-built 1923 Voisin sporting victoria, built in France

Below: A car seldom seen in America is the Belgian-built Minerva. The custom body on this 1928 model was designed by the American designer Floyd Derham, and is known as a convertible town cabriolet

Right: By the time this 1909 Packard helped establish a new sales record for the company, Packard autos enjoyed an international reputation for outstanding precision workmanship

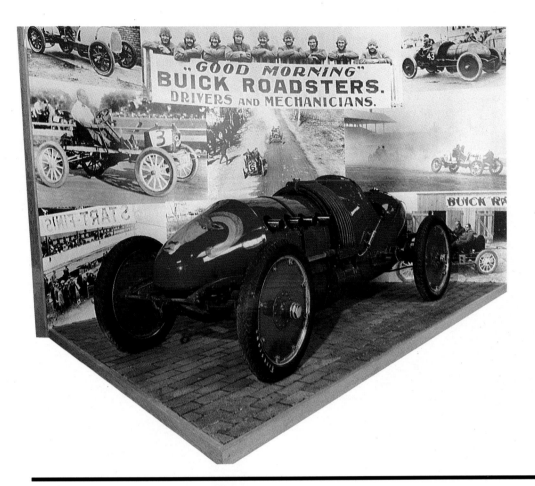

ALFRED P. SLOAN MUSEUM

1221 East Kearsley Street, Flint, Michigan 48503. Telephone: 313-762-1169.

Location: Flint is approximately 50 miles northwest of Detroit. Drive northwards on Interstate 75 to Interstate 475, and continue north to the Court Street exit. Turn right on Court Street and follow the signs to the Flint Cultural Center where the Sloan Museum is located.

Advanced racing car design is exemplified by the 1910 Buick Bug. The Bug is powered by a massive 622 cubic inch four-cylinder engine

The Alfred P. Sloan Museum, opened in 1966, commemorates the automotive history of Flint, Michigan.

At the turn of the century Flint was referred to as 'Vehicle City' because of its prosperous horsedrawn vehicle industry. In 1903 the Flint Wagon Works began automobile production after buying the Buick Motor Company of Detroit. By 1906 over 1000 cars a year were coming out of the Buick factory and by 1910 that figure had increased to over 30,000, making Buick second only to Ford in terms of car production. In 1913 the first Chevrolets were built in Flint and seven years later both Buick and Chevrolet were building over 100,000 cars a year.

The collection of over 80 cars begins with several exhibits pertaining to Flint's horsedrawn vehicle era between 1885 and 1900. During 1901 the first automobile factory was founded in Flint by the Flint Automobile Company. The product was called the Hardy Flint roadster, after the owner's name, but output reached only a little over 50 cars during the company's three-year history. Somehow a 1902 model of this horseless carriage survived and is prominently exhibited.

Although the Buick Motor Company had initially built experimental motor cars in Detroit, production was first initiated in 1904 when the company was moved to Flint. A reconstructed model of a 1904 Buick Model B, built by the Sloan Museum from miscellaneous parts and engineering drawings, shows how this motor car had already evolved beyond the horseless carriage stage. Later in 1904 the controlling interest in Buick was purchased by William 'Billy' Durant, owner of Flint's largest carriage manufacturer, the Durant-Dort Carriage Company. Under Durant's control Buick became an industry leader. The 1905 Buick Model C tonneau on exhibit is one of 750 built that year.

When Buick introduced the Model 10 in 1908 it met with immediate success. The price of this three-passenger runabout was $900 – almost half the price of its competitors. Powered by a 22.5 horsepower four-cylinder motor, Buick described the Model 10 as 'a gentleman's light four-cylinder roadster'. The combination of low price and good publicity from Buick's racing successes made it a top seller for three years while the company challenged Ford for the leader-

Left: **General Motors' first experimental vehicle is referred to as the Buick Y Job. The styling of this automobile influenced GM design for almost 20 years**

Below: **The Sloan Museum contains a unique collection of one-of-a-kind prototype and auto show cars from the 1950s, which provide a revealing insight into auto design during that period**

ship in sales. Two Model 10s are displayed in the Sloan Museum – a 1908 roadster and a 1910 touring. Because of the financial strength of Buick at this time, Durant took the opportunity to form a combine of automotive manufacturers in 1908 which would alter the course of the entire industry. The result was the formation of General Motors, which in time became the world's largest industrial entity. Major vehicle manufacturers included in the corporation along with Buick were Cadillac, Oldsmobile and Oakland. Chevrolet was added several years later.

An example of the first Chevrolets produced in 1912, the Chevrolet Classic Six, is featured in the Sloan collection. At the time the only model available was a huge touring car priced at $2150. Also exhibited is a 1912 Little which was built by the Little Motor Company of Flint. After it was bought up by Chevrolet in 1913 Little's name was replaced by Chevrolet on this lightweight car designed to compete with the Ford Model T. Subsequently the bigger, more expensive Classic Six was eliminated. By 1915 Chevrolet was tenth in production with output reaching 13,000 that year, but by 1920 it had soared to over 120,000 and Chevrolet was the third most popular car in America. A 1915 touring and a 1920 roadster are also among the exhibits.

Through the 1920s Flint thrived on the production of automobiles with Buick and Chevrolet ranking among the world's biggest producers. General Motors grew explosively and the man at the wheel was Alfred P. Sloan. The progress of Buick and Chevrolet through the 1920s and 1930s is demon-strated by the cars on display. Several smaller car manufacturers continued to build cars in Flint throughout this period and Dort, Flint and Paterson are represented here.

In addition to the vehicles which made Flint a booming automotive town in the pre-1939 era, the Sloan Museum offers a unique collection of one-off General Motors prototype and experimental models. The oldest is a 1939 Buick 'dream car' known as the Y-Job. This design exercise influenced GM styling for almost 20 years. From the 1950s are several exhibits of futuristic designs which reflect a Flash Gordon spacecraft-like theme. Innovative features incorporated into these designs include power seats, built-in power jacks at each wheel for lifting the car during tire changes, television cameras replacing rear view mirrors, aluminum and fiberglass bodies, radar devices, integrated bumpers and sliding parallel doors. Additional show cars and prototypes provide rare glimpses into creative automotive thought in the modern era.

Each year the museum hosts the Sloan Museum Summer Fair, a two-day car show and automotive swap-meet featuring approximately 1000 antique and special interest cars. The event is always scheduled for the fourth weekend in June. Proceeds from the event are used to make acquisitions and restorations which will benefit the museum's automotive collections.

Below: **This 1912 Chevrolet represents the first year of Chevrolet production. The only model offered was the touring model equipped with a six-cylinder engine**

Above: **The Flint was manufactured between 1924 and 1927 by Durant Motors in the town of Flint, Michigan. A 1925 six-cylinder sedan, as shown, was available for less than $2000**

Best
truck (1910)

Buick
Model B (reconstruction) (1904)
Model C touring (1905)
Model 10 roadster (1908)
Model 10 touring (1910)
Model 60 bug racer (1910)
Model touring (1911)
Model C-25 touring (1915)
Model D-35 touring (1917)
center-door (1918)
Model K-44 roadster (1920)
Model 25-48 opera coupe (1925)
Model 28-S Club coupe (1928)
Model 59 estate wagon (1950)
XP-300 convertible (prototype) (1951)
Model 56R 2-door sedan (1953)
P-4003 'Wildcat II' (prototype) (1954)
Centurion sedan (prototype) (1956)
Pace Car (1975, 1976, 1981, 1983)
LeSabre (last rearwheel-drive) (1985)
Model 36 victoria coach (1932)
Y-Job (prototype) (1938)
XP-8 LeSabre (GM prototype) (1951)
XP-810 Silver Arrow Riviera I (prototype) (1963)
Silver Arrow Riviera III (prototype) (1971)

Cadillac
touring (1912)
touring Model 61 (1921)
Cyclone convertible (prototype) (1959)
Corvair 'Super Spyder' (prototype) (1962)
Corvega (Cosworth engine) (prototype) (1971)

Chevrolet
Model C touring 'Classic Six' (1912)
Model H-4 touring 'Baby Grand' (1915)
Model 490 touring (1920)
chassis (1922)
Superior Series K touring (1925)
Superior K sedan (1926)
National AB coach (1928)
Independence AB coach (1931)
roadster deluxe (1932)
Impala sedan (1962)
Corvair Monza 105 sedan (1969)
Monza 2+2 hatchback (1975)
Chevette (1976)

Covert
Motorette roadster (1902)

Detroit Electric
Model 90 (1922)

Dort
Model 19T sedan (1922)

Flint
'Hardy' roadster (1902)
Model 40-B sedan (1926)

Flint Motor Wagon
truck (1914)

Ford
Model T touring (1923)

General Motors
Phantom (prototype) (1977)

GMC/BTV
truck (1977)

Hispano-Suiza
Model H6 sedan (1924)

Little
Model 4 roadster (1911)

McLaughlin
Model K45 touring (1920)

Marquette
Model 30-30 (1930)

Marr
cyclecar (1914)

Monroe
(1915)

Paterson
Model 6-47 touring (1919)

Peugeot
Bébé roadster (1914)

Pontiac
2-door sedan (1927)

Pontiac Motor
highwheel (1907)

Randolph
truck (1910)

Stanley
Steamer Model 72 B touring (1917)

Whiting
Model A roadster (1911)

BROOKS STEVENS AUTOMOTIVE MUSEUM

10325 North Port Washington Road, Mequon, Wisconsin 53092. Telephone: 414-241-4185.

Location: 12 miles north of downtown Milwaukee on Route 141 (Port Washington Road). The museum is on the west side of the highway, just south of Donges Bay Road.

Brooks Stevens began his interest in automobiles at a very young age. His father was a pioneer inventor of the preselective gearshift during the 1920s. As a boy Stevens accompanied his father to the annual automobile shows, which inspired him to later pursue a career in industrial design. Although he has been involved in numerous aspects of that profession, his first love is for challenges resulting from automotive design.

During his career Stevens has led engineering and design teams which consulted on projects by Willys-Overland, Kaiser-Frazier, Studebaker and American Motors. In the mid-1960s he founded his own auto company to produce the limited edition car he called the Excalibur.

The collection of cars which now comprises the Brooks Stevens Automotive Museum was begun over 50 years ago when Stevens acquired a much coveted 1929 Cord Cabriolet. Stevens later customized the Cord through modifications such as skirting the fenders, slanting the windshield, adding distinctive headlights and a huge fin on the back, and applying a special two-tone paint scheme. The car remains in this condition as part of the collection today. Through the years, as he continued to add more cars to the collection, an impressive array of antique, classic and sports and racing cars was assembled. To house the growing collection and to share it with the public, Stevens designed, built and opened the museum which was opened in 1958.

Approximately 75 cars are included in the Stevens collection. Beginning with the oldest car, a 1905 Cadillac one-cylinder Roadster, the museum features a selection of both American and European autos. The pre-1920 motorcars are all from American manufacturers with rare and unusual examples from Metz, Velie, Paige and Marmon. The 1914 Marmon race-about roadster, for instance, is one of only six built and is based on the same engine and chassis as the Marmon Wasp, which won the inaugural Indianapolis 500 race. Excellent European luxury cars from the 1920s are represented by Rolls-Royce, Bugatti, Hispano-Suiza and Mercedes-Benz. The Rolls-Royce is a Silver Ghost phaeton model originally owned by King Alfonso XIII of Spain. The Mercedes-Benz SS-180 illustrates the legendary supercharged sports racing cars which gained considerable attention around

the world in the late 1920s.

Illustrating the most fashionable motorcar designs of the 1930s are creations such as the custom-built, one-of-a-kind 1930 Cord coupe, a statuesque twelve-cylinder Packard dual cowl phaeton from 1934, the elegant 1935 Mercedes Benz 500K Phaeton, a curvaceous 1938 Talbot Lago coupe, and the sporting SS-100 roadster of 1939.

The majority of cars in the Brooks Stevens Museum are from after World War II. Most of these selections consist of two categories: European sports and special interest vehicles, and American prototypes and production vehicles which Brooks Stevens and his associates designed and built. Demonstrating the English sports car ideology of the 1950s are examples such as the MG TC and Jaguar XK-120. Exhibits reflecting the Italian design at this time include an Alfa Romeo touring coupe and a Ferrari 250 Europa.

Stevens' designs have been incorporated into the styling of a number of automobiles, many of which are exhibited. The 1948 Willys Jeepster is an early example of Stevens' association with the Willys Corporation. Later in his career he became instrumental in the designing of many Studebaker and American Motors cars. Several examples of his innovative thinking include two 1964 Studebakers – the boulevard cruiser known as the Gran Turismo Hawk, and the 'Skyview' station wagon featuring a roof which slides forward to allow extra cargo space.

Stevens was also involved with creating several show car designs. These were innovative automobiles produced only for auto shows to demonstrate future engineering and styling features being developed. For instance, the 1956 Cadillac 'Die Valkyrie' sedan featured a removable hard top. Also exhibited is the Scimitar, a car designed for Olin Aluminum Company in 1959. The entire body was built of aluminum and also features the removable hard top. The one-of-a-kind 'Sceptre' coupe was designed in 1966 to replace the Hawk in the Studebaker line, but unstable company finances forced its cancellation.

Yet another Stevens-designed show car built as a possible performance/touring model was originally known as the Studebaker SS. Before it ever made an auto show appearance, the car was renamed the Excalibur SS, and Brooks Stevens had become the originator of a new breed of automobile which he re-

Preceding pages: **A one-of-a-kind custom coupe body was placed on this front-wheel-drive 1929 Cord Model L-29. It was designed and built as a show car for the stylish European** *concours d'élégance* **circuit**

The Hispano-Suiza is certainly among the most admired cars of its day and since. The status and stature of this marque is illustriously demonstrated by this elegant 1927 town car

Alfa Romeo
  touring coupe (1950)
Buick
  touring (1913)
Bugatti
  speedster Brescia Model (1926)
Cadillac
  roadster (1905)
  2-door (1926)
  'Die Valkyrie' sedan (1956)
  limousine (1960)
  roadster (1905)
Cord
  speedster L-29 (1929)
  coupe L-29 (1930)
Detroit
  electric (1914)
Deutsch
  Bonnet coupe (1956)
Erskine
  Studebaker (1929)

Excalibur
  SJ-100 roadster (1952)
  XJ-R sports car
  XJ-S supercharged (1953)
  GT Hawk sports car (1963)
  Mk VI (1963)
  SSK prototype No. 1 (1964)
Ford
  victoria (1956)
Frazer
  convertible sedan (1951)
Gutbrod
  Superior (1953)
Hispano-Suiza
  town car (1927)
Indianapolis
  race car (Studebaker) (1933)
Isetta
  coupe (1955)
Jaguar
  XK-120 roadster (1950)

Marmon
  raceabout roadster (1914)
  special HCM Prototype V12 (1933)
Mercedes
  500K phaeton (1935)
Mercedes-Benz
  sport sedan (1938)
  phaeton (1928)
Metz
  roadster (1910)
MG
  TC Midget roadster (1949)
Packard
  phaeton dual-cowl (1934)
  Twin Six phaeton (1920)
Paige
  Daytona roadster (1919)
Premier
  touring (1921)

Rolls-Royce
  phaeton (1925)
  Silver Wraith (1954)
Scimitar
  (1959)
SS
  100 roadster (1939)
Talbot Lago
  coupe (1938)
Velie
  touring car (1918)
Willys
  Jeepster (1948)
  Aero 2600 sedan (1963)
X001
  rear-engine Hoffman sedan (1935)

ferred to as a contemporary classic.

The Excalibur borrows many of its styling features from the famous Mercedes-Benz SSK of 1927-30. Much of this identity is captured through the use of the familiar Mercedes-Benz radiator design and the external exhausts which snake outward from the side of the hood. It originally was built on the supercharged Studebaker engine and chassis. Later models, however, featured General Motors components. The evolution of the Excalibur is followed in museum exhibits of the car, which is now in its fifth series of technical updating. Approximately 3000 have been built in the family-run factory since 1965.

Right: **Brooks Stevens designed, built and raced this Excalibur Hawk in 1962. The Excalibur racing cars were successful in Sports Car Club of America racing from 1955 through 1964**

Below: **A handsome competitor in the 1914 sporting car field is this fine Marmon speedster. Fast, light and expensive, the speedster is one of only six remaining examples of this high quality sporting breed**

The Brooks Stevens Automotive Museum displays an auto seldom seen in America, the 1938 Talbot Lago Coupe, designed and built in Paris by the custom coachbuilders Figoni and Falaschi.

THE SWIGART MUSEUM

Route 22 East, Huntingdon, Pennsylvania 16652. Telephone: 814-643-3000.

Location: On Route 22 just four miles east of Huntingdon. Less than an hour's drive from the Pennsylvania Turnpike in central Pennsylvania. Huntingdon is just east of Altoona and approximately half way between Pittsburgh and Philadelphia.

The Swigart collection began in the mid-1920s as one man's effort to preserve a vanishing portion of Americana. At the time William Swigart began collecting automobiles the automotive industry was just 25 years old and technology had progressed mightily since the turn of the century. Many car manufacturers were already out of business at that time and many older cars had already become obsolete. In most cases the aged automobile became scrap iron or was dismembered to provide the needed part for some other apparatus around the farm. Fortunately, Swigart realized the automobile industry was evolving quickly and the past was being lost. His fondness for pre-1914 automobiles is evident in the collection he assembled over 20 years.

The Swigart collection emphasizes the era when America was first becoming a mobile society. Unquestionably the automobile brought a profound change in the lifestyles of most Americans. More than the ability to travel to and around town, it provided the freedom to travel across the continent. In its brief history the family car had become the preferred mode of transportation.

However, as the automobile became increasingly the product of mass production, many smaller companies were unable to compete and ceased production. By 1930 the Big Three manufacturers were selling nine out of ten cars in America – the world's largest market. Between 1923 and 1927 the number of automobile companies was reduced from 108 to 44. The products of those manufacturers that failed were referred to as orphans. They most often were unwanted items. The focus of the nation was on the future, and most people believed Henry Ford when he said, 'the past is more or less bunk.' Rather than discard the automotive past, Swigart decided to preserve it.

Many early auto manufacturers were derived from businesses such as machine shops, bicycle or buggy manufacturers. Studebaker, in South Bend, Indiana, was the world's largest producer of horse-drawn vehicles before turning its efforts to automobiles and the Pope Manufacturing Company of Hartford, Connecticut was America's largest bicycle producer. The collection features autos from both these companies.

The first auto builder to develop a large-scale production effort was the Olds Motor Works, a company with experience in building stationary engines.

Numerous examples from obscure American manufacturers are represented in the Swigart collection. This 1920 model is the only known survivor of the Carroll automobile, which was built in Ohio

Although the first car was completed in 1897 it wasn't until the introduction of the famous curved dash Oldsmobile in 1901 that the company became a force in the auto industry. The curved dash model became the most widely sold auto from 1903 to 1905 when it sold for $650. The Swigart collection includes models from 1902, 1903 and 1904. William Swigart has driven the 1903 model on 15 Glidden Tours and claims it is among the best one-cylinder performers in existence.

The selection of one- and two-cylinder cars in the Swigart Museum is probably the most diverse in the United States. Included among the exhibits are several of the most popular autos at the turn of the century. The 1900 Locomobile steamer was second in total sales that year. (The following two years Locomobile would be the number one car in America.) An example of the 1903 Cadillac rear entrance tonneau model is also exhibited. Although this was Cadillac's first year of production, more than 1500 cars were built, placing the company third in production that year. Other Cadillacs in the collection include one-cylinder models from 1904 and 1905, and a four-cylinder model from 1909. By that time Cadillac sales had climbed to over 7500.

The demand for automobiles during the first decade of the twentieth century sparked phenomenal growth in the numbers of cars being built and the number of companies offering vehicles. Other than Henry Ford's Model T mass production techniques, most auto manufacturing procedures remained slow and quite reminiscent of methods used in the carriage trade. Although production capabilities remained limited for most, competition was keen and much local and regional brand loyalty existed. Along with the successful cars which Swigart collected, such as the 1904 Rambler (third in sales) and the 1904 Franklin (fifth in sales), there are also many examples from long-forgotten companies such as Crestmobile, Jewell, Mora and Sears. The Sears car, for instance, was manufactured for the famous Sears Roebuck Company and sold through their stores and catalogs.

Above: **The 1930 duPont Le Mans speedster was based on the duPont racing car which was entered in the Le Mans 24-hour race of 1929. It was produced in very limited quantities before the company closed down in 1933**

Right: **This 1914 Grant represents the first year of production for the Grant Brothers Automobile Company. The firm lasted eight years before failing in 1922**

Although the collection is distinguished in its presentation of the automobile during its formative years, it also features examples of outstanding vehicles from the classic era. Famous marques represented in the collection include Pierce-Arrow, Packard, Marmon, DuPont and Duesenberg as well as several others. In addition to the approximately 100 cars on exhibit, the museum also features huge collections of license plates, horns, lights, automobile nameplates and other accessories.

Incomplete list

Black
highwheeler (1909)
Buick
Model F (1905)
touring (1908)
Brush
roadster (1906)
Cadillac
(1903, 1904)
rear-entrance tonneau (1905)
touring (1909)
Carroll
(1920)
Chalmers
touring (1912)
Crestmobile
(1900)

duPont
dual-cowl phaeton (1930)
Le Mans speedster (1930)
Franklin
roadster (1904)
Jewell
(1906)
Lincoln
Continental (1947)
Locomobile
steamer (1900)
Mitchell
roadster (1902)
Mora
(1909)
Oldsmobile
curved dash (1902, 1903, 1904)
Limited (1910)

Pierce-Arrow
roadster (1919)
Rambler
touring (1904)
Reo
Model G (1905)
Scripps Booth
town car (1916)
Sears
autobuggy (c1900)
Studebaker
electric (1908)
Tucker
sedan (1948)
Winton
(1900, 1901)

Opposite: **The evolution of horse-drawn vehicle to horseless carriage was a gradual process. The Black Manufacturing Company sold this highwheeler type farm wagon in 1909**

Above: **From 1903 to 1905 the curved dash Oldsmobile was the most widely sold automobile in America. At its peak in 1905, approximately 6500 cars were sold**

Left: **Pierce-Arrow autos developed a reputation for high quality craftsmanship and conservative design during their 30-year history from 1909 to 1938. Their trademark was the headlight mounted in the front fenders, as demonstrated by this 1919 model**

TEXAS SCIENCE CENTER AUTOMOTIVE COLLECTION

Durango and South Alamo Streets, San Antonio, Texas 78299. Telephone: 512-226-5544.

Location: The Texas Science Center is in HemisFair Plaza in downtown San Antonio. From Interstate 281 (McAllister Freeway) exit on Durango Street. Drive west on Durango 3½ blocks to HemisFair Plaza across from the Four Seasons Hotel.

A 1933 Duesenberg Model J, America's most expensive motor car. The factory designed and produced the engine, chassis, fenders, radiator shell and bumpers which cost approximately $8500. The body, which had to be made by a custom coachbuilding firm, added another $4000 to $10,000 to the final price

Through the years since the initial cars were brought together, this collection has been known as the Liston Zander collection, the Witte Museum, the San Antonio Museum of Transportation and, now, the Texas Science Center. In the 1940s Liston Zander was a well known automobile collector. His association with the Witte Museum was instrumental in establishing an automotive collection as an adjunct to the art and natural history collections for which the Witte is famous. A number of the autos in the original museum collection were donated from Zander's own collection. He also persuaded other collectors to donate autos to the collection. When the number of cars outgrew the Witte Museum facilities, the collection gained its own identity as the San Antonio Museum of Transportation. At this time, the cars were relocated in their present facility with four separate showrooms.

Recently the auto collection has become the focal point of what is known as the Texas Science Center. As a result, the automobiles are exhibited to illustrate the relationship of the automobile and technology. Through the various displays, the cars demonstrate the science of automotive engineering. The exhibits accurately present the automobile as the invention which has had the most profound effect on the industrialized world. What better way to study the progress of technology than through the history of the automobile.

The entire transportation collection numbers over 60 vehicles including a dozen horse-drawn carriages dating from 1850-90. Automobiles range from pre-1900 to the late 1960s.

From the pioneering years the exhibits include rare cars such as an 1899 Locomobile steamer, a 1906 Pungs Finch and a 1906 Columbia. The Pungs Finch roadster is the only example of that marque remaining. Its engine is a monstrous 684 cubic inch four-cylinder model capable of 50 horsepower. The Locomobile steamer was among the most popular cars sold in America during its production from 1899-1902. During that time the company built over 5000 steam-powered cars. The Columbia is a seven-passenger touring model which was bought at the Chicago Auto Show of 1906 and then driven to southern Texas. Due to its weight and wheel type, the

auto was unsuitable for Texas roads and the car was subsequently stored until the 1940s. It was then repaired and driven on a number of tours before becoming a part of the collection.

Examples of automobiles which have attained legendary status include marques such as Alvis, Auburn, Duesenberg, Pierce-Arrow and Rolls-Royce.

The 1934 Alvis Speed 20 represents the classic English combination of a snappy six-cylinder engine, excellent handling and brakes, along with high quality workmanship. Vanden Plas, the custom coachbuilder, designed and built the coupe-style body. While the Alvis cost approximately $4000, the 1933 Auburn speedster on exhibit was priced at almost half that amount. This Auburn features the V12 engine which propelled the car to the American Stock Car speed records of that time. Because of its status as a custom built motorcar, Duesenberg was ineligible to compete in speed tests against production vehicles. Undoubtedly though, the Straight Eight Duesie was the fastest car on the road. The 1933 torpedo convertible coupe on exhibit boasted 265 horsepower, over 100 more than the Auburn or any other contemporary.

A car of exceptionally high quality was the Pierce-Arrow, which was produced between 1901 and 1938. The Model 66 of 1917 which is on display was the official car of President Woodrow Wilson during World War I. Priced at $6500, it was among the world's choice luxury automobiles. The Rolls-Royce Silver Ghost was the epitome of conservative luxury cars from 1906 to 1926 – the second longest con-

tinuous run of any model in history. The 1926 model on display was manufactured in the company's American facility in Springfield, Massachusetts. Its custom-built roadster body, which cost approximately $13,000, is powered by an almost silent six-cylinder engine of 454 cubic inches.

The vehicle with the longest production run in history, the Volkswagen 'Beetle', is also exhibited with a model from 1949. Also from the post-World War II era is the rear-engined Tucker, the three-wheeled Messerschmitt, the luxurious Lincoln Continental Mark II and the exotic Lamborghini P400 Miura. Throughout the collection each exhibit makes a vivid statement regarding the evolution of automotive technology. The science of automotive engineering is in focus here.

From 1920 to 1932 Rolls-Royce built motor cars in Springfield, Massachusetts as well as in England. This custom roadster features a body crafted by Brewster & Company on the Rolls-Royce Silver Ghost chassis

Above: **Locomobile built steam-powered automobiles from 1899 (when this example was made) to 1903 before switching to the internal combustion engine. The steamers were designed by the famous Stanley brothers who produced a steamer of their own**

Preceding pages: **The V12 powered Auburn Boattail Speedster set 36 stock car speed records in distances from one to 500 miles. Its top speed was over 100 mph**

Ahrenes
  fire pumper (1892)
Alvis
  (1934)
American-La France
  fire truck (1930)
Auburn
  boat-tail speedster (1933)
Bugatti
  (1938)
Buick
  Model F (1910)
Chevrolet
  Bel-Air (1957)
  Corvair convertible (1969)
Chrysler
  LeBaron (1963)
Circa
  Fagoel bus (1920)
Columbia
  Mk XLVII touring (1906)
De Dion Bouton
  (1901)
Dodge
  touring (1930)
Duesenberg
  Model J Rollston body (1933)

Edsel
  4-door (1959)
Ford
  Model T fire truck (1927)
  Model A roadster (1930)
  Model A 2-door sedan convertible (1931)
  Model A 2-door deluxe phaeton (1931)
  Woody wagon (1940)
  Model T couplet (1915)
  Model TT truck (1923)
  Model T roadster (1923)
Fuller
  (1910)
Georges-Richard
  roadster (1903)
Holsman
  Model 3 runabout (1905)
Lamborghini
  P400 Miura 6 (1967)
Lincoln
  Continental Mk II (1956)
  Continental (1964)
  Continental limousine (1965)
Locomobile
  steamer (1899)
Mercedes
  (1953)

Messerschmitt
  KR200 (1955)
MG
  TD replica (1979)
  TC (1948)
Moon
  Model 6-30 touring (1916)
Monte Carlo
  prototype (1961)
Oldsmobile
  curved dash (1903)
Overland
  (1918)
Packard
  Model 3-38 touring (1915)
  sedan (1949)
Pierce-Arrow
  Model 66 touring (1917)
  Model 80 brougham (1925)
Pungs Finch
  (1906)
Rolls-Royce
  Brewster-bodied sedan (1926)
  Springfield Silver Ghost Piccadilly Roadster (1926)
  20/25 (1929)
Saxon
  (1917)

Sprint
  dirt track racer (1948)
SS
  Model SS-1 coupe (1933)
Studebaker
  (1924)
Stutz
  Blackhawk sedan (1933)
Texan
  Model B-38 touring (1920)
Texas Longhorn
  (1939)
Tucker
  (1948)
Velie
  (1920)
Volkswagen
  Beetle (1949)
Woods
  electric victoria (1906)
manufacturer unknown
  streetcar (1886)

THE VOLO ANTIQUE AUTO MUSEUM

Location: From Chicago, take Interstate 294 north to Highway 120. Follow Highway 120 west approximately 13 miles.

27640 West Highway 120, Volo, Illinois, 60073. Telephone: 815-385-3644.

At the Volo Antique Auto Museum the fine selection of cars are not merely on display, they are for sale. Naturally, this collection is an ever-changing one as cars are sold and replaced; however, approximately 100 cars are always exhibited. The display models generally provide an accurate barometer of popularity in the collector car field.

Brothers Bill and Greg Grams preside over the antique and special-interest car showrooms, which have been open to the public since 1974. They own about half the collection themselves and the other half are privately owned cars which are for sale on commission. The expansive Volo complex was formerly one of the biggest dairy farms in the area which was acquired by the Grams family in 1963. A large auction barn was soon renovated, providing plenty of room for antiques of all descriptions to be displayed and sold. Today the auction barn houses approximately 65 pre-1948 autos.

The majority of cars here date from the late 1920s to the late 1940s. Generally the convertible models easily outnumber the sedans, though a wide variety of manufacturers is customary. The widespread popularity and loyal following for Fords, Buicks and Chevrolets ensure these are the most commonly seen makes.

In 1932 Ford introduced the first low-priced eight-cylinder car, a roadster costing $460 and a top-of-the-line convertible sedan costing $650. These early Ford V8s, particularly those of 1934-6, created a following which remains strong 50 years later.

During this era Buick remained the most popular mid-priced ($1000-2000) motor car. In 1931 a straight-eight engine replaced the six. Even though sales fell dramatically during the worst years of the Depression, Buick remained at the top of their class.

From 1927 to 1945 Chevrolet outsold the competition in America in all but three years. Even the Ford V8 couldn't match the appeal of the sturdy Chevrolet six-cylinders.

Many of the more flamboyant motor cars are regulars in the Volo showrooms. Frequently displayed are the most elite cars of the 1920s and 1930s, such as the V12-powered Packards, Cadillacs, Lincolns, Pierce-Arrows, Franklins and Auburns, or the V16 cars of Cadillac and Marmon. Other famous marques likely to be found here are Stutz, Duesenberg, Cord, La Salle and Chrysler. Hand-built custom-designed bodies are featured on many of these models. Competition for the luxury car market was intense at this time: in the history of the luxury automobile these were the golden years which have never been surpassed.

Included in the display of pre-1948 vehicles are ten or twelve examples of the high-quality cars of the brass era. Big and powerful touring cars that offered the most luxury and performance in the years before World War I are generally exhibited.

In a second showroom the Volo Museum displays their selection of cars produced after 1948. Under normal conditions this building presents a diversity of modern machinery. Like the antique and classic cars, these late-model cars are chosen for their popularity in today's collector car market. The emphasis is clearly on high-performance versions. The American muscle cars of the first three decades after World War II are the most frequently seen. Corvette is the undisputed leader in this category. The fiberglass-bodied sports car tradition that Chevrolet began in 1953 now has a legion of admirers that is continually growing. Ford's Thunderbird models, especially the 1955-7 models, provide another perspective of the American sports car of this era. The fastest stock cars of the day are well represented in the Volo collection.

In addition to Corvette and Thunderbird there is always a supply of high-performance cars, particularly those that guaranteed over 400 hp, like the Chrysler Hemi, the Cobra Jet Ford and the Chevy 454. Volo also presents the unique practice of offering personalized high performance cars known as street rods. An entirely different form of customizing is apparent in the replicars (modern replicas of classic car designs), such as the Auburn boat-tail speedster, the Mercedes-Benz 500K and the Duesenberg dual-cowl phaeton. Also exhibited are the specialized products of modern limited-run firms such as Excalibur, Zimmer and Avanti. This diversity provides a demonstration of design evolution which is virtually untouched in most collections.

The Volo Museum hosts three annual car shows during the summer. A sports car show open to all post-World War II performance cars is annually

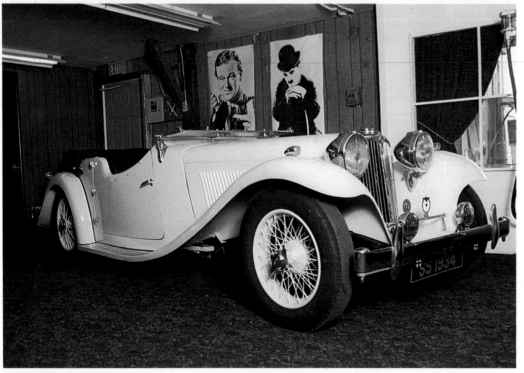

scheduled for Father's Day in June. A show for street rods and customized cars is set each year on the second Sunday in July. The third weekend in August marks the annual antique auto show, featuring the pre-World War II autos. Each show attracts approximately 200 cars on the Volo Museum grounds.

Left: **The SS 1 sports car was introduced in 1932. Because of an underslung suspension, the SS 1 was able to take advantage of a low and racy profile. Within a few years it was being referred to by a name familiar to today's auto enthusiast – Jaguar**

Right

Above: **The 1935 Auburn boattail speedster was powered by a supercharged 150 hp straight-eight motor. Each car contained a dash plaque notifying the owner that the car had a top speed of over 100 mph**

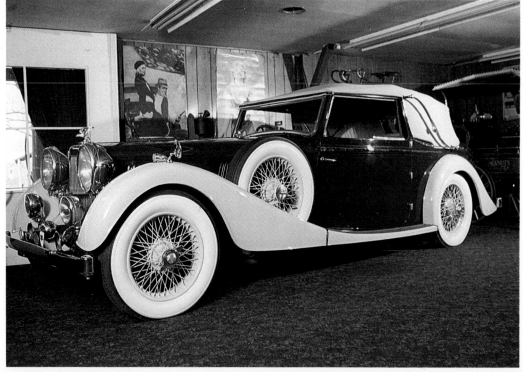

Left

~~*Below:*~~ The Packard radiator design became a universal symbol for quality and provided instant recognition for the marque for much of its existence. This 1931 Packard convertible features distinctive Wood lights as an alternative to the standard headlights

Right: This 1939 Alvis represents the British version of the 1930s concept of a sports touring car. From their launch in 1920, Alvis cars developed a reputation for careful craftsmanship

Index to collections and collectors

A
Alcan Hall of Fame 125
Alfa Romeo Museum 77
Alfred P. Sloan Museum 179
Ålholm Automobile Museum 38
Allan Söderström Automobile 96
Annual Grand Classic car show 173
Arts et métiers museum, Paris 56
Auburn-Cord-Duesenberg Museum 130
Auto und Technik Museum, Sinsheim 60
Automobile and Technical Museum, Sinsheim 62
Autotron Drunen 87

B
Bad Oeynhausen 73
Beaulieu 125
Behring Museum 134
Bellm's Cars and Music of Yesterday 137
Birdwood Mill National Motor Museum 9
Biscaretti Museum 81
Briggs Cunningham Automotive Museum 147
Briggs, Peter 16
British Motor Industry Heritage Trust Museum 108
Brooks Stevens Automotive Museum 184

C
Canadian Automotive Museum, Oshawa 26
Carlo Biscaretti di Ruffia Automobile Museum 81
Château de Rochetaillée 42
Classic Beauty Collection 175
Collezione Quattroruote 84
Compiègne Castle 52
Concours d'élégance (Crawford Museum) 143
Conservatoire national des arts et métiers 56
Crawford Auto-Aviation Museum 143
Cunningham, Briggs (Museum) 147

D
Daimler-Benz Museum 66
Deutsches Auto Museum 71
Donington Collection 112
Dresden Transport Museum 59

E
Eric Rainsford 9

F
Ford, Henry (Museum) 151
Frederick C. Crawford 142

G
George E. Gilltraps 13
German Motor Museum 71
Ghislain Mahy (Collection) 22
Gilltraps Auto Museum 13
Gilmore-Classic Car Club Museum 157
Gilmore, David 157
Grams Brothers 197
Grand Salon Showroom (Merle Norman Collection) 175
Greenfield Village 151

H
Harrah's Automobile Collection 161
Henri Malartre (Museum) 42
Henry Ford Museum and Greenfield Village 151
Hoosier Auto Show and Swap Meet.173
Houthalen Motor Museum 22

I
Imperial Palace Auto Collection 156
Indianapolis Motor Speedway Hall of Fame Museum 172
Innes, J.F. 27
Innes Collection of Motion Picture Cars 29

J
Jack Kaines 9
Johan Raben-Levetzau, Baron 38
Jysk Museum, Gjern, Denmark 39

K
Kaines, Jack 9

L
Langenburg 71
Len Southward Museum 91
Len Vigar 9
Lennart Svedfelt 99
Lips' Autotron 88
Liston Zander Collection 192
Luigi Fussi 77

M
Mahy, Ghislain (Collection) 22
Malartre, Henri (Museum) 42
Merle Norman Classic Beauty Collection 175
Midland Motor Museum 116
Milestone Cars (Car Show) 173

Montagu Motor Museum 125
Moscow Polytechnical Museum 106
Musée nationale de l'automobile (Schlumpf) 47
Musée nationale des techniques 56
Musée nationale du Château de Compiègne 52
Museum of British Road Transport 119

N
National Automobile Museum (Schlumpf) 47
National Motor Museum, Beaulieu 125
National Museum, Compiègne Castle 52
National Museum of Science and Technology, Ottawa 30
National Museum of Technology, Prague 33
National Technical Museum, Paris 56
Nethercutt, J.B. 175
Norddeutsches Auto-Motorrad und Technik Museum 73
Norsk Teknisk Museum 94
North German Motor and Technical Museum 73
Norwegian Technical Museum 94

O
Old Car Festival, Greenfield Village 152
Oshawa (Museum) 26

P
Provincial Automobile Museum, Houthalen 22

Q
Quattroruote Collection 84

R
Raben-Levetzau, Baron Johan 38
Rainsford, Eric 9
Ralph Engelstad 166
Red Barn Spectacular (Car Show) 157
Roberts, T.A. (Bob) 116

S
San Antonio Museum of Transportation 192
Schlumpf Collection 47
Sinsheim 62
Sloan Museum 179
Söderström, Allan 96

Southward, Len 91
Stevens, Brooks 184
Studley Castle 108
Svedino's Car and Aircraft Museum 99
Svedfelt, Lennart 99
Swigart Museum 187
Swiss Transport Museum, Lucerne 103
Syon Park 108

T
Tatra Technical Museum 35
Technisches Museum für Industrie und Gewerbe in Wien 19
Texas Science Center Automotive Collection 192

V
Verkehrshaus der Schweiz 103
Verkehrsmuseum Dresden 59
Vienna Museum of Industry and Trade 19
Vigar, Len 9
Volo Antique Auto Museum 197

W
Wheatcroft, Tom 112
William F. Harrah Automobile Museum 161
Witte Museum 192

Y
York Motor Museum, Perth, Australia 16

Z
Zander Collection 192